CHIEF COMMUNICATIONS OFFICERS AT WORK

TRUSTED ADVISORS THAT BUILD,
INFLUENCE, AND PROTECT
ORGANIZATIONAL REPUTATIONS

Tabita Andersson

Apress®

Chief Communications Officers at Work: Trusted Advisors That Build, Influence, and Protect Organizational Reputations

Tabita Andersson
Henfield, West Sussex, UK

ISBN-13 (pbk): 979-8-8688-1855-4		ISBN-13 (electronic): 979-8-8688-1856-1
https://doi.org/10.1007/979-8-8688-1856-1

Copyright © 2025 by Tabita Andersson

This work is subject to copyright. All rights are reserved by the Publisher, whether the whole or part of the material is concerned, specifically the rights of translation, reprinting, reuse of illustrations, recitation, broadcasting, reproduction on microfilms or in any other physical way, and transmission or information storage and retrieval, electronic adaptation, computer software, or by similar or dissimilar methodology now known or hereafter developed.

Trademarked names, logos, and images may appear in this book. Rather than use a trademark symbol with every occurrence of a trademarked name, logo, or image we use the names, logos, and images only in an editorial fashion and to the benefit of the trademark owner, with no intention of infringement of the trademark.

The use in this publication of trade names, trademarks, service marks, and similar terms, even if they are not identified as such, is not to be taken as an expression of opinion as to whether or not they are subject to proprietary rights.

While the advice and information in this book are believed to be true and accurate at the date of publication, neither the authors nor the editors nor the publisher can accept any legal responsibility for any errors or omissions that may be made. The publisher makes no warranty, express or implied, with respect to the material contained herein.

>Managing Director, Apress Media LLC: Welmoed Spahr
>Acquisitions Editor: Shiva Ramachandran
>Development Editor: James Markham
>Project Manager: Jessica Vakili

Distributed to the book trade worldwide by Springer Science+Business Media New York, 1 New York Plaza, New York, NY 10004. Phone 1-800-SPRINGER, fax (201) 348-4505, e-mail orders-ny@springer-sbm.com, or visit www.springeronline.com. Apress Media, LLC is a Delaware LLC and the sole member (owner) is Springer Science + Business Media Finance Inc (SSBM Finance Inc). SSBM Finance Inc is a **Delaware** corporation.

For information on translations, please e-mail booktranslations@springernature.com; for reprint, paperback, or audio rights, please e-mail bookpermissions@springernature.com.

Apress titles may be purchased in bulk for academic, corporate, or promotional use. eBook versions and licenses are also available for most titles. For more information, reference our Print and eBook Bulk Sales web page at http://www.apress.com/bulk-sales.

If disposing of this product, please recycle the paper

*This book is dedicated to my long-suffering husband, whose support has been unwavering throughout a period where most of my spare time has been spent in front of my laptop. A huge thank you goes to each CCO that I interviewed for the book.
I enjoyed doing the interviews and hope you will enjoy the result. Apologies to our dog, who had to give up some walks while I was interviewing and writing.*

Contents

About the Author		v
Preface		vii
Chapter 1:	Monika Schaller, *Chief Communications Officer SAP*	1
Chapter 2:	Jessica Alm, *Chief Communications Officer Essity*	13
Chapter 3:	Karen Kahn, *Chief Communications Officer Intel*	25
Chapter 4:	Andrew Geldard, *Chief Communications Officer Willmott Dixon*	37
Chapter 5:	Pernille Sahl Taylor, *Chief Communications Officer Handelsbanken UK*	51
Chapter 6:	Jennifer Temple, *Chief Marketing and Communications Officer Hewlett Packard Enterprise*	59
Chapter 7:	Nicola Green, *Chief Communications and Corporate Affairs OfficerVirgin Media O2*	73
Chapter 8:	Stacey Jones, *Chief Communicator Honeywell*	85
Chapter 9:	Amalia Kontesi, *Chief Communications and Marketing Officer NATO Innovation Fund*	99
Chapter 10:	Heather Campbell, *Chief Communications and D&I Officer Eurostar*	111
Chapter 11:	Ryan Curtis-Johnson, *Chief Communications Officer Valuable 500*	125
Chapter 12:	Laura Brusca, *Chief Communications Officer Forbes*	137
Chapter 13:	Amy Lawson, *Chief Communications, Brand, and Corporate Affairs Officer Sage*	149
Chapter 14:	David Burnand, *Chief Marketing and Communications Officer Staffbase*	161

Chapter 15: **Dan Charlton,** *Chief Communications Officer Sussex Partnership NHS Foundation Trust* 171

Chapter 16: **Joanne Trout, Chief Communications** *Officer Omnicom Group* 183

Chapter 17: **Craig Spence,** *Chief Brand and Communications Officer International Paralympic Committee* 195

Chapter 18: **Lucy Henry,** *Chief Communications Officer Avanti Communications* 209

Chapter 19: **Paul Barrett,** *Chief Communications Officer Davie Group* 219

Chapter 20: **Katherine Neebe,** *Chief Communications Officer Duke Energy* 229

Chapter 21: **Christian Stein,** *Chief Communications Officer Renault Group* 241

Chapter 22: **Kate Humphreys,** *Chief Communications Officer Banijay* 251

Chapter 23: **Amy Bunn,** *Chief Communications Officer McAfee* 263

Index 275

About the Author

Tabita Andersson is a senior communications, brand, and marketing leader in the B2B industry. For over 25 years, she has worked in-house, with agencies, and as a freelancer to provide communications support, advice, and leadership to build and protect company brand and reputation. She is passionate about the role communications play in helping a business thrive and how it can help C-level executives connect the dots inside and outside their organisation.

Throughout her career, she has seen first-hand how difficult it is for talented communications professionals to make it to the C-level and beyond. At the same time, with the world becoming more volatile and the number of disparate stakeholders growing by the minute, the importance of having a trusted reputation is becoming a vital part of ensuring success for strategies aimed at growing or protecting businesses.

Preface

I still remember the first executive team offsite meeting I attended as newly promoted senior vice president of communications and brand. We sat around the boardroom table. As people around the table spoke about their subjects, I started to feel smaller and smaller. Imposter syndrome took hold. Why was I feeling this way? What was my role? When was I supposed to speak? My mouth went dry, and I struggled to speak up for the first time in my career.

After more than 20 years of working in various roles within communications and marketing, I was very proud of my promotion. I felt my role and contributions were valued, and when my boss retired, I was more than ready to take up the reins and lead reputation and brand. He had been the first Chief Communications and Brand Officer for the company I was working for, and I had a strong desire to cement the role and continue building an excellent reputation. I've always had a passion for how what we do in communications contributes to an organisation's overall health and success.

I stepped back and made a point of truly listening and learning from the conversations. Little by little, my impostor voice started to subside, but something was still missing. Apart from my now-retired ex-boss, I had no role models. Most of my background had been in the technology sector, and I'd never seen communications make it to the boardroom. My instinct is to pick up a book whenever I want to understand something, so I went hunting for a book where I could read about the CCO role and figure out what was missing in my toolkit of skills. After browsing all the usual online book outlets, I couldn't find what I was looking for. This is when the idea of this book was born.

This book is written for two types of people and anyone else who's curious about organisational reputation. First, it is for all younger communications professionals who want to listen to good role models, people who have been in our shoes, and who have made it to the top table. As a profession, we must show it's possible to aim for the C-level, regardless of where we might have started.

Second, it's written for all Chief Executive Officers (CEOs) and other C-suite executives who struggle to understand the value our role brings to the table. My husband once said to me, "Why is it that whenever a new executive starts, the first thing they do is try to take over your function? Why is your role not respected, despite having worked in communications for 20 years and being the expert?" Many communications professionals laugh when I tell the story, recognizing the dilemma. I desire that CEOs and other C-suite executives who read this book will understand the role better and make a different decision, paving the way for many more communications leaders to be appointed, promoted, and respected for what they bring.

Reputation belongs at the top table. Many CCOs have worked hard to elevate the role. It's time for the next generations to cement their role in the boardroom. This book helps bring CEOs and CCOs closer together. It helps everyone understand the other person's perspective, values, and motivations. As a result, I hope CCOs will feel validated, motivated, and excited about the future.

When I prepared to interview the CCOs you will hear from in this book, I touched base with a retired CEO who played a big part in my career. His first CEO job was in the 1970s, when there were no communications tools and people were still using the monograph! Even so, building trust and reputation was always one of his keys to success. "The trust of an organisation is critical to success in the CEO role," he said. "Consistency and responsiveness, especially to colleagues, are imperative to running a business. A good CCO will help you deliver your message with thought, care, and honesty so the message lands in the best way possible. CCOs can help mitigate and manage crises in a way no one else in the C-suite can." His advice to CCOs and CEOs: "Trust and respect each other equally. There's no time to debate when there's a crisis, so you need to be ready to act."

Throughout the interviews, three top skills and attributes a great CCO displays shone through more clearly than others, apart from the obvious functional skills within the disciplines:

1. Critical thinking
2. Courage
3. Curiosity

The stories in these interviews give examples of CCOs who displayed these attributes and explain why they believe these key skills are intrinsically linked to the role's success.

If you're a CEO reading this book, you might ask why you need a CCO and what value they will bring to your leadership team. These interviews may be surprising, but very insightful. Some of the themes that come up again and again include

- Trust
- Partnership
- Seeing around corners
- A multitude of perspectives
- Joining dots

What results from strategic communications and a communications professional at the top table? A business with an excellent reputation where loyal employees want to go above and beyond, where loyal customers want to return, and where investors want to invest. Too lofty a goal? Let me know what you think after reading the interviews.

These CCOs come from various industries, different sizes of companies, and across business-to-business and business-to-consumer organisations. They include CCOs who work for non-profits, iconic brands, and lesser-known niche companies. The majority report to the CEO, a few to other C-suite executives. Each has a story to tell.

Everyone is passionate about their role in the success of their company. Everyone has a role to play in the boardroom. That doesn't always mean you see everything they do. For example, many commented on how the best crises are when there are no crises, and where they have been able to steer their organisation away from potential damage. That's invaluable and immeasurable. So, why wouldn't you want a CCO at your top table?

Tabita Andersson

July 2025

LinkedIn: linkedin.com/in/tabitaandersson/

CHAPTER 1

Monika Schaller
Chief Communications Officer SAP

Monika Schaller is the **Chief Communications Officer** for **SAP** (NYSE: SAP), a global leader in enterprise applications and business AI. Organisations have trusted SAP for over 50 years to bring out their best by uniting business-critical operations spanning finance, procurement, HR, supply chain, and customer experience.

Monika has more than 20 years of extensive experience in all aspects of communications and is a seasoned communications leader with deep expertise in global communications, political strategy, and crisis communications management. Known for her drive, energy, and positivity, she is a highly respected people leader who is passionate about compelling storytelling, which lies at the heart of great communications.

She joined SAP from Deutsche Post DHL Group, where she led Corporate Communications, Sustainability and Brand. In this role, she was instrumental in enhancing the company's reputation and positioning. Before this, Monika led corporate communications for companies such as Goldman Sachs, Citigroup, and Deutsche Bank. As part of her leadership roles in corporate communications, she also led strategic communications for executive Boards, helping them navigate multiple crisis situations. Monika started her career working for Bloomberg News, reporting from various locations, including New York and Tokyo, after a period as a sales trader at CA Investment Bank in Vienna.

© Tabita Andersson 2025
T. Andersson, *Chief Communications Officers at Work*,
https://doi.org/10.1007/979-8-8688-1856-1_1

Born and raised in Vienna, Austria, she holds a degree in Business Administration from the Wirtschaftsuniversität of Vienna.

For more information about SAP, visit sap.com.

Monika's LinkedIn profile: linkedin.com/in/monikaschaller/

Tabita Andersson: First, can you tell us a little about your career in communications? How did you start, and what does your career path look like?

Monika Schaller: I came into communications by chance. I started out in banking and worked as a sales trader early in my career. Then I joined Bloomberg, where I was a TV presenter covering financial markets: equities, derivatives, ETFs, and so on. I was based in Frankfurt, worked in London and New York, and later spent time in Tokyo.

After three years at Bloomberg, I got a call from a headhunter who asked if I wanted to build the communications function at Citigroup in Germany. At university, there was no such thing as studying communications as a discipline, so I didn't plan this path. But once I got into it, I realized I had found my true professional passion.

Tabita Andersson: How do you think that type of background, perhaps somewhat less traditional, helped you in your communications career over the years?

Monika Schaller: It helped enormously in terms of understanding content. I've spent most of my career, more than 20 years, in investment banking. I worked for Goldman Sachs, Citigroup, and briefly Deutsche Bank. Goldman Sachs, in particular, shaped my thinking. You could say my DNA is shaped by Goldman.

But the key takeaway is: it's always been about content and relationships. You can be a great communicator, write beautiful plans, and still fail—unless you understand what you're communicating. Content is king.

Tabita Andersson: What advice would you give yourself if you could go back to your early communications career, perhaps when you switched to Citigroup, having the benefit of hindsight and knowing what you know today?

Monika Schaller: I'd tell myself to trust my gut more. Like everyone, I've made poor decisions along the way. Sometimes I did things because others expected it, not because I believed in them. And those weren't always the best choices.

Tabita Andersson: How do you think communications professionals who are newer or younger in their careers could do that? Because it is so easy to fall into the trap of listening too much and wanting to please everyone.

Monika Schaller: That's very true, and there are a few layers to it. Some people naturally want to please others, but when you're early in your career and not yet established, it's hard to push back. You're still figuring things out, and it can feel risky to defend your own opinion.

The danger is, you become just an execution tool. That's a risk for the profession. Communications is no longer a support function. It's a real advisory role, just like finance or sales.

That's something I try to instill in my team: we're here to advise the business, not just to do what we're told. If you understand that from day one, it changes how you approach every meeting and every project.

I see myself as an advisor to the Executive Board and the Supervisory Board. But it's important to remember: giving advice doesn't mean it's always followed. That's okay. Decisions are often based on information we don't have. Our job is to offer perspective, flag consequences, and help shape the best possible outcome.

Tabita Andersson: Do you think these attributes help with working at the C-level? How do you work successfully in that advisory capacity with other executives?

Monika Schaller: Definitely. I work with a very strong group of executive and supervisory board members. They expect sound advice, and they respect pushback—as long as it's grounded.

But to get to that level, you need to earn their trust. You have to operate on equal footing. We're not here to say yes to everything, that's not the job. We're here to spot the issues early, bring solutions, and make sure leadership sees the full picture.

Tabita Andersson: You talk so warmly and excitedly about your role, so what do you enjoy the most about being a chief communications officer?

Monika Schaller: A crisis. Honestly: I love a crisis. I love tough situations. That's when communications shows its true value.

At Citigroup, I was still young and learning. Then I moved to Goldman Sachs just when the financial crisis started, and it felt like we were constantly in crisis mode. The pressure was enormous, but we navigated it successfully. That experience shaped me.

To this day, what excites me most is not knowing what will happen. If I wake up in the morning and can already predict my day—that's not a good day. I like the unexpected.

Tabita Andersson: I think many communications professionals are similar. At a senior level, you almost have to really enjoy a crisis because otherwise, you wouldn't be able to cope with it. You have to be calm under pressure consistently and work through a crisis with a clear head.

Monika Schaller: Exactly. The more hectic things get, the more you need to stay calm and grounded. When everyone around you is stressed, your job is to absorb that energy and bring clarity.

And that's also why communications needs to be different from other executive functions. A good communicator won't act or think like a CFO or a CEO. We bring a different lens and that's what makes the whole leadership team stronger.

Tabita Andersson: That's very true; we need to be able to debate different sides of the same problem or the same action. So, what do you think are some of the most important traits of communications leaders that you look for in your team?

Monika Schaller: First, you need to understand content, create plans, and execute tactics. That's the foundation.

Second, leadership. It's about how you treat people. Give them room to grow. Let them try things. And yes, let them make mistakes. Not the same mistake over and over, but we have to learn by doing.

Third, listening to your stakeholders is key. This is a people business, even as technology changes how we work. AI is the latest shift—and it's significant—but we've seen many waves of change over the years. None of it replaces the core of communications: passion, empathy, and trust.

Last but not least: team culture. I value loyalty. I've seen too many people use their access to power as currency. That's dangerous. In my team, I want people I can trust—and who trust each other. And we stay ego-free. Success isn't about personal credit. I have no patience for people who claim other people's achievements as their own. That has no place in my team.

Tabita Andersson: So what advice would you give to someone who's new at the most senior communications leadership level, who is just moving into a Chief Communications Officer role and taking that step up in terms of leadership?

Monika Schaller: Build your networks, both inside and outside the company. You need strong relationships with stakeholders: journalists, analysts, influencers, policymakers. These are the people you grow with over time. I've built my career alongside people who started out as reporters and are now editors-in-chief. Having people you trust and can collaborate with makes a real difference. And inside the organisation, it's just as important. Surround yourself with colleagues who share your values and can help move initiatives forward.

Tabita Andersson: You've touched on internal communications a little. How do you, and why do you think it's important that internal and external communications are aligned? What kind of value does that bring to an organisation?

Monika Schaller: Internal and external communications need to be aligned—especially when it comes to reputation. For me, internal is external. And vice versa. That said, I strongly believe they require different skill sets. But the messages must be consistent. I always say: whatever we write internally, assume it could be on the front page of the Financial Times tomorrow. That standard keeps us sharp and focused.

Tabita Andersson: As a publicly listed company, do you think that mindset is even more important than perhaps a private company that has a bit more leeway?

Monika Schaller: Absolutely. As a listed company, the scrutiny is different. Every communication can be interpreted externally, even if it was meant for an internal audience. The lens is sharper, and the stakes are higher.

Tabita Andersson: Also, on the point about leading communications for a publicly listed company, how do you balance the needs of shareholders vs. other types of stakeholders because you have other pressures as a publicly listed company, working with investors and shareholders in a different way than you do in a private company. So, how do you balance that?

Monika Schaller: At the end of the day, your most important asset is your people. But I believe in treating all stakeholder groups with equal respect. The difference lies in how we package the messaging, not in the underlying value we place on each audience.

Tabita Andersson: It builds the same reputation consistently but targets the message to each audience so it works for that audience.

How do you work and align messaging and communications across the organisation? SAP is a really large global organisation with over 100,000 employees and countless customers around the globe. How do you work with other functions, such as brand, marketing, sales, and product?

Monika Schaller: We align closely across the board. Everything starts with company strategy. From there, we define our communications strategy, typically over a three-year horizon, and develop yearly tactics within that framework. On a day-to-day basis, we work with Government Affairs, Investor Relations, and Strategy. But for key moments like Sapphire (flagship customer event) or major product launches, Marketing and Brand becomes a critical partner. In tech, this close alignment between Marketing and Communications is even more crucial than in other industries.

Tabita Andersson: Yes, when you get the right processes in place, they are easy to align. So, thinking about your team, how do you structure your communications team to best support such a large global business?

Monika Schaller: I take a fairly classic approach. We're structured into external communications, and what I call "employee and transformation communications." I changed the name because "transformation" better reflects the dynamic nature of our industry. We also have executive communications, a content team and colleagues focusing on for major company moments like Sapphire, TechEd, COP, the World Economic Forum—just to name a few. In total, we're about 300 people, around half based in Germany. About 35% are in the United States, which is a critical market. The remainder of the team are spread across Europe, Asia, and Latin America. This set up allows us to support the business in almost every country SAP is represented and operate in a "follow the sun" approach, enabling 24/7 availability.

Tabita Andersson: Further to that thought, what are some of the macroeconomic and geopolitical trends that you see influencing how we do communications more now than perhaps, say, ten years ago?

Monika Schaller: The overall discourse has changed quite dramatically. There's a noticeable difference between how US and European companies engage in public conversations. As communicators, we constantly navigate when to speak out and when to stay silent. What position does the CEO represent? What's truly relevant to our business?

My approach is pragmatic: companies should take a public stance when an issue directly impacts them. We speak up when there's a clear company-related connection. But I don't believe in making statements on every issue just for the sake of visibility. That can quickly undermine credibility.

Tabita Andersson: How can communications help a company through a crisis situation?

Monika Schaller: It starts with protecting the company's reputation—by providing guidance, by advising leadership, and by helping employees understand what's happening and get through it. Communications plays a key role in making sense of complex situations and turning that into clear, actionable messaging for leaders. That's our job: to advise the CEO and the Board with sound judgment.

In a crisis, tone really matters. You can't overreact—but underreacting is just as bad. And especially at Board level, you need to manage emotions. Not everyone will agree with every word, but they all need to be prepared to stand behind the message.

Tabita Andersson: You mention that a lot of this type of communication advice is done by the gut; it's a bit of a red thread throughout our conversation!

Monika Schaller: It really is. Or in other words: It all comes back to experience. In a crisis, gut instinct plays a big role. There is no "one-size-fits-all" approach and no shortcut through a crisis.

Some people just have a stronger instinct for consequences. I sometimes hear a sentence and immediately know it will cause issues, even if I can't explain exactly why. That's instinct. Part of it comes natural, but about 30% comes from experience.

And that's where experience helps. The more you've seen, the better your intuition becomes. Every experience adds to your ability to make the right call in the moment.

Tabita Andersson: As a result, do you think one of the key skills for a communications professional is being able to connect the dots because that's what drives and builds that experience and gut feeling?

Monika Schaller: Absolutely. If you're doing product comms, you need to be good at pitching, understand the product, know the journalists—and then go.

But if you're protecting a company's reputation, it's the small things that matter. One word can make a huge difference. That's where instinct and experience come into play. It's something you develop over time, and some people are naturally better at it than others.

Tabita Andersson: What are some of the biggest challenges that you see for the Chief Communications Officer right now as a profession?

Monika Schaller: We're in a perfect storm. The media landscape has changed dramatically, and the rise of non-traditional platforms has diluted quality.

Fake news is still a major issue and we didn't manage it well early on. That's led to a decline in trust across society, media, politics, and business.

At the same time, we're facing economic pressures. Budgets are tight, headcount is shrinking, and hiring the right talent is harder than ever.

We also see a shift in generational expectations. Many young professionals have different ideas about performance, effort, and feedback—and communications is still a business that requires resilience.

All these factors combined make the role more demanding than it's ever been.

Tabita Andersson: Taking into account all those external and internal factors, how do you build a great reputation for an organisation? What are some of the key things that you look at in your role and function to prioritize?

Monika Schaller: At SAP, we have a unique opportunity to shape industries and improve lives and that's a powerful foundation for reputation.

In Europe, we're well positioned. We have strong credibility and relevance. But in the United States, we're a smaller player and need to work harder to explain our value and the role technology plays in solving real-world problems. That's what builds reputation: relevance, impact, and consistency.

Tabita Andersson: SAP has got a fantastic reputation in Germany and Europe and has been a leader for such a long time. How do you keep up that momentum? How do you continue building that and not letting it wane away?

Monika Schaller: When Christian Klein became sole CEO five years ago, he initiated a major transformation: from on-premises to cloud. It was painful. The day he announced it, the share price dropped 20%.

But today, we're seeing the results. We have proven that we are a true cloud and growth company—all built on Business AI. Strong earnings, growing investor confidence, and positive media coverage—all show that we made the right call.

Still, we can't rest. Past success doesn't guarantee future success. If we don't transform faster than the market, we risk falling behind. Reputation is built through delivery and we have to keep delivering.

Tabita Andersson: Looking forward, how do you think communications needs to change and adapt in the next two to three years to better collaborate with the organisation in the way we are working and advising and keep improving?

Monika Schaller: We need to adjust to the new external reality. Traditional tier-one media outlets are still going strong, and we will continue to rely on them. Despite the growth of AI, social platforms, and new media formats, I believe trusted journalism from established publications will remain essential.

When I started in this field, trust was everything. It was about relationships and credibility. Then came the era where anyone could publish anything, often without oversight. But with AI on the rise, concerns about data integrity and misinformation are putting trust and the people behind it back in the spotlight.

At the same time, we need to meet younger audiences where they are. They want fast, informal, social-first content. So while traditional media remains key, we also need to double down on emerging platforms.

Another shift is how stakeholder groups are converging. Employees, investors, politicians–they increasingly expect similar transparency and speed. That's why I believe in one unified communications strategy, adapted to each audience. This clarity and consistency will be more important than ever.

Tabita Andersson: You've mentioned AI a couple of times. How has AI impacted your role and the team, and what do you do so far? How do you think AI will shape out in the future?

Monika Schaller: AI has already impacted all of us. With budget and cost pressures increasing, many companies immediately asked: how can AI help us reduce costs? That's the reality we're in.

But I see AI as an opportunity, not a threat. It can transform jobs, not eliminate them. Many colleagues wondered if they'd still be needed. My answer is always yes. AI can take care of repetitive tasks no one enjoyed. That frees us up to be more creative and strategic.

At SAP, we've built our own GenAI Hub, a platform that connects to multiple large language models and is customized to our needs. We're feeding it with our own content: CEO speeches, earnings calls, journalist profiles, and more. This lets us generate communications that actually sound like us.

Say we need a LinkedIn post about sustainability, the tool pulls from real, relevant materials and drafts in our tone. That's incredibly powerful.

The real challenge in large organisations isn't lack of information, it's finding the right piece when you need it. This hub helps us surface the right message, in the right voice, at the right moment. That improves speed, accuracy, and consistency.

Tabita Andersson: That sounds really exciting. It's not something a lot of companies are doing at the moment, so you're really at the forefront of using AI to improve communications, and that is super exciting.

Monika Schaller: It won't be perfect from day one, and that's fine. As we say, "garbage in, garbage out." The quality of the tool depends entirely on the data you feed it. But SAP has a rich base of communications material, so we're starting from a strong position.

I also want to mention tools like Microsoft Copilot. I recently used it to summarize a long email chain and within seconds, I had the key takeaways. That's real productivity.

Yes, some people hesitate because they think AI is too complex. But like the iPhone did with mobile tech, AI is becoming intuitive and accessible. You don't need to be technical, you just need to be curious and open.

Tabita Andersson: There is a different side to AI as well, in terms of the big systems out there, like ChatGPT or Claude, etc., the training of the LLMs and the possibility of hallucinations that could potentially be a reputational issue, though, for some organisations, if those systems are not trained on the right content, on the trusted content that's been checked. Do you see that as a potential reputational risk for organisations going forward?

Monika Schaller: Absolutely. Hallucinations and false information are a real risk. But this brings us back to the fundamentals of communications.

AI is a fantastic tool to get you started, but you still need someone to validate the facts. Just like in traditional journalism, there has to be a layer of quality control. Someone has to check the output. That's not a downside, that's a responsibility. You still have to use your brain, and frankly, that's a good thing.

Tabita Andersson: If you look back at the chief communications officer as a profession, what are some of the things that we've not done very well, and what do you think we can learn from that going forward?

Monika Schaller: I think we've often undersold ourselves. Measurement has always been a challenge. We need KPIs, of course, and without them, the Board won't fully value our work. But unlike sales or finance, the impact of communications isn't always directly measurable.

Some of our most valuable work happens behind the scenes: in what doesn't get published, in reputational risks we prevent before they surface. That's incredibly hard to quantify.

Early in my career, communications was often an afterthought. When there's a crisis, legal is called in. When there's a strategy project, consultants like McKinsey or BCG are brought in. But communications? Many people thought they could do it themselves.

In Germany, we say there are 84 million football coaches. In a big company, it can feel like there are 100,000 communications experts. We should have positioned ourselves more clearly and confidently.

The good news is, things are changing. Today, we have a seat at the executive table. We're involved early. Our voice is heard. But looking back, I wish we had pushed for that visibility and influence sooner.

Tabita Andersson: How do you think we can do that better going forward? Because I totally agree with you. I've come across the same challenge throughout my career.

Monika Schaller: It comes with experience, self-confidence, and delivering results. Trust is key. If the Board sees that your advice adds value, you move from being an advisor to becoming part of the inner circle.

We don't perform miracles. But we can shift a story from A to B. And that distance, that delta, is where our impact lies. That's how you prove your worth.

Tabita Andersson: If that's the case, how do you actually demonstrate and prove that value above and beyond KPIs because we all have the usual kind of KPIs, data, and metrics? Sometimes, though, it's the value that we provide above and beyond the metrics. How do you convince executives to follow your advice?

Monika Schaller: I remember a case right after I joined SAP. A Board member had issued a public statement that could have been damaging. I was pulled in to advise on the response.

Because there was trust in my judgment, we worked through the situation together. We aligned on what to say, how to say it, and how to manage the fallout. The end result was a solid statement, handled proactively and the issue was closed. That's what being on the front foot looks like. That's how you show value.

Tabita Andersson: Do you have any final nuggets of advice for aspiring communications professionals?

Monika Schaller: Trust your gut. Don't let others talk you out of your instincts. This job isn't rocket science, it's about relationships, understanding content, and loving what you do. I've always loved my job.

But the hardest shift for me was moving from head of media relations to leading the full communications function. I love media—I still talk to journalists regularly—but stepping back from that day-to-day work was tough.

I had to realize that media relations is just one part of the whole picture. Leading the function means thinking more broadly. That was my biggest transition, and the most rewarding.

Tabita Andersson: That's great advice for those of us who grew up in the PR and media relations world, who still have that passion and excitement when we see a new piece of media coverage. Here at Clarivate, we recently had a piece in *The Economist* this year, which I was super proud of. It's sometimes really hard as a leader not to just focus on that because you've got a big team, but actually, when you put your PR hat on, that piece of coverage on the front page of *The Economist*—it is just such an amazing achievement. And it's sometimes difficult for the rest of the team to understand how difficult it is, but it's also so amazing.

Monika Schaller: Totally. And that brings us back to KPIs. A salesperson has a KPI tied to revenue. An athlete has a time or score. An investment banker is measured by how much money they bring in. A journalist has their byline.

And for us in communications, it's those quiet wins. For instance when a board member departs unexpectedly or a supervisory board change hits the media, and I've made all the calls behind the scenes to ensure it lands right. There's no name on it, no signature, but I know it was the work of us, the communications department. That's our KPI.

CHAPTER

2

Jessica Alm
Chief Communications Officer Essity

Jessica Alm is the **Chief Communications Officer** for **Essity**, a leading global hygiene and health company. Listed on Nasdaq Stockholm and employing 36,000 people, Essity is the home of global brands such as TENA, Tork, Leukoplast, and Libresse.

The name Essity stems from the words "essential" and "necessities," and the company offers products and services within hygiene and health that make a difference every day in people's lives across 150 countries worldwide.

The company's purpose is to break barriers to well-being for the benefit of consumers, patients, caregivers, and customers across the globe, as well as for the benefit of society and the planet. As a business, by gathering insights, sharing experiences and partnering with other organisations, the company provides knowledge and promotes a public dialogue about societal challenges relating to hygiene and health.

For more information about Essity, visit essity.com.

Jessica's LinkedIn profile: https://www.linkedin.com/in/jessica-alm/

Tabita Andersson: To start with, can you tell us a little bit about your background. How did you start in communications and what does your career path look like up to today?

Jessica Alm: Sure, my career path might not be as straightforward as that of some other communications professionals. I started by studying for a master's degree in geology.

I grew up on a farm outside Uppsala in Sweden, and I was always interested in natural science topics and how things work, so that's why I decided to study geology, which I really enjoyed. My second topic was chemistry. I studied everything from how the Earth's processes work, like earthquakes, erosion, groundwater supply, and cartography, to climate change issues. Then I realized that in Sweden, most of the jobs relating to geology are in mining or hydrology, which are very rare and mostly located in the northern part of Sweden. In short, you can say it was a difficult job market to enter.

At the same time, I had always enjoyed writing and telling stories, so I applied to journalism at Uppsala University. It was a difficult program to enter, they only took on 20 students each year, you had to have a master's degree already, and you had to complete a practical test as part of your application, so I was fortunate to be accepted.

It was such an interesting education because we did a lot of practical exercises, everything from radio to television, and many of our teachers were active journalists. At that time, I realized that very few journalists have the opportunity to go deep into a topic, and I think it's even trickier today. As a person, I like to understand how things work and go deep into a topic. Just as I had completed my studies, I noticed a job that seemed to fit me like a glove. It was a job as a communicator at the Swedish Agriculture University. At the time, they had different centres of expertise for different topics, centres that gathered researchers and PhD students. This particular job was at the centre of excellence for sustainability questions in agriculture.

So that's how I started in communications, and I worked there for five years at the beginning of the 2000s. It was a perfect school for communications. I had the opportunity to do everything, from building web pages to setting up events to help the researchers get funding and helping PhD students write copy or do presentations.

I have then stayed in communications. My next job was with Sandvik, the global engineering group, and I worked for them for 17 years in different positions. I started off in internal communications, then went into marketing communications, and then, quite young, I took up the position of overall Executive Vice President for Communications. Sandvik is a large company that is present in 150 markets and has 45,000+ employees. In 2023, I started here at Essity as Chief Communications Officer (CCO) and part of the group executive management team.

Tabita Andersson: How do you think your role has changed between where you are now and when you started, and how does your current CCO role compare with your CCO role at Sandvik?

Jessica Alm: I think the field of communications has matured a lot since I started, especially from the company's point of view. In the early days, I would be hired to do a tactic such as an internal magazine, but we always ended up needing a layer of strategic communications within the company because we needed to explain the strategy or major changes and what was expected from the business. Of course, we still use internal channels, they are important tools but communications has become much more connected to what we need to convey from a company point of view and therefore you need to think internally, externally, omnichannel, etc., at the same time.

If I look back 20 years, I think the field of communications was quite immature. As the CCO role has developed, I think what's included in the scope has become much more natural, such as leadership communications, corporate branding and public relations which can convey what the company actually does, where we are heading and what its purpose is.

If we think back, even just a few years ago, not all companies spoke about their purpose. Now, it's almost a given for everyone to do so to create engagement and trust. So, I think the scope of communications has become more clearly defined, which also has a lot to do with the changes in our external environment. Today, companies need to be much more transparent and open and having established internal and external communications channels is expected.

Tabita Andersson: You mention changes in our external environment. What are some of those changes that you have seen impact the scope of communications and help it become part of everyday company life?

Jessica Alm: I think the world now expects more open communication. The media environment has helped to develop and put pressure on companies to become more open.

You can look at any sphere, like politics or business, and today, you more or less don't see anyone responding to anything that wasn't sourced or thought through from a communications point-of-view, but if you go back, say, 10 or 15 years ago, conversations were more unstructured. At the same time, channels have shifted, there's an openness on social media and increasing pressure for 24/7 availability. All of that puts pressure on having a more open but also structured way of handling communications. You can no longer wait three days to respond to something, and I think that pressure increases when you work for a global organisation.

Tabita Andersson: Thinking about the different changes the communications profession has been through, what keeps you in the role? What do you enjoy the most about being a Chief Communications Officer?

Jessica Alm: For me, it's probably related to who I am as a person. I really enjoy trying to understand things. I like to be able to see the broad perspective while having an opportunity to go deeper into what it means.

For me, the CCO role has to do with both where the company is heading and how you help support that from a brand point of view and the company position. How do you tell that story, how do you engage people around that, and how do you help close those gaps by using communications? I really enjoy working in that strategic direction.

At the same time, the CCO role can also be very operational, handling presentations, building channel presence, and enabling materials that are needed to bring people on board with the company's direction or strategy.

Tabita Andersson: What do you see as the biggest challenge for Chief Communications Officers and the communications function?

Jessica Alm: What we try to balance very much with my team is to set up a good structure and common objectives and ways of working, and then at the same time, you have to be very agile to the world around you. I think it's a balance between having a structured approach based on the company's direction and objectives and the impact you want to have on your target audience. You need to be rigid about your priorities but, at the same time, be very responsive to whatever is going on around you.

Tabita Andersson: On that topic, what is your opinion on how you manage the disparate priorities of different stakeholders, especially as a publicly listed company, with shareholders and investors as well as the usual target audiences? How do you manage the balance between them?

Jessica Alm: To me, it is not contradictory in any way. I think shareholders have very similar interests to many of the other stakeholders we manage, such as attracting talent, building public affairs relationships, or, for that matter, customers and consumer aspects.

I think shareholders are happy if the company is performing well; talent wants to join companies that are performing well, and it's very similar. So, the message is the same: it's about generating value.

Of course, you also have to set your priorities, which audience is of priority and then approach each audience with what is attractive to them and, in our case, what's most relevant in each market. Not every market is the same for us; in some, we need to build more public affairs relationships, in some, we need to generate more talent, and so on.

Tabita Andersson: How about your team? What does your team structure look like, how has that changed over the last three years? Will it change in the next three years?

Jessica Alm: If I go back to my previous employer first, we tried to create a very clear line of functional responsibilities. We had the brand and the content, trying to bring together all content planning across internal and external communications in a 360 approach. A job that I think has increased in importance over the last three to five years in corporate communications. Then, of course, the priority of efficiency in the communications channels, I think, is key, and then internally, it's about employee engagement, making sure people can access relevant information, but it's also about how you engage people, enabling employees to be your company and brand ambassadors. Additionally, ensure solid external communications and media relations.

So, if I look at my team now, we are organized around key functions. We have internal communications, public relations, and media relations, and we have an organisation that handles brand and content. Then, in our communications leadership team, we work to set common objectives for the entire corporate communications function—globally. In addition, we have in-country communications. We are quite lean as a communications function with limited resources from a group function and business unit point of view, so we are quite dependent on the country's communication resources for crisis communication, internal communication, leadership communication, PR, training, etc.

Tabita Andersson: Does that align with your overall House of Brand strategy and multiple product brands in so many different countries?

Jessica Alm: Yes, if I compare with my former world at Sandvik, which is a very decentralized B2B company, they still had a group brand and then a variety of brands because the type of customers and demands were very different depending on whether they were in mining or, say, metal cutting or construction. In that case, we were very dependent on the business unit's communications resources, and we removed the country layer because it didn't bring so much added value, because communications was more related to the business than the geography.

Here at Essity, we have more cross-synergies in the markets and a global brand-building and innovation organisation with shared benefits. Therefore, it has made much more sense for us to have common resources in the countries.

Tabita Andersson: What's your philosophy for building a team and attracting talent? What are the kinds of things that you look for in up-and-coming leaders and the rest of the team?

Jessica Alm: When it comes to my closest direct reports, even if they have their areas of expertise, like brand or PR, they also need to be well-equipped to understand and have an interest in the full corporate communications field.

A former colleague of mine once instilled in me, and I still think it's one of the best concepts for describing a good communications person: "You need to be a strategic worker." You must be very strategic in everything you do. At the same time, you must be able to deliver. That goes for the leadership roles as well.

Some people in communications are really good at communicating themselves, but that, to me, is not the same as being really, really skilled with your communications toolbox, which I think is what's needed to be successful.

Tabita Andersson: Do you think that's different from some of the other C-functions as well? If you think about the Chief Communications Officer as opposed to, say, a Chief Marketing Officer or a President of a business unit, do you think that's one of the things that sets the CCO apart a little bit?

Jessica Alm: Good question! If I look at my closest colleagues in the executive team, I think many of them are strategic workers. But you're probably right if I go all the way through my function, not only for the CCO role but for the communication role, it's probably the same wherever you look; I could pick more or less anyone in my team who has to have a strategic point of view but being able to deliver operationally at the same time. If I, for example, take the person who manages our website, the person has to be able to understand how to build and structure content from an audience point of view while setting the strategy for developing the web as a channel. To me, a good communicator needs to understand the strategic approach and be able to deliver on your everyday tasks.

Tabita Andersson: That's also very useful from a leader's perspective because, as a communicator, you need to connect the dots and have that overall picture of where the business is going and how it all fits together.

Let's switch subjects a little. What does a typical day look like to you?

Jessica Alm: That's such a good question. And such a challenging question. If there's one thing I would highlight, and perhaps this is related to who I am as a person, but on a daily basis, I focus a lot on the team. On team delivery and what's needed from the team, it might be a press and media situation, a brand development positioning project, or a campaign. Every day brings a different focus, but the common thread is the team performance and thinking about how we make sure we're always on track and, of course, align that with what we want to achieve in the long term.

Tabita Andersson: So, to build on that, how do you build a successful reputation for a global company? What are the tactics, the techniques and the channels you use? How would you explain what reputation building is to someone who doesn't know what goes on behind the scenes? I think a lot of what we do happens in the background, and people just see the end results.

Jessica Alm: Yes, I think one of the most important ways to build a reputation in a structured way is to have agreement across the company about what you are trying to leverage as a brand with your reputation. To me, ideally, you have full alignment between the brand and the kind of reputation you want to see. Since this has been my first year as CCO at Essity, we have spent quite some time thinking through this from a communications perspective, looking at the toolbox we have access to and figuring out how to better align channels and messages across the company, triggered by our business strategy. The brand reputation is, of course, about your purpose, vision, strategy, and how you bring it all together. Then you package that from a communications point of view, telling a story, bringing it alive and making it differentiated so that people can trust you. It takes a lot of thought to align every action and every element that you communicate. Be it an internal piece of content, a marketing campaign, or a media article—the message must be consistent and aligned to build a great reputation.

Here at Essity, we started with very broad communication and a lot of good activities, but as we move to build a trusted reputation, it's more about being selective and narrowing down what you do because you want to lead with the right key messages. Otherwise, you become more or less everything and nothing really specific.

Building reputation is about consistency and removing what shouldn't be in the story.

Tabita Andersson: Are we seeing a trend of narrowing down and personalizing communications to be much more targeted and specific now and perhaps even more in the future?

Jessica Alm: Yes, I think so, because there are things that are just taken for granted, right, things we should do as a globally responsible company. Things all of us should do. We are all trying to deliver great performance, grow the business, be profitable, compliant, sustainable, and lead with innovation. All of us, right? But reputation is about the difference between us and everyone else in how we do these things and/or what we do.

Tabita Andersson: And that is becoming much more important in an even more competitive and global world.

How do you think communications as a function and the CCO as a role can best work at a business executive level with your C-level peers?

Jessica Alm: I think it's very similar to other functions. It's about understating what's key to the company and what's key to the direction you're taking, and then you bring your functional expertise to the table.

Even though the communications function has matured a lot over the last few years, I think there's still a bit of immaturity in the role because a lot of senior people haven't been fully educated on the value communications brings to the table and how that's done. In other words, how you measure success. I mean, take Finance for example, of course not all of us are educated on all financial aspects, but all know that the Finance function is naturally part of the executive leadership team and acknowledge the value it brings. It of course also has to do with connecting it clearly to the company's financial performance, regulatory aspects, etc. All understand that this requires a skill set, competence to do things right, etc.

For communications, I think it's still, in some cases, related to seeing the clear value relating back to communications efforts. This is what we as a profession are still developing. If you look at different businesses across the world, overall, we're probably around 85% there. It's come a long way from where I believe it was when I started many years ago—there are more ways to measure value, more research studies that are available today within the field of communications, etc.

Tabita Andersson: Linked with that, I also think there's an element of commercial awareness that I see communications professionals needing to develop along the way. If you want to help the business and be able to advise, you need to understand how the business works.

Jessica Alm: And be selective. It's so easy to go wrong on communications and spend a lot of effort on something that is not worth anything, or very little, to the business.

Tabita Andersson: On that note, how do you think other executives, your peers and colleagues, can help the Chief Communications Officer be successful in their role?

Jessica Alm: I think it comes back to setting clear expectations for strategic priorities, knowing what's key to the business, and helping everyone understand. The clearer everyone is, the easier our job is!

Tabita Andersson: A topic in communications we either tend to love or hate is metrics and measurements. It's become much more sophisticated, I think, in our field over the last five years or so. How has the use of data impacted you and your team in the last two to three years?

Jessica Alm: Yes, I think, as we touched upon, what is positive is that much more of the communications efforts can be measured today. You can also cut the data to be more specific, even down to an audience level in some cases, to understand if you have achieved what you aimed to do.

One example is our employee engagement survey, which many companies do. When I joined Essity, we didn't have what I think is a crucial question in the survey: Does my manager communicate effectively?

We implemented it very quickly when I joined here, and it's so beneficial to have a key measurement of leadership communication even if peer-to-peer networks and other channels are growing in importance. I think highlighting highly relevant measurements helps bring attention to how good your communications are and helps you set benchmarks.

The same goes for external communications. There are, for example, good KPIs for the brand and how it resonates with audiences that you can put in place and then measure consistently to gauge your progress.

Tabita Andersson: So, do you measure your reputation and brand as well as internal communications?

Jessica Alm: We do, but there is still much we can improve in exactly how we measure tactics and track progress, particularly in relation to our communication efforts and systems. It is a real challenge, and many times, the choice to measure more involves costs. I think a tricky part for us is still to see exactly how we impact general awareness and how we impact our audiences. There are still layers in measurement effectiveness that we would like to improve.

Tabita Andersson: Isn't that type of measurement something we can improve as a profession as well, not just on an individual company basis?

Jessica Alm: Yes, I think what we see now is that what is added to our toolbox is artificial intelligence, which can help us put layers into our measurements with connections and analysis behind them. Adding tools like this will be very helpful for us to understand further how we are working as a function, but at least to me, it is still early days and an area we are exploring further

Tabita Andersson: I agree with the potential. How do you think artificial intelligence (AI) will impact the communications profession and your role going forward?

Jessica Alm: I think it will have a lot of impact. First, we are already seeing some impact with AI supporting content development and idea generation. I think it will soon move to create more efficiencies, improving the output of different channels, adjusting messages to different audiences, and automating tasks, which I think is good for our profession.

With that said, I think you will always need to have a kind of real craftsmanship to be able to quality-check and take responsibility for content. As we go forward with AI, I believe it will put the same requirements on most professions and for us in communications, it will probably transition our jobs to become even more relationship-related and focus on the human aspect.

Tabita Andersson: Yes, I would agree with that, and I would say that stakeholder relationship management will become much more important going forward because it's less about content and more about the human side of what we do.

Thinking about the profession again, what mistakes do you see many communications professionals make when they're creating a strategy to advise the business or perhaps going in new to a role?

Jessica Alm: That is such a good question. What I see happening sometimes is also part of being human. I think some are too quick to action, and it's easy, especially in the field of communications, although I'm not foremost referring to communications professionals. I think there's a lot of eagerness overall to communicate, share information, and be responsive. As humans, we're often quick to action. However, and especially in a communications leader role, I think one of the most important things to do is to not be the first to take action or be the most action-oriented person. At least not before doing your homework. We have to be the ones who actually think, okay, let's wait a moment and think about what we are trying to achieve, what's the impact, what's the structured approach, what's the audience, is it relevant, etc., because it's so easy to jump to action. I honestly don't think that's helpful at all for our profession because it often only contributes to what we already see—information overload!

Tabita Andersson: I think that's great advice. Stop and think. I often say that to my team as well. And that's the strategic piece of what we do and the strategic part of communications that makes it so valuable.

Jessica Alm: Yes, because the challenge is not to be creative and come up with ideas, right? You can come up with 500 different ideas to communicate something or reach out to a person or whatever it is. That's not the challenge. The challenge is to do it in the smartest, most efficient way, based on the need, not on anything else.

Tabita Andersson: I agree, and I think we've probably both seen too many people, too many communications professionals, jump the gun and then have to go back. Then you end up having to unravel everything and just end up in a worse situation than you were in the first place, so yes, I think that's great advice.

Jessica Alm: I have a great team here at Essity, but at the same time, one thing that we've worked a lot on was exactly that in our communications strategy. To explicitly state that we focus on the impact of what we do, we don't jump straight to activities; we focus on the impact.

Of course, we shouldn't sit and do nothing because that could also be misunderstood. However, in our field, just because we've done something one way in the past doesn't mean doing it in the same way again will be the best course of action. It's much more about understanding the situation, knowing why you're doing something, and making sure it's right for the right impact reasons before you act on it.

Tabita Andersson: With your experience in communications and at a senior leadership level, what nuggets of advice do you have for aspiring communications professionals?

Jessica Alm: If I had to pick one, it would be to stop and think. Also, leverage your business acumen. Of course, you're not going to be an expert on business management but use the experience you've built up and apply your functional expertise.

Then, I would say stay calm and focus on the impact of actions, not the actions themselves.

Lastly, remember your audience. This sounds so basic, but it's often just about getting the basics right, and it's easy to forget those if you jump to actions too quickly.

CHAPTER 3

Karen Kahn
Chief Communications Officer Intel

Karen Kahn is the former Senior Vice President and **Chief Communications Officer** for **Intel** (Nasdaq: INTC), an industry leader creating world-changing technology that enables global progress and enriches lives. Inspired by Moore's Law, the company continuously works to advance the design and manufacturing of semiconductors to help address our customers' greatest challenges. By embedding intelligence in the cloud, network, edge and every kind of computing device, Intel unleashes the potential of data to transform business and society for the better.

For more information about Intel, visit intel.com.

Karen's LinkedIn profile: linkedin.com/in/karenhkahn

Tabita Andersson: Why did you chose communications as a career?

Karen Kahn: At my core, I'm a writer—and that identity was cemented early in life through a pivotal moment. As a painfully shy eighth-grade student, I rarely spoke up in class. One day, an English teacher accused me of plagiarizing a writing assignment because it was too strong to be mine—or so she thought. After confirming it was my work, she asked me to read it aloud to the class. That moment changed everything. I found my voice—literally and figuratively. From that day forward, I became "the good writer," and that label stuck.

That experience didn't just give me confidence—it gave me a direction. Storytelling has been the thread running through my entire career. Whether I'm shaping a corporate narrative, leading through a crisis, or advising a CEO, it always comes down to this: understanding the essence of a complex situation and translating it into clear and compelling communication.

I studied journalism at the Newhouse School at Syracuse, then earned an MBA at Boston University. The MBA grounded me in financial fluency and strategic thinking and gave me the tools to engage as a business leader—not just a communicator.

I began my career in journalism, writing for *Inc. Magazine*, *The Wall Street Journal*, and *Frontline* on PBS. These were intense, competitive environments that taught me how to think critically, ask the right questions, and write under pressure. But more than that, they instilled in me a sense of precision, discipline, and accountability—qualities that shaped me as a future leader.

Over time, I realized I wasn't as drawn to pure reporting as I was to more nuanced, complex storytelling. That's what led me into communications. I started on the agency side (Weber Shandwick then Fleishman Hillard), where I learned the value of hustle, collaboration, and delivering client value in high-stakes, high-pressure environments. I grew quickly—not just in responsibility but in perspective. I built and led teams, grew major accounts, and learned how to drive both performance and purpose. But I also began to feel the limitations: the more I was promoted, the further I got from the work I loved. I was told, *"Why do you want to be a mechanic when you're so good at running the garage?"* I couldn't help myself—I have always liked being hands-on.

That's what led me in-house—and it's where I've built the most meaningful part of my career.

I've now spent the last two decades leading corporate reputation and brand at companies like Sun/Oracle, Broadcom, HP Inc., and Intel. Each role has pushed me to grow in new ways. At Sun/Oracle, I learned how to navigate in a powerful, founder-led environment where every word mattered. At Broadcom, I operated in an M&A-intensive culture that demanded strategic rigor and clarity under pressure. At HP, I stepped into true enterprise leadership—joining the ELT and learning how to find my voice in a room of very seasoned, deeply technical executives. I had to learn quickly that I didn't need to be the expert in finance or supply chain—that my value came from helping shape how the company showed up to the world.

This was a real turning point for me as a leader. I went from seeing myself as the person behind the scenes to realizing that communications is a strategic function that belongs at the centre of decision-making.

At Intel, I've taken that even further—stepping into the role at a time of corporate transformation and volatility, and serving as a trusted partner and advisor to the CEO and board. It's not just about messaging. It's about influence. It's about helping a company find its voice—and its direction—through uncertainty.

If there's a constant in my journey, it's that I've always been drawn to transformation. I thrive in moments of complexity, change, and reinvention. And I've grown the most as a leader when the stakes were highest—when the narrative needed to change, the culture needed to shift, or the organisation needed to rally.

Looking back, the leadership lesson has been clear: communications isn't a support function—it's a strategic one. It's not about being the loudest voice in the room. It's about being the clearest. The most trusted. The one who can see around corners, ask the right questions, and bring people along.

That's the kind of leader I've become—and it's the kind of leadership our profession demands more than ever.

Tabita Andersson: There are a couple of things that struck me about your career path in terms of skill set. You mentioned not having so much of an ego. Do you think that's a soft skill that's needed for a good communications leader, and what other skills do you think are important?

Karen Kahn: I don't lead with ego—and I think that's one of the most defining aspects of how I show up as a leader. That mindset has shaped the kind of teams I build and the people I attract. Someone once said to me, *"I'd rather work with a work horse than a show horse,"* and that's always stayed with me. I see myself as a workhorse—someone who leads from the front, stays close to the work, and is more focused on outcomes than optics. That approach has not only served me well, it's created the foundation for trust and credibility with my teams and peers.

There are CCOs who thrive on visibility—on being part of the industry circuit, building their personal brand, and cultivating influence in that way. And I genuinely respect that. But for me, influence has always come from listening, learning, and delivering. I've always gravitated toward people who think differently—engineers, scientists, operators, even skeptics—because those are the people who sharpen your thinking and expand your worldview. I get more energy from learning than from showcasing what I already know.

I've never needed to be the smartest person in the room. What I've tried to be is the most prepared, the clearest thinker, the one who can connect the dots, distill complexity, and guide others through uncertainty. And I've been fortunate to work in cultures—like HP and Intel—where substance matters more than style, and humility is valued over bravado. Those environments reward clarity, empathy, and grit.

That's also what I look for in the people I hire and promote. Grit. Angela Duckworth described it as passion and perseverance toward long-term goals, and I see it every day in the people who bring their best—even to the unglamorous work. The ones who care deeply about doing things well, who are relentlessly curious, who don't quit when it gets hard. That's the kind of talent I invest in, because those are the people who drive lasting impact.

In today's environment—where trust is fragile, change is constant, and communications is increasingly strategic—I believe a low-ego, high-curiosity mindset is not just a leadership style. It's a competitive advantage.

Tabita Andersson: Your background was in journalism. Do you think that was a good start and that your time as a journalist helped you on your career path?

Karen Kahn: My background in journalism gave me a strong foundation—but more than anything, it gave me confidence. I learned how to talk to everyone and anyone—from CEOs to academics to everyday people with compelling stories and insights. Journalism forced me to listen deeply, to distill complexity, and to write with clarity and precision. And most importantly, it trained me to never settle for the first answer. That mindset has been invaluable in corporate communications.

That said, I don't believe there's one "right" path into communications. In fact, I'm often more intrigued by people who *didn't* follow the traditional trajectory. I've worked with former lawyers who are exceptional storytellers, marketers who've made the pivot because they wanted to engage with deeper corporate issues, and people from public policy, investor relations, and even science backgrounds who bring fresh thinking into the discipline. Some of the strongest communicators I've hired had no formal training in communications at all—but they were relentlessly curious, strong critical thinkers, and had a deep instinct for narrative and influence.

That kind of functional diversity makes the team—and the function—smarter. It brings a richness of perspective that helps us avoid groupthink and approach reputation, brand, and stakeholder trust with nuance.

For me, coming from investigative journalism, the skill I still value most—and actively seek in others—is rigorous thinking. Writing, in my view, is the clearest expression of thought. I can tell immediately, by how someone writes, how they think. Are they clear? Are they structured? Are they persuasive? Do they ask good questions? In journalism, asking the tough questions isn't combative—it's how you get to the truth. That's the same approach I bring into the corporate world. I'll often start a conversation with, *"Help me understand why we're doing this,"* or *"What's the underlying assumption here?"* That kind of inquiry sharpens our strategies and ensures we're not just going through the motions.

Because if all we do is execute what we're asked to do, we'll never be seen as strategic partners. But if we lead with curiosity, ask smart questions, and challenge constructively, we become true counselors to the business. That's where the real value of communications shows up.

Another essential skill is understanding business. And that doesn't necessarily come from having an MBA. I've seen plenty of people with advanced degrees who still don't grasp the language of business. If you want a seat at the table, you need to understand how your company makes money, what your customers care about, what value looks like to them. Whether you're at a public company or not, understanding financial drivers, market dynamics, and product strategy is non-negotiable. Great communicators don't just craft messages—they understand the business deeply enough to shape meaningful ones.

Tabita Andersson: Commercial awareness is something I see lacking in some of the more junior communications professionals. How do you help communicators build that real commercial awareness?

Karen Kahn: The first thing I look for in someone on my team is their ability to start with a clear "why." If you don't understand the purpose behind a piece of work—what problem you're solving, what behavior you're trying to shift, what outcome you're driving—it's impossible to build a coherent strategy. Communications isn't about checking boxes; it's about shaping perception, building reputation, and moving stakeholders to believe or do something differently. That requires clarity of purpose from the outset.

But purpose alone isn't enough. I also expect a data-driven thesis. What is the hypothesis you're operating against? What are you trying to influence—and how will you know if you've succeeded? You need to define the desired impact up front and ensure the effort aligns with the level of investment. If we're spending time, budget, and executive energy on something, it must ladder up to a meaningful business outcome.

At Intel, we brought on Meltwater to strengthen our analytics capabilities—specifically around brand and reputation impact. The goal isn't just to collect metrics but to extract insight. What are we measuring? Why does it matter? If a campaign performs well, *why* did it work? What variables drove performance—creative? Timing? Channel strategy? Paid amplification? And critically, how did it influence our business goals?

This kind of thinking applies at every level. When I work with junior team members, I pay close attention to how they define success. If they're still saying, "*We secured 50 media stories*" or "*We had strong social engagement,*" I know they're stuck in a volume-based, tactical mindset. That might have been fine ten years ago—but not today. Today, we need to look at reach, tone, sentiment, resonance, engagement, conversion, and overall impact across the PESO model—paid, earned, shared, and owned. That's how we build integrated, credible programs that drive reputation *and* results.

And you don't need to be a senior leader to think this way. In fact, some of the most exciting talent I've worked with are junior communicators who bring that mindset from day one. I often find that people with strong agency backgrounds—especially those who've worked at firms with disciplined strategic planning and measurement frameworks—bring that kind of intellectual rigor. They understand that our role is not just to "get coverage" but to counsel, shape, and influence.

That's what separates executors from advisors. And that's ultimately how we earn trust, credibility, and a seat at the decision-making table.

Tabita Andersson: Do you also think we, as communications professionals, have become a lot better at using data? If I think back 10–15 years ago, data for comms was very basic. We were counting clips and looking at Advertising Value Equivalency (AVE) rates, and we've come such a long way in the last 5–10 years to be able to move to look at the impact of what we do, so we can move on from counting output and the number of press releases you've put out.

Karen Kahn: Absolutely—it's all about shifting from an *output* mindset to an *outcome* mindset. When I joined Intel, I inherited teams that were running at full speed, but often on what I call the hamster wheel—churning out activity without a clear link to impact. It happens a lot in-house, especially in large, complex companies going through transition. The instinct is to keep producing: more press releases, more content, more updates. But at some point, you have to stop and ask, "*What are we actually delivering?*"

I believe in doing fewer things—and doing them better. Focusing on real outcomes, not just activity. And sometimes, that means going back to basics: what are we trying to influence, who are we trying to reach, and how are we measuring success?

For me, especially in a company like Intel, it's also about understanding where communications fits in the broader business ecosystem. I think of it as a Venn diagram—communications sits at the intersection of government affairs, investor relations, marketing, HR, and culture. We're the connective tissue across all those functions. The real value comes when we align our programs with those areas, amplify their work, and contribute to strategic outcomes—not just generating comms for the sake of it.

That's what makes the work more meaningful—and more impactful. And yes, thankfully, as an industry, we've come a long way in the last 10–15 years. We now have the tools and data to track influence, not just output. That's a huge step forward.

Tabita Andersson: On your point about working with different stakeholders across the business and being in a publicly listed company, we also have additional investor and financial analyst audiences; how do you balance all those different priorities when planning and executing communications programs?

Karen Kahn: It depends on the plan you're executing and the phase the business is in. Right now, Intel is in the midst of a corporate turnaround, so nearly everything in motion is investor-centric. Communications are heavily focused on mitigating negative surface area—minimizing distractions so the strategy and business performance can shine through.

That said, priorities shift depending on the moment. For example, a few months ago, our communications were centreed around the CHIPS and Science Act—the US government's investment in semiconductor manufacturing. At that time, our work was more aligned with government relations, and we had to approach the market together, united in our messaging. That required building trust with a different stakeholder circle. So again, it all depends on where the business is headed and what it needs in that moment.

What I always come back to are four essential questions: What are we trying to achieve? Who are we trying to reach? What do we need them to believe? And how do we want them to feel? That last one can sound a bit soft, but it's foundational. It's where my background as a writer and storyteller comes in—bringing humanity to how a company communicates. You have to write like a human, not a corporation, and truly understand how people feel about your brand.

When I was CCO at HP, it was a different story because consumers had a strong emotional connection to our products. For better or worse, people felt something about their PCs or their printers. That kind of emotional connection matters, even when the story is driven by data

At the end of the day, effective communication—especially in a public company—means combining data, rigor and empathy. You need to understand the business imperative, ask the hard questions, and build programs that not only inform but also connect. That's the heart of what we do as CCOs. It's what makes the role so powerful—and frankly, so fun. We sit at the intersection of everything: strategy, culture, reputation, and customer experience. It all comes back to how you show up and communicate as a brand.

Tabita Andersson: As you mentioned, it's a fun job; what part of it do you think is the most fun?

Karen Kahn: What I find most rewarding—and frankly, most fun—about being a Chief Communications Officer is the opportunity to operate at the highest levels of an organisation, where communication truly shapes strategic direction. Having a seat at the senior leadership table doesn't just offer visibility—it provides a unique vantage point into the business, enabling me to influence decisions that drive growth, protect reputation, and fuel long-term value.

Like many CCOs I admire, the role places me in the centre of complex, high-stakes environments. Whether it's steering through organisational transformation, navigating geopolitical risk, responding to shareholder and public pressures, or repositioning products in dynamic markets, each day brings a fresh challenge. That constant problem-solving is what keeps me energized.

But what makes the role truly meaningful is the people. I get to collaborate with exceptionally smart, driven individuals who are as committed to excellence as they are to purpose. The creative side of the job—shaping narratives, inspiring action, and imagining what's possible—is where the real magic happens. It's not about executing a checklist. It's about pushing boundaries to spark innovation, build trust, and create lasting impact. That's when the work becomes not just exciting—but deeply fulfilling.

Tabita Andersson: What's your advice on how communications can help in these situations when companies are going through a turnaround or a tough situation, especially when you have a large workforce so you are also trying to bring everyone along on that journey?

Karen Kahn: It's hard—no doubt about it. But these are the moments when communications has its greatest impact. Just a few weeks ago, I led strategic communications for an unexpected CEO succession. It was high-stakes, high-pressure, and exactly the kind of moment where communications becomes the tip of the spear. Rolling out strategic news to multiple stakeholders—employees, investors, media, partners—requires clarity, speed, and trust. Good, bad, or messy, we're in the middle of it, helping the organisation make sense of change and chart the path forward.

One of the most critical roles a CCO plays during a turnaround is drawing a clear line between what's a communications issue—and what's a business issue. You cannot message your way out of a broken strategy or poor execution. If you try, you lose credibility fast. I've had people say, *"Karen, can't we just shift the narrative to something more positive?"* But here's the truth: the only thing that changes the narrative is performance. Four straight quarters of exceeding expectations—that's the story. Financial results *are* the narrative. Everything else is noise.

Just yesterday, we reviewed a chart mapping financial performance, stock price, and employee morale. They moved in lockstep. When the business struggles, morale follows. No internal campaign or email can paper over that reality.

So, what can communications do? We can tell the truth. We can be the ones in the room who say what others won't: what actually moves the needle, what employees need to hear, and how leaders must show up. Not with platitudes—but with authenticity. Our role is to push for real voices, real stories, and real leadership presence. We help shape not just *what* leaders say, but *how* and *when* they show up—and whether they connect.

These moments of disruption—a turnaround, a leadership shakeup, an identity crisis—are inflection points. You can fill them with corporate fluff, or you can use them to spark real momentum. Not everyone will come along, but if you lead with purpose and honesty, you'll bring enough people with you to start turning the tide.

Being a CCO is exhilarating when the company is thriving. But it's essential when the company is struggling. That's when you earn your seat at the table—not by spinning stories, but by speaking truth to power, championing integrity, and helping the organisation find its voice when it matters most.

Tabita Andersson: Spinning on that, what advice would you give to a new CCO who has just stepped into that situation? I remember taking that step up to the most senior level. It's quite a big step, and it's not easy to be prepared or even know what it involves because there's not much written about how to make a successful transition because part of it is exactly what you've been talking about, speaking honestly and directly with potentially some very powerful and influential executives that you are now sitting next to. What is your advice to someone in that situation, going through, or just starting on that journey?

Karen Kahn: It's a great question—because that step up is significant, and there's very little guidance on how to make it well.

When I was promoted to the executive leadership team (ELT) at HP, it was a hard shift. When I looked around at my peer group, I had impostor syndrome. I wasn't the deepest in finance, product, HR, operations, or any of the traditional domains. I sat there thinking, "*I don't know what they know.*"

I remember having that exact conversation with the CEO—who, funnily enough, now sits on Intel's board and remains a close friend. He said to me, "*Karen, that's not why I promoted you. They know those things because that's their job. Your job is to help us figure out how we show up—inside and out—and you're great at that.*" It was a turning point. I realized I didn't have to know everyone else's domain—I had to own mine. But finding that confidence took time.

In my first year on the ELT, I was quieter than I wanted to be. I needed to listen, learn, and observe, but I also held back more than I should have. In hindsight, I know I was playing small—something many women do. I underestimated how critical communications was, and how central it is to everything: brand, reputation, employee engagement, ESG—you name it. Once I found my voice, the function started growing because people began to realize the value of what we do.

For new CCOs stepping into that top seat for the first time, my advice is: *find your confidence early*. I worked with an executive coach for three years when I joined the ELT, and it was one of the best investments I made. It helped me stop projecting my own perfectionism onto others, and start holding my team to clear, consistent expectations rather than compensating for them.

My old CEO once told me, "*I never have to be hard on you because you're harder on yourself than anyone else ever could be.*" And he was right. That drive for excellence is what defines me—but it also taught me that I had to expect that same standard from others, not carry the burden alone.

Two years ago, I was inducted into PRWeek's Hall of Fame. It was funny, because I'd spent much of my career saying, *"I'm not a PR person—I'm a CCO, I run communications."* But looking around the room, I saw peers I respect deeply—heads of corporate affairs, real leaders in our field. In the video they played, someone I'd worked with said, *"Karen's the kind of person who can say 'this isn't good enough' in seven different languages."* I loved that, because it reflects what I believe: excellence matters.

Communications is not a dumping ground for people who didn't make it in marketing, or who aren't strong writers. It is not a place for mediocrity. If you want a seat at the table, you have to keep the bar high. Hold yourself to it. Hold your team to it. Because when done well, communications is at the centre of how a company thinks, leads, and transforms.

Tabita Andersson: That's a great point; we should all aim for excellence in everything we do. Looking at the CCO role from a different perspective, what advice would you give a CEO or one of your executive peers on how to work successfully with your CCO?

Karen Kahn: It's interesting that you ask this, because I just had a conversation with one of my peers about this very topic! When it comes to working with a CCO, the most important thing is building a strong, genuine relationship. And that relationship can't be transactional. It's not just about reaching out when there's a crisis, a speech to prepare, a program to launch, or an event to execute.

You have to invest in the relationship consistently, even when things are calm. In big companies, your reputation is your currency, and that doesn't happen overnight. It's about creating a two-way relationship based on mutual trust and understanding. This foundational trust is crucial—it allows you to navigate both the big moments and the smaller, everyday decisions with clarity.

Another key aspect is aligning on what's needed, expected, and desired. One of the reasons I have strong relationships with my executive peers is because I'm always thinking about their reputations and their personal brands. People often come to me asking for advice, *"Do you think this is the right approach for employees?" "Should we communicate this differently?" "What's the long-term impact of this decision?"*

I begin by asking a lot of questions. What do you want people to feel after this announcement? What's the emotional trajectory over the next few weeks? What are we really trying to achieve here? Communications is not a "quick hit" solution—it's a layered, strategic approach. It's about building trust, credibility, and emotional connections over time.

So, my advice to CEOs and executive peers is this: Take the time to build a thoughtful, ongoing partnership with your CCO. Don't wait for a crisis to establish this relationship. Be prepared to engage in deeper, strategic conversations that go beyond just executing the task at hand.

Tabita Andersson: Building that trusted advisor relationship and helping people figure out what the real problem is, coming back to what we said earlier about how there are things communications can't solve, and unless you know what the real problem is, you can't apply the real solution.

Karen Kahn: There's no one-size-fits-all solution, and you can't simply expect to change people's minds overnight. To truly address the problem, you need to understand the full scope of the situation, and that begins with data. You have to benchmark where you are and gain a clear understanding of the current state before deciding where you want to go. Without that, you won't have a reliable way to measure success or understand whether your efforts are making an impact.

The key is asking the right questions—what is the real challenge here? What are we trying to achieve? Communications isn't just about delivering information; it's about understanding the human element. People are emotional beings, and you need to navigate both the rational (the data and facts) and the emotional (how people feel and believe) aspects of any situation.

Only once you grasp where you are, both in terms of data and emotional sentiment, can you create an effective communication strategy that moves people forward and delivers real, meaningful results. Without this understanding, any solution you apply will lack direction and purpose.

Tabita Andersson: Is there any gold nugget of advice you want to add?

Karen Kahn: The best advice I've ever received is deceptively simple: *find work that you love*. Not every day will be perfect, and not every task will inspire you—but pursue work that speaks to your core values and leverages your natural strengths. Work consumes a significant portion of our lives, so choosing a path that feels meaningful can have a profound impact on long-term fulfillment and happiness.

If you truly want to excel, commit to working hard—relentlessly hard. Push beyond your perceived limits. Outwork your peers, outlast the challenges, and outgrow your failures. This lesson was instilled in me by my father, a son of immigrants, who showed me the power of grit and resilience. When I stumble or fall short—individually or as part of a team—I view it as a chance to grow. I often ask leaders a question: *"Do you love to win or hate to lose?"* For me, it's the latter. That mindset keeps me learning, striving, and evolving, no matter the setback.

Perhaps most important of all: attitude matters. People gravitate toward those who are positive, curious, and always learning. Bringing joy, optimism, and hope into the workplace is not just good for morale—it's a powerful force for influence and change. Being a force for good, both in work and in life, is a legacy worth building.

CHAPTER 4

Andrew Geldard

Chief Communications Officer Willmott Dixon

Andrew Geldard is the **Chief Communications Officer** for **Willmott Dixon**, the UK's leading independent construction and property services company. The company aims to deliver brilliant buildings, transform lives, strengthen communities, and enhance the environment so our world is fit for future generations.

In 1852, John Willmott undertook his first contract for £1. Since then, Willmott Dixon has grown into a £1 billion business that remains privately owned, family-run, and dedicated to leaving a positive legacy in its communities and environment.

For more information about Willmott Dixon, visit willmottdixon.co.uk.

Andrew's LinkedIn profile: linkedin.com/in/andrew-geldard-a950371/

Tabita Andersson: As someone who has worked as a Chief Communication Officer for a while, what does the role mean to you?

Andrew Geldard: The variety of the role is so great. One minute, when I spoke to a friend who has an art gallery in Soho about an exhibition, I came up with ideas to better promote our brand in that setting. The next minute, we've just done a show for Amazon Prime called Unsigned. I know the film director, and he approached me to say they were doing a show and needed a concert venue. They had identified a place that was run down. Many smaller concert venues have become tired, run down, and dilapidated, especially during Covid, which is thwarting the musical industry because it's stopping smaller acts from coming through. The new artists and musicians need the smaller venues to get started and grow their fan base. I thought it would be a great idea to provide a platform for new, unsigned musical talents that would have a platform to shine and perhaps even be seen to get signed and go on to do bigger things. That would also be good for our brand and the community, so I said, "Yes, let's do the film." We assembled the team, fitted out an old venue in Kentish Town and brought it back to life to be used in the film. You even see me in the film, in the audience!

That's just one of the Arts we support as an organisation because giving back to the community is essential. For us, being a good community resource and encouraging people to thrive in the communities where we work is important. At the same time, it's great for our colleagues. It helps everyone build a sense of pride in our organisation and what we do for people. It's one reason why Willmott Dixon was ranked Europe's fourth best company to work for by the Financial Times, and declared best big construction company by the Sunday Times' Best Places to Work guide in 2025.

For me, that exemplifies the Chief Communications Officer (CCO) role; it's about driving huge positive impact by taking advantage of opportunities.

Tabita Andersson: What characteristics do you think a good CCO needs?

Andrew Geldard: The ability to mold and bend to adapt and meet an organisation's constantly changing needs. A good businessperson and communicator will always think about what they can do to bring the most value to the business, spotting opportunities and making things happen that create business advantages. Don't wait to be asked, you need to be proactive, to think how to best move forward, or achieve something. Be in tune with the company and bring value to the senior team. By that, I mean being in tune with business demands, requirements, objectives, goals, and strategies and using what you can do to help the business accelerate and achieve its targets.

It's not about sitting down and waiting for the next assignment; it's about proactively looking to move the dial with your intelligence, abilities, experience, and vision. It's about thinking about what you can bring to the table to help take the business forward, being creative, and coming up with fresh, new ideas. It's about being able to adapt, be flexible, adopt new ideas, move forward with the latest technology, and do it in a way your senior team thinks, "Wow, that's brilliant, we wouldn't have done that otherwise."

To give an example, one of the problems I was recently thinking about was "how do we share and support learning among our team" and "how do we support learning among our senior female leaders" because one of our business objectives is to try and encourage more women into senior roles.

Overall, this is a big issue in the construction industry as it has traditionally had a very set demographic, which we are trying to change. It is slowly becoming a more diverse and inclusive industry, but we need to continue the journey where more women progress into more senior roles. One of the ways we are addressing this problem is through activities like having a senior women's leadership network, and one of the activities I brought to the table is a series of webinars with business leaders internally and externally. I've interviewed one of our senior female police commissioners, a female ex-minister of parliament and a female CEO of a large corporation, among others, giving them a platform to share their insights, knowledge, and story to inspire and equip the next generation of leaders. We've also run webinars on topics such as unconscious bias and imposter syndrome to help motivate leaders from across the organisation. This helps by giving leaders a space to hear and learn from others to continue their leadership journey. The webinars have become very successful as they are cost-neutral, the technology is here, so it's easy to set up, and I run them myself. I do the interviewing, we do some light editing, and then post. It is simple to do but has been very effective because we can cover a whole range of issues, from optimism bias to how to turn around projects that seem to be heading for disaster.

You can watch one example here https://youtu.be/ykC_aB4MdyE

Tabita Andersson: That sounds like an easy and effective win. Can you give us another example of the type of stories you have covered and how effective these have been?

Andrew Geldard: Another angle was to use them to comment on what's happening around us. For example, we commented on the UK national budget. When the budget was announced last time, a top commentator and I did an analysis, which was released both internally and externally. We had about 400 people listening live, and we've had several hundred more views on it afterward on YouTube. It went down really well. We even got good traction with customers who could register and watch it live, and their feedback was that they found the analysis very helpful to their businesses. It helps build brand loyalty and supports how we are perceived as relevant in the market by customers.

We did something similar with the Procurement Act, which came into force in Q1 2025. I interviewed a top lawyer and then worked with colleagues in the marketing team to drive footfall. It turned into a great webinar, with a good volume of people watching it live and on-demand. As a result, I plan to continue broadening out the series of webinars and learning opportunities this year as part of our larger strategy around predictable profit and sustainable growth.

Tabita Andersson: You mentioned your company strategy for profit and growth. How does communications as a function help drive these strategies and help a company through periods of perhaps less strong growth?

Andrew Geldard: It's well documented that Willmott Dixon's growth was hit by Covid, with flat turnover for the past few years. We're now back on track to being a strong business in terms of growth and revenue, and one of my goals as CCO has been to ensure that our goals of predictable profit and sustainable growth are part of our company vocabulary, so we are all pulling in the same direction.

I believe the role of communications when a company goes through these ups and downs is twofold. Firstly, we need to put the best words into the company vocabulary to articulate what the company needs to achieve. For us, it's the fact that we exist for profit. We build brilliant buildings for our customers, we have a purpose to give back to society, but we can only do this by being profitable. So, when our Chief Executive Officer and his senior leadership team, our divisional managing directors, etc., all talk to their teams, they have to be able to speak to the fact that we need to deliver predictable profit, which has to permeate everything we say and do. I've made a big thing about this in the past 12 months, in regular business briefing updates, which I choreograph for my CEO that is then sent out to the business.

These used to be sent out as emails, but today, we send them as short videos because they are more personal and it's an easier format to consume. We've had feedback from our colleagues to say they get much more from the videos. I shape the narrative, and my CEO works with it and add his own tweaks to suit his words; we then get to a point where we're both happy with the final script, so we set a time for recording. We tend to nail it in about an hour as he has the script and autocue and delivers it in less than ten minutes. After that, we edit and add imagery and graphics in-house to make it more engaging rather than just him being a talking head. We like to keep the briefings fresh and dynamic to build engagement over time.

Tabita Andersson: How do you measure the engagement with these video briefings?

Andrew Geldard: I look at the analytics. We have roughly 2,000 people in the business, so when I send out a link to the video via an all-staff email, we get around half of all employees watching it there and then. We also post a link to the video on our intranet so that you can watch it on demand in your own time if you can't watch it immediately, and we send it to shareholders. If we add the number of people watching offline to the online number, it's usually around 75%, which is good for a large organisation. We also post the script of the videos in a condensed, bulleted format. These are the key messages that our CEO wants to put across. I circulate them to our senior leadership team so they can repeat the same messages and reaffirm the keynotes in their local communications. That way, we're all on point and consistently have the same messages. These are the same messages we keep reiterating.

This year, these messages have been very positive; we've talked about growth, we've been able to talk about a record order book, new orders coming in, and achieving our goal of predictable growth and profit. We also talk about where we want to be and the emerging market trends, such as Net Zero, which is a big area for us and where we have positioned ourselves as a big contractor to deliver Net Zero combination buildings. There are many market opportunities for us now that we have to develop further skills to take advantage of. Also, overall, this helps us build a feel-good factor because we want our people to feel engaged and part of the process. We want them to feel part of something big.

Another key message we want to convey is that when you work at Willmott Dixon, it should feel like a lifetime career. In internal communications, we weave this message into everything we do. For example, tomorrow, I'm sending out a story about all the promotions we did at the beginning of the year. This is not typically a big announcement; it could easily become routine or short, but around 5 to 6% of our workforce receive promotions at the start of each year. We want to celebrate this, but also reinforce the fact that there should be no other company on their mind where they want to work. We want our people to feel that their career aspirations are met here at Willmott Dixon, and that's a big issue for retention because we want to retain the best people. After all, that's good for the business, but it costs a lot more if we replace people regularly. We need stability for the company to thrive.

I mentioned that I believe the role of communications when a company goes through ups and downs is twofold. Firstly, we have to put the best words into the company vocabulary to achieve what we need to do. Secondly, we have to keep repeating the key messages we want to convey. One of the tactics I'm using for this is to roll out an insights video series, which is part of our predictable profit strategy, where we are demonstrating the outcomes that drive growth. For these videos, we interview our delivery teams about their building projects, what happened, why they're successful, what they learned, and what lessons they would pass on so they don't make the same mistakes again, and we capture key details that may otherwise get lost. These are half-hour interviews broken into bite-sized segments that all colleagues can view on demand. It's so easy for our teams to finish a project and then move on, but by capturing learnings on video, we can share best practices and knowledge much more widely than before. We also have a Willmott Dixon University, which is cool as we try to encourage more learning throughout the organisation.

Tabita Andersson: We've discussed different communications tactics and strategies, and you mentioned the move from email to video. As you have been in your CCO role for a few years, how have you seen how people consume content change? Do you think it's changed dramatically in the last 10–15 years, and how have we as communicators had to adapt?

Andrew Geldard: I think the advent of the smartphone brought on the change. People are always time-poor. They also have a low attention threshold. You are no longer prepared to cut through stuff that's not relevant, interesting or useful to you personally. People do not owe you their attention; you have to earn it.

Looking at our most recent business update with the CEO, we found that when we got to about seven minutes into the video, there was a steep 20% drop-off rate. I thought to myself, I wonder why this is, and then I realized that at this point, the CEO had started to talk about something that probably wasn't particularly interesting to the larger part of the audience. It was interesting to us, but looking back, perhaps we shouldn't have included that particular section. Looking at the metrics and analytics, we can immediately tell what content people are engaged with and where they drop off. We could tell that the first seven minutes were excellent, consistent engagement with no peaks or troughs, but then the engagement really changed, and that's now something we need to learn from and use so we can adapt and tailor our content better the next time. It means I can go back to our CEO, show him the data, learn from it, and we can then work on something more engaging.

Going back to how people consume information and how this has changed, people are time-poor and have a very low threshold for boredom. They will switch off once they decide they are no longer interested, or it is not relevant. I think a trap that's easy for communicators to fall into is thinking that we know what people want to see and read, but actually, it's up to them. As communicators, we have to see things from their perspectives. We have to learn how to make the content as interesting and valuable for them as possible.

It's exactly the same thing as engaging with customers. We have to see the world through their prism. It doesn't matter if you're a customer, a stakeholder, or an employee; everyone has their own challenges, perceptions, wants, and needs. A company telling them how successful they are is not a big thing for them, but if a company can engage them about ideas and areas that will help them improve, that matters, and suddenly we become interesting and helpful. Whether providing knowledge or information or solving a problem, it matters if it's relevant to that audience.

Tabita Andersson: Let's pivot to talk about technology and perhaps the role Artificial Intelligence (AI) will play for us in communications. What's your opinion? Can you share any examples of what you are doing in this area?

Andrew Geldard: AI is such a buzzword, but seeing what it might bring to our profession is exciting. I'm currently trialing a new AI solution, working with a US-based company on synthetic data. We've had real-world data for a while, but it's difficult to acquire, expensive, lengthy, and time-consuming to curate. How cool would it be if you could easily get hold of synthetic data, which is 95% accurate, at a fraction of the price and time than real-world data?

One of our companies is a housing repairs and maintenance business. Its new strategy is based on the three pillars of net zero, minor capital works and major maintenance projects. Its customer base consists mainly of local authorities and housing associations. They have a fantastic list of around 1,000 organisations of people they work with, and I'm now working with a technology company to use this data to build synthetic customers. Once completed, we can start talking to them and build our knowledge about how to best work with real customers. It means we can more quickly and accurately build up personas and then ask them how they would buy a particular product or look for a solution to whatever problem they may have. You can ask them anything, and they reckon it's over 90% more accurate than a real person's answers. That said, this is a trial, so we will see what comes from it in a few months.

Being opportunistic is an important facet of being a Chief Communications Officer. AI presents a great opportunity, but CCOs should always be harvesting new ideas, tactics, and technologies and then sifting through them to develop solutions that make a difference. The sifting is crucial because we only have so much bandwidth to do things, so we have to be very determined and focused.

One of my personal mantras is to try to do the role of two or three people at half the time. I want to do that because high productivity is one of the keys to success in this role and is also good for the business. In communications, we seldom have access to big budgets or big resources, so we always have to be more resourceful. We have to use technology such as AI to help us figure out how to do things better and smarter, so we don't waste time going down blind alleys.

For me, being a good CCO means coming up with creative ideas and creative solutions to problems. I don't feel comfortable spending huge amounts of money just because the business can. I believe in establishing business cases and rationale for areas with the most return. For example, we've recently supported a campaign around diversity and inclusion in an industry publication called Construction News. It's a nominal five-figure, but we get a very clear return on that investment, a wide range of activities such as profiling, networking, recruitment, promotions, etc., that are all aimed at driving awareness in the right area for us. We've already seen how people have been recruited on the back of it, which is excellent and aligns with our brand values.

Aligning campaigns and programs around brand values and what reputation you want to build in the marketplace is key for us. We want to be seen as a forward-thinking company that's embracing diversity and inclusion, and is a great place to work, a place where people thrive, develop and grow their careers. Attracting the right talent is a massive issue for us in construction, and there's a skills crisis. There's only a finite number of skilled people out there, and for us as an industry, we're battling with recruiting more people and encouraging more people to train in the trade skills we need. Encouraging more people to join the construction industry has always been an issue, and we now discuss how we need to look at the next generation of talent coming through and choosing construction vs. other sectors, like PR, marketing, law or accountancy. It's a battle. We're doing okay, but we need role models. One of the opportunities I'm looking at is how we create these role models and the excitement about working in our industry. I believe the clue is in dealing with some of the perceptions and stereotypes. It's not about working long hours; it's about showing all the different roles and disciplines you can work in within construction. There are so many opportunities in HR, design, project management, or whatever you may want to choose. We also offer a very agile way of working where you don't constantly get stuck in one place; we're trying to create an environment where people feel they can have a good work-life balance.

This is one of the things we've learned from the COVID pandemic. To encourage more women and more people from all parts of society, you need to have a more agile, more flexible workplace so people feel like they can balance other challenges in life, such as childcare. One of the issues we often get, particularly with women, is that when they have families, it tends to be the women who disappear from the workplace for a few years. How can we make it as easy as possible for them to balance childcare so they can still maintain a career? This is one of the main reasons we see a drop-off of women moving into senior roles, because they take a few years out and then play catch-up. It's an area we need to address. In addition, we may also want to look at a four-day working week in the future and how we manage agile working on sites. Currently, remote working on-site is difficult; managing people remotely is hard. We've done some trials but have found that people have to become more productive, leaner with their time, conduct more focused meetings and have great team ethics.

It's working for us, given that the FT ranked us as the fourth best company to work for in Europe in 2025.

Tabita Andersson: We've talked a lot about internal communications aimed at colleagues and building a workplace brand, but how about managing reputation from an external perspective, from a customer viewpoint? How do you build a reputation as a leading construction company that wants to attract the right type of customers?

Andrew Geldard: We've been talking quite a bit about trying to get key messages weaved into our language, mentality, and culture because one thing a CCO can and should do is influence the thinking of the business. When it comes to customers, they want you to win; they want you to be successful. You don't want to work with customers who don't care if you lose money, so the language we use externally for customers and potential customers is equally as important as internally.

We still see high-profile insolvencies in the construction industry, so we need to communicate the risk profile and risk allocation on projects. We want our customers to think we are a fair and highly sustainable business with a rich and proud heritage. We've been around for a long time, next year we celebrate our 175th anniversary, and that's important in our industry because our customers want to work with a company that they can trust and depend on, a company that is in tune with its values, which for us is social mobility and purpose.

One of the things I've worked very closely on is our purpose. We wanted to be seen firmly as a purpose-driven business, not just to our people but to our customers. We were talking about purpose at a time when it wasn't that much in vogue, 20 years ago, and we set some stretching targets around the pillars of our purpose, such as sustainable development, zero waste, and reducing landfill. The good thing about setting targets is that it establishes and shows who we are. It tells the world what we stand for and that we are a responsible business. We've been here for 175 years and want to continue to be here for a long time into the future, meaning you have to be responsible and consider the legacy. What legacy will you leave for future generations? The purpose permeates a lot of what we say and how we operate as a business because we want to leave a world and a society that's fit for future generations to thrive in.

Being purpose-driven is a big thing in business, generally now. Twenty years ago, when we started talking about it, others were talking about turnover growth and other financial terms without thinking about the legacy we're leaving that will create significant opportunities for future generations to thrive. This is something we've worked hard on building, and we found that particularly younger people like to work for a business that's in tune with its purpose. When I look at surveys among young people, they often reply that working for a company with a purpose is more important than money. Obviously, money is essential, and you have to provide the right package, so we're not out-turned on that. However, people like to feel they are part of creating something that will contribute to a better future. Especially now, with climate change and other environmental concerns, we don't know how our actions will impact our future. We are starting to see migration movements based not only on economics but also on climate change, with people moving from places that are no longer hospitable or habitable. Here at Willmott Dixon, we continually think about our role, how we are either complicit in the change or what we can do to mitigate some of these outcomes.

Tabita Andersson: Those are some bold statements and significant challenges. How do you work with your peers in the C-suite to tackle these issues? Some senior executives may not agree that these are valuable conversations and are stuck in their old, financially driven way of thinking. How do you navigate that situation?

Andrew Geldard: Setting the principles and values comes right from the top. The executive chairman and CEO set the tone and take the lead, and then everyone else buys into it. We have a strong leadership team with a solid focus on sustainability and ESG, and we have started to have more diversity on our Board of Directors, which is important to us because of the family dimension of our business. Our Executive Chairman is the fifth generation that runs our business, so if you come to work here, you will work with a company that is 100% focused on what the legacy of the business will be for the future. So, it's not necessarily about convincing other executives to value the same thing; it's about ensuring our behaviors, policies, and actions align with our values. It's about ensuring that what we're doing will be a testament to the business, so it's a happy medium between doing the right thing and ensuring it works for us and our customers.

Tabita Andersson: That makes sense. Building on that, what advice would you give to other executives on the leadership team on how to best work with you and the communications function?

Andrew Geldard: Tell a cohesive story. It's one of the things that has grown in importance, and the use of storytelling as part of business strategy has grown exponentially over the past ten years. Today, you can't just get on with business-as-usual activities and not consider how your actions affect or impact people, the workforce, and other stakeholders. You have to make sure you bring people along with you constantly, and that's down to telling the story. It's about keeping people engaged and feeling part of something brilliant that impacts society.

Going back to your question about the CCO role and the value that the communications function generally plays in support of the business, going back 25–30 years ago, communications was seen as dealing with the press. We have a press office, and they deal with anything relating to the media. In fact, I was once classified in a structure chart under the term "media relations," no personal name, just that. Back then, companies held conferences and needed help with messaging, so the press office got involved because communicators were good at joining the dots. For me, the key thing here is joining the dots. There are so many dots around a business that need joining up, and the communications team is best placed to be curious, spot the dots, and join them. By joining up the dots, the messages, and the stories, you create something even more powerful than what you have. That's why I say to anyone in this role that being able to join the dots is a powerful skill to have because no one else in the business can do that, and that's the valuable part you bring to the table.

At the CCO level, you have to continuously consider the value you add and spot the gaps and opportunities. About 80% of what I do is bringing new ideas to the table rather than having people ask me to provide services. My role is advising and counselling on what we should be doing, how we measure it and how it dovetails into the ultimate, overarching business priorities of a brilliant, engaged, and motivated team creating fantastic products that people love, which brings more repeat customers and delivers profitable financial performance. All of these things are the essence of a business; everything else we do feeds into that essence, so we need to constantly think about how we add value to this process.

Here at Willmott Dixon, we have distilled this into three principles that we constantly connect everything back to: having a lifetime career, brilliant buildings for our customers, and predictable profit for the future. In communications, I believe it's our job to connect everything we do to these principles.

Tabita Andersson: Let's move to a slightly different topic regarding skills and expertise for communications professionals. What areas of learning and development do you think more junior colleagues should look for when trying to build their careers?

Andrew Geldard: I always recommend understanding the business first if you are in a junior communications role. Understand the drivers and the language of business rather than being on the periphery. It can be very easy to think that it's up to the commercial people, it's up to the executives or the CEO to know the language of the business, and we're just here to serve them and do what they tell us. But I believe you have to be seen to understand the language of business, profit and loss, whether a business makes money or not.

In addition, also understand the value of data and how you can use data to inform decisions. I've been doing this much more recently, trying to understand the data around projects in more detail, which projects make money, which ones don't, which sectors are more profitable, and then understand the trends. As a communicator, it's my job to bring these trends to the front, to inform people and say we looked at the data, and here's what we saw and need to explore. Being able to ask those questions and bring those observations to the table to help drive the business is an important skill. Sometimes, it's easy for communicators to believe in their hype and think we need to go big with our tactics. Still, it's important always to question yourself and be curious because that's how you come up with something that will add real value to the business rather than just accepting it as it is and not challenging things.

Tabita Andersson: That's great advice for junior and senior communications professionals: always be curious and always question.

Andrew Geldard: Being proactive and on the front foot also helps bring visibility to your actions. For example, at the start of the year, I sent my CEO a note to say, these are our priorities right now; this is what we're working on, and boom, he phoned me, and we had a great chat about the plans, and he felt comfortable to sign off on our focus. It just showed that you need to be constantly on the front foot, having a sense of proactiveness. I also put together a schedule for the year, telling everyone about the upcoming activities, so I'm on it immediately, informing teams about how the year looks, all the key milestones externally and internally, all corporate dates, business briefings, etc.

Visibility is key because sometimes, you can get consumed and think you're doing a great job in this role. You're happy about it and pleased for the team, but if people aren't seeing that success and not feeling it, that's a shame because you're not getting the respect and appreciation you deserve. I would always make sure that part of the job is to promote being a community. A communications person is not only making things happen but also is responsible for making the job visible, presenting it, and selling it clearly. We should never assume that people will consume what we do because everyone is always busy and has different priorities, and it's not their job to know what's happening. Therefore, I think we must blow our trumpet without being too much in people's faces, just to make it clear what we're doing and what value we're bringing.

For example, we put together a report at the end of the year that encapsulates highlights and statistics. Still, I also think it's important to share successes during the year as a reminder of the value you bring to the organisation and share with multiple stakeholders, not only the Board and the CEO but also throughout the organisation with all the people you want on your side because we want colleagues and leaders at all levels to be your advocates. Being mindful of how we serve people across the business and what ideas we bring ensures that they stay engaged and learn about our fantastic service.

For me, junior communications professionals need to understand and build their networks, the drivers behind the perception of a successful service and how to make an impact. Here at Willmott Dixon, for example, we have a great team of regional managing directors, and I make sure that I have a good working relationship with them. In communications, we can't operate in isolation; we have to be ever-present so our stakeholders can see that we're real team players.

Something else we do here at Willmott Dixon that contributes to engaging colleagues is an annual "Above Beyond Award." Our chairman, who was previously our CEO, came to me with the idea for the awards, and he wanted peers and colleagues to nominate their colleagues who have been going above and beyond in their work, those who are exceeding expectations. He and I came up with the idea that anyone can nominate or be nominated, and the award is the amount of money that corresponds with the year, so last year, it was £2,024 per winner, and they get paid in November, right before Christmas, which is brilliant. After the idea was planted, my team was then tasked with working out the plan for how to get it implemented and rolled out.

This aligns with a trend I've seen recently: the morphing of the CCO and Chief of Staff roles, which is an interesting concept. If you look at the wide variety of roles across the business, many aspects, like Chief of Staff, could easily be assimilated into the CCO role. If you want to be progressive and look into the future, you could even argue that roles relating to people, culture, and ways of working could be morphed. Even looking at client retention and customer experience, you could create a super area where a chief operator and communications officer look at all these areas. Communication is at the core of all of these areas. As I work very closely with our CEO, there are lots of things I do that would probably fall under the traditional Chief of Staff category, but because I'm in the room and I have the skills and abilities, I'm picking up responsibilities beyond traditional communications, especially when it relates to culture, which is very much driven by and a large part of what we do in internal communications.

Tabita Andersson: Yes, I've seen that in recent years with communications being part of the Chief of Staff agenda. I also tend to pick up things like organizing the senior leadership kick-off meetings or events, because we happen to be good at doing events. Like you, I've also seen the role bridge the gap with Chief of Staff responsibilities more now than ever before.

Andrew Geldard: If we look to the future regarding productivity, efficiency, and leanness, CCOs should also be used as Chiefs of Staff because they get things done. It means the CEO or Chairman of the Board can come and ask for communications tasks to be done, and we can just easily roll with it. To give you an example, my CEO recently shared with me that he'd seen some interesting films about shared learning, and he wanted to know what we could do about it, so it became my responsibility to figure out what we could do. I took the task away, looked it up, and had conversations with several other functions. We could have gone down the road of building a new platform and involving a big team, but it was getting too complex. After investigating the various solutions, I returned to our CEO and said I'd create our own content and roll it out in a straightforward way. That's how Project Insights was born, which we talked about earlier. It's a simple solution to a potentially complex problem, and one way that communications can bring value.

In terms of encouraging the future generation, I would say to anyone who wants to develop and grow, just look at what the business wants and needs, what dots you can join up, and what things you can bring that no one else brings. That will nail your personal value and the value of the communications function.

CHAPTER 5

Pernille Sahl Taylor
Chief Communications Officer Handelsbanken UK

Pernille Sahl Taylor is the **Chief Communications Officer** for **Handelsbanken UK**, a relationship bank with a decentralized way of working, a strong local presence due to a nationwide network of branches, and a long-term approach to customer relations. Handelsbanken specializes in providing banking and wealth management services to private and corporate banking customers. Handelsbanken was established in Stockholm in 1871, and its home markets are Sweden, Norway, the Netherlands, and the UK. It also has operations in Luxembourg and the United States.

For more information about Handelsbanken, visit Handelsbanken.co.uk.

Pernille's LinkedIn profile: linkedin.com/in/pernillesahltaylor/

Tabita Andersson: Handelsbanken is a decentralized organisation focused on building trust and relationships with local customers. How are you set up to manage communications?

Pernille Sahl Taylor: We did a small restructure in the team at the beginning of the year, which reflects better how we currently work as a team and how communications as a function has evolved in Handelsbanken over the years. We have an internal communications team that manages employee communications; we have a corporate and customer communications team that looks after all external communications, public affairs, PR, and customer communications; we have a brand communications team that covers copywriting, graphic design, our website as well as brand and branch communications. In addition to this, we have a strategic lead on content who looks after all our content, including social media.

In summary, we look after all communications activities across the bank, internally and externally, as well as the brand. Even though we are a decentralized organisation, we have some centralized pillars—our brand is one of those along with our HR and credit policies.

Historically, branches have been empowered to do the marketing they deemed necessary in their local area to attract the right kind of customers, while operating within a framework of centralized brand guidance and policies. However, we are now at a stage on our growth journey in the UK where we need to raise more awareness of our bank with our target audiences. We are a bit of a hidden gem, and we want to tell more of our target audiences who we are and how we might be able to help them. We have therefore embarked on more centrally driven marketing activities, collaborating very closely with our branches in a way that sees us looking after activities that drive brand awareness and consideration and the branches doing what they are experts at—building and nurturing customer relationships through local networking activities. Any marketing activities will always be very focused and targeted as we're not a mass-market bank. We will always be aiming to strike the right balance between raising awareness of who we are and driving the right type of traffic through to the branches. Fortunately, the technology and data we have available today enable us to do marketing in a very targeted way to reach our specific customer target audiences. So, that's what we're starting to do now, which is really exciting. We're in the process of planning a campaign that will help us raise brand awareness with our target customers and hopefully boost growth.

Tabita Andersson: How exciting! It's always thrilling to start a new big campaign and see the eventual results. How do you align your marketing activities, such as the new campaign, with building the reputation in the market that you need? You mentioned not being a mass-market bank, which means you need to build a reputation as something niche or specific. How do you go about doing that above and beyond the campaign and traditional marketing activities?

Pernille Sahl Taylor: What you want is marketing and PR (public relations) working hand in hand. While marketing can be used to raise brand awareness and raise the profile of the brand, we drive trust and credibility in our brand through our PR activities. For us, this means promoting the expertise we have in the bank. For example, by promoting the expertise of our Chief Economist and our UK Economist and other bank spokespeople in the media. We also draft op-eds (a written piece typically opposite an editorial page that has an opinion or comment on an issue relevant to the readership audience) on behalf of our experts in the bank to pitch to the media. The themes we work with range from specific financial expertise to promoting the values of our relationship banking approach. This all helps to promote our brand with our target audiences alongside the great work our branches do in their local communities to build relationships with existing and new customers. For us, it's about empowering all of us in the bank to do what we do best and then collaborating effectively to drive growth.

Tabita Andersson: As you go about raising your profile and building that trusted reputation, how do you cut through the noise? It's becoming much more difficult with the amount of content that's now available, and even more so with the use of AI tools to get the attention of customers and potential customers. How are you cutting through the noise from a banking perspective, and how do you think that's changed over the last couple of years and will change in the future?

Pernille Sahl Taylor: That's a really good question. Customers today are hyper-connected. They are always on; they are always connected through their mobiles and other devices. You will need to reach them where they are and through the networks they're part of, physical and online, or other providers will move in and build meaningful relationships with your customers. So, we look at where our customers are and where we can best target them. After that, we look at what makes us stand out from our competitors.

You're right; it's a very noisy environment. We are a relationship bank, and we value human interactions, the ones we have with our customers and colleagues. But now we live in a world where human interactions are becoming increasingly rare, across all kinds of sectors, not just the banking sector. Engagement with customers are often online or through chatbots. To some extent, that erodes the platform on which we operate, but it also makes us more unique. So, it's an opportunity for us to capitalize on this change and communicate our proposition, why we believe customers still value banking with a human touch. Of course, customers want self-service and to do their banking whenever they want, but occasionally, they may also want to speak to a human and that's where we come in. We want it to be our customers' decision when, where, and how they want to interact with us. It's then about taking that proposition, promoting those unique selling points that we feel we have, and finding the points of differentiation to create a sharpened customer proposition to communicate to your target market. I believe that the market is big enough for all of us to operate in and use our different unique selling points. What we are seeing is that there are other providers also promoting relationship banking, but their propositions are still slightly different, so it's all about finding that differentiation, honing in on that and then communicating that targeted, sharpened proposition to your customers. I think that's especially important now in such a noisy environment.

Tabita Andersson: Would you agree that communications can play such a key role in terms of finding and honing the message and then figuring out the right places where an organisation should be seen?

Pernille Sahl Taylor: Yes, absolutely, and I'm lucky to work in a business where there is a lot of appreciation of the importance of communication and marketing in driving growth. As a function, we are helped by that appreciation alongside the technology and data available to demonstrate the effectiveness of our work. I mentioned earlier how we are planning a targeted marketing campaign to raise brand awareness. The contents of the campaign have been influenced by "test and learn" initiatives, where we were able to demonstrate through data that certain types of tactics were particularly effective for driving growth with our target audiences. Having this type of data is particularly important for me to share with the rest of the management team so that we can make an informed decision on what we choose to invest in.

Tabita Andersson: Talking about data, the use of data in how we measure communications has changed dramatically in our profession over the last 5–10 years. How have you seen it change in your role, and what do you think is going to happen in the next few years with the advent of AI and other tools coming to market? How do you think we can continue to build on the great work we've done so far to improve how we measure what we do and how we use the data we're now collecting?

Pernille Sahl Taylor: I believe it's just going to become more important. Data will always be important, but what you do with it is what matters. You will always need human judgment. For us, that means we will always be cross-checking what the data is telling us with the experience of our branches—does the data match with what they are seeing in their local communities? That way, you have both your quantitative and qualitative insights to inform your decision-making.

Similarly with AI, which is a hot topic at the moment. We have started to explore this and how we could work with it in a good way. We are keen to test and learn. From research I have seen, most communications professionals are doing that at the moment. There is so much that AI could help us with going forward in terms of content creation and driving efficiencies by automating certain processes, but there are also a number of risks to consider. For example, AI is only as good as the data it pulls—"garbage in, garbage out" as they say! Experimentation with AI is important for continuous learning, and in that experimentation, paying attention to areas including alignment with business goals, internal culture, skills and expertise, ethics and trust, and data management and protection.

We have established a working group in the Bank to explore how best to use AI to drive efficiencies while maintaining our low risk tolerance.

As a relationship bank with a human-centreed approach and values of trust and respect for the individual, proceeding with AI would need to focus on how AI could augment both the employee and customer experience. Dr. Fei-Fei Li, who is known for her pioneering work in AI, puts it beautifully when she talks about AI needing to "augment humanity, not replace it."

Tabita Andersson: Let's pivot to talk about the Chief Communications Officer role and your career path. Can you tell us about your background and how you got to your current CCO role at Handelsbanken?

Pernille Sahl Taylor: I studied media communication studies in Denmark, and I then moved to the UK when I was just about to write my master's thesis. While I was studying, I started to work for a PR agency a couple of days a week, which led to a full-time job. I worked for a few agencies and then had almost 13 years at a consultancy called Lansons, primarily working with financial services companies. I was heading up the broadcast, PR, and content production department, and conducted a lot of media training. At the time, Moneysupermarket.com was one of our clients, and I went on a six-month secondment with them as their head of communications. That gave me a taste for working in-house. I really liked how close you get to issues in an organisation and how that company is run.

When I returned to Lansons, I continued doing media training, and one of the businesses I worked with was Handelsbanken. I had media-trained all its senior management, which meant I was familiar with the culture and values of the Bank, so when I was asked if I might be interested in taking on the role of the Chief Communications Officer when it became vacant, it didn't take me long to say yes. I went for a few interviews, and the rest is history, as they say. Doing the six-month secondment with Moneysupermarket was a good move. It gave me broader communications experience, which put me in a position to go for this role.

Tabita Andersson: What advice would you give to more junior communications professionals who are perhaps in the early stages of their careers and looking at what they need to do to grow their careers? Would you advise having experience from both sides of the fence, agency and in-house, is a good way of growing?

Pernille Sahl Taylor: The best thing you can do is to broaden your skill set. It gives you more strings to your bow and will make you more attractive to potential employees, as you will be more flexible and adaptable to changing circumstances in an organisation. We are living in a world that is constantly changing, so continuous learning is important, not just when you're in the early phases of your career but throughout your career.

For example, last year, I took a course in digital marketing at the Said Business School, Oxford University, to broaden my skills and capabilities. I found it incredibly rewarding, and having some working experience behind me enabled me to apply that to my studies, and similarly, I was able to apply what I was learning to my work.

Here at Handelsbanken, we are encouraging colleagues to develop a growth mindset and make sure that they expand their skills and capabilities. I talk to my team about thinking in terms of a 75/25% approach. If you imagine that 75% of your work is focusing on your core skills and capabilities, what about the rest? How can you use the last 25% to expand your skills and capabilities? Maybe it's deepening some of your skills or knowledge in certain areas, but it could also be about acquiring new skills that will enable you to do your existing job better. To me, it's this constant stretching of yourself that gives you a fulfilling career. It is also good for the organisation, which will be able to deal with evolving business and customer demands without having to recruit a whole new set of people. Expanding skills and capabilities and developing a growth mindset is good for both the organisation and its employees.

Tabita Andersson: I agree, and the pace of change is so much faster now than it used to be. With that in mind, what talents and attributes do you look for when you're looking for new people for your team? Do you think those attributes have changed over the last few years because of everything we've gone through and because of the evolving role of communications within an organisation?

Pernille Sahl Taylor: We're a values-driven organisation, so it's very important for us that the people we recruit feel they can work for an organisation like ours with values of empowerment and trust and respect for the individual. We empower people in Handelsbanken to make decisions in their area of expertise, but that empowerment comes with individual responsibility and accountability, and that may not suit everyone. For me, it's about finding people who thrive in this kind of environment first and foremost because if they don't, then it will be difficult for them and for us, so it has to be the right kind of match in values. We spend a lot of time making sure that there's a good fit.

I would be looking at whether the candidate has a growth mindset. Is it someone who's willing to learn, who is curious and who has the appetite to keep on learning and acquiring new skills? I would also look at whether they would be able to fit in with the team and if it's someone we could all work with. Those human skills and personal interaction skills are important.

Of course, having the right skills for the job is necessary, but it's all those other human attributes that will get you the job.

Tabita Andersson: If we go back and talk about the CCO role. You've been in it for a few years now. What changes have you seen in your role and in what you're doing now since you started in-house as CCO?

Pernille Sahl Taylor: I've been at Handelsbanken for eight years now, and there's been constant change. I started at a time when the bank had decided to create a subsidiary in the UK. This meant applying for a banking license, which wasn't something anyone had ever done before for a bank already in motion. It meant that professionally, it was a very interesting and stimulating period. We then went through a few years where we were consolidating expertise in certain areas, which again brought change, and it really has been constant change ever since. So, my role in communications has been constantly evolving.

I have seen a shift in the way organisations communicate with their employees and drive employee engagement. COVID definitely played a part in this shift. There was a move toward well-being before COVID, but the pandemic really accelerated this. Also, flexible working has become much more prevalent, and I don't think that would have happened to the same extent if it hadn't been for COVID. I think there was a real social paradigm shift in how we work as a result.

We already talked about the rise of data and the use of data in our work, and the way technology is enabling us to be hyper-targeted in external communications is also a shift I've seen happening in the last few years. It's improved how we engage with existing and potential customers for sure.

Tabita Andersson: Have you also noticed the role becoming more strategic in that we have to get involved in a lot of the conversations on a board level, for example, advising leaders on how the organisation should reply to something or not reply, what we should say or not say externally and internally?

Pernille Sahl Taylor: For me, that's perhaps harder to compare because I stepped straight into the role as CCO here at Handelsbanken, so I've always been part of the management team and part of the conversations about wider business issues and aligning communications with our business priorities.

As a CCO, you are responsible for the long-term reputation management, communications strategy and implementation for a company or brand. Communications is central to everything a company does. In a fragmented media environment where everyone can be a news provider, building trust and a good reputation becomes very important for brands. Communications, as opposed to marketing, can build this trust and credibility, so I think that is why the communications function has become more important. But as I said earlier, you need communications and marketing to work hand in hand to drive growth and success.

Tabita Andersson: You mentioned that you've always worked as part of the senior leadership team at Handelsbanken. How do you work with your peers and the other senior leaders within the organisation, and what advice would you give them on how to best work with communications and brand to be most successful?

Pernille Sahl Taylor: You collaborate most effectively if you understand each other's business areas. When you're part of a management team, you have to be able to understand a little bit of everything, and you have to be able to contribute to conversations and discussions about areas and topics that may not be within your core expertise. You will be expected to have a view on them. Additionally, you will need to understand your colleagues' different personalities and preferences for engaging. Some people are very analytical and detail-oriented and may want things laid out in certain ways; others will be more about the bigger picture. Gaining an understanding of each other will enable better collaboration and create a high-performing team, as will everyone being united around a shared vision and purpose. Communications can help drive engagement with the key business priorities across the organisation. Open and transparent communications and bringing in communications and brand early on in projects will mean that we are able to do our job more effectively.

Tabita Andersson: Do you have any gold nuggets of advice that you would like to add?

Pernille Sahl Taylor: The key to success for me lies in continuous learning. I love a quote from Søren Kierkegaard, the Danish philosopher who said: "To dare is to lose your footing momentarily. To not dare is to lose yourself." You have to dare to put yourself out there where the ground may be a little bit unsteady because that's when you develop the most professionally and personally. So that's my personal motto!

CHAPTER 6

Jennifer Temple

Chief Marketing and Communications Officer
Hewlett Packard Enterprise

Jennifer Temple is the **Chief Marketing and Communications Officer** for **Hewlett Packard Enterprise** (NYSE: HPE), a global technology leader focused on developing intelligent products and solutions that accelerate business outcomes for customers. The company innovates across networking, hybrid cloud, and AI to help customers develop new business models, engage in new ways, and increase operational performance. HPE employs more than 60,000 people worldwide.

For more information about HPE, visit hpe.com.

Jennifer's LinkedIn profile: linkedin.com/in/jennifersmithtemple/

Tabita Andersson: Thank you very much, Jennifer, for joining me today. I'd like to start our conversation with your career background. How did you end up in your current role, and where did you start?

Jennifer Temple: Often, I tell people that I think I'm one of the very few people who actually majored in communications in college, and 30 years later, I'm still practicing communications! I'm practicing what I studied to do, which seems rare today. But what really sparked me was that I grew up with a teacher as a mom and a doctor as a dad. Both professions are all about helping people. In a way, that's how I define my role; it's about helping brands and

---

© Tabita Andersson 2025
T. Andersson, *Chief Communications Officers at Work*,
https://doi.org/10.1007/979-8-8688-1856-1_6

leaders articulate to the world what the world would lose if we didn't have those brands or those leaders. So, I do feel that, in a way, communications is a proud type of service profession.

It's also a never-dull profession, which I like. No two days are alike!

Upon graduating from the University of Michigan, I immediately went to my first communications job, which was to open the Edelman Sacramento, California office. Edelman, the largest privately held communications firm at the time, didn't have a Sacramento office, and as a California native, I was excited to return "home" from Michigan after spending my school years there. It was really helpful to go immediately into communications on the agency side after graduation because you learn a lot about the craft at an agency. You're dealing with multiple constituents. You have to be very flexible and nimble. You're leading the art of the message. You're learning the importance of frequent stakeholder engagement. All of those things you learn while working as an agency professional, I think, really helped pave the way for my career.

Since then, one of the hallmarks of my career has been juggling across industries. I've worked in politics, for example. After my time at Edelman, I went back into the California Governor's office and was an assistant press secretary. After that, I moved to San Francisco and worked in investment banking for a privately held bank that was then acquired by a national bank, which ultimately ended up as part of the Bank of America. When I left investment banking, I went to real estate and then went back into an agency. From there, I went to consumer banking at Wells Fargo, and then I came here to HPE. So, I've worked for privately and publicly held organisations.

Nothing has intimidated me in terms of subject matter expertise or having a chance to work in small or large companies. The one thing that has been the same about all of these roles is that they have been with brands that have something to tell or share with the world, and I've helped shape that story. I really love to jump in and create and shape narratives to earn respect and trust as a brand.

It's been a magical career, I think, and I've certainly got a lot more gas in my tank. There's a lot more I want to do, but what I've done so far has been really refreshing and invigorating.

Tabita Andersson: That's amazing; you've worked in communications on both sides for business-to-business (B2B) and business-to-consumer (B2C) organisations, and then within the political environment, too; that's quite special. What are some of the differences you've seen between the different industries from a marketing and communications perspective? I'd like to hear your opinion on what commonalities or differences there are.

Jennifer Temple: There are certainly some differences, but B2B companies could and should take a page out of the B2C book. Too often, we say we're different; this doesn't work for us because we don't sell to the end consumer. But everyone wants to fall in love with a brand and feel like a brand embraces their own values or will help you accomplish your goals, so there are a lot of similarities in how we're marketing and how we're telling our story.

Certainly, in the B2B space, you're dealing with different levels of sophistication of technology, which means there are certain buyers who speak a slightly different language, and you have to be able to tell a credible story about the features and functionalities of what you make and sell. At the end of the day, we're all storytellers. There's a consistency in what we all do.

I think repetition is important. It doesn't matter if you are selling to consumers or businesses; the affirming set of qualities and experiences that make your brand beloved are similar. You have skeptics and critics both in the B2B and B2C world. It can be easy to say that consumer businesses, like financial services or healthcare, are so personal to the end user that it makes them even more fraught with risk and reputation calamity, but the same could be true about a piece of technology that's meant to work in a high-performance computing centre that fails and suddenly planes can't land, or something doesn't work. I think we all have to continue to carry favor, engender trust, and keep to our word. So, I see a ton of similarities across industries.

I've tried to think more like a consumer in my B2B jobs. Consumers benefit from our technology, even if we're selling it to someone who then makes that possible.

Tabita Andersson: That's a great point, and it aligns with some of the other conversations I've been having. At the end of the day, we're dealing with people, communications and brands. It's about storytelling. It's about people. Those components are the same regardless of where you work; you're still talking to people and communicating a message.

Jennifer Temple: I think we're all growing more sophisticated in the way we're approaching communications.

Tabita Andersson: I agree, and that's because the technicalities of the role are the same regardless of the organisation. We all have the same channels and technologies available to us as tools for our jobs. It doesn't matter if you work in B2B or B2C; it's more about the story and message that is slightly different depending on your audience.

Is there something in your background, perhaps unrelated to marketing or communications, that has really helped you in your career?

Jennifer Temple: From a personal perspective, I would say one thing is having climbed Mount Shasta, which is a 14,000-foot-high mountain in Northern California, right in my own backyard growing up near Redding,

California. I summitted it with my dad when I was 25. I then climbed it again just a few years ago with my son, right before I turned 50. The summit experience, getting ready for the climb, and doing it with two people who are so special to me, was incredible. For me, there's a lot in those experiences that reflect in the way I show up as a leader. When I climbed and summited in my earlier years, it felt like it was mostly about skills. I was in really good physical shape, and I had trained a lot, so the physicality, skill, and talent that were required were really important. Then, when I was 49, I wasn't as fit physically, and I perhaps didn't have the same talent or agility that I once had, but I had the mental capacity to do it.

Setting lofty goals, whether personal or professional, and listening to both is a great learning experience. I think about what talents, skills, and traits I need to have and how I need to learn to think differently about problem-solving. What do I need to mentally prepare? What's getting in my way?

From a personal standpoint, I reflect a lot on those experiences, and it creeps into the way I try to lead and encourage people to take risks or do things that scare them.

Professionally, I've also loved doing so many different roles because the accumulation of experiences has afforded me a really rich career, instead of feeling stale or bored at any point. One of the things that's helped me the most hasn't been about the practice of communications but more about the lens through which I see opportunity.

Tabita Andersson: Would that be the advice that you'd give someone more junior who is perhaps just starting a career in communications and wants to shape their path?

Jennifer Temple: Definitely. In fact, it's advice I give a lot. I love people who are ambitious and who are currently at point A, and they want to be at point B. Then they're at point B and want to be at point C. I just love that hunger and appetite. Instead of thinking about our careers as ladders, where you're constantly climbing and getting anxious if you're not a manager, or a director, or a VP, my advice is to hunt for something you've never done before. Maybe it's a lateral move; maybe it's outside of communications for a stint to learn the business. Maybe it's something adjacent to communications, like government affairs or investor relations. All of that experience adds up and accumulates into something special. I tell people to, instead of thinking of their career as a ladder, think of it as a mosaic of different tiles or a patchwork of quilt squares that can be stitched together into something special. In the end, it will be a really rewarding career.

Tabita Andersson: You mentioned the value of learning the business. Do you think that's something that communications professionals haven't done so well in the past, or need to do better? To understand the ins and outs of the business and not necessarily just what you do, but how you do it as well?

Jennifer Temple: I think learning the business is fundamental. I don't know that I'd say communicators haven't been good at it. Historically, I think if we've suffered from something, it's been a view of ourselves as being either subservient to the business or adjacent to the business, or somehow not having a seat at the table. I think it's essential that we view ourselves as one of the business decision-makers at the table. The lens through which we see the world might be different than the engineer, or the person charting out the product roadmap, or the people thinking about talent needs, but we're very much in the mix.

However, we can't really put ourselves in the centre of the conversation if we don't do the work and learn about the business. We should almost, in a way, treat learning the business as though we are in business school to learn about the industry or the company that we're supporting because then we can make some really astute recommendations along the way, like how certain decisions may result in a trade-off in sales or pipeline or help (or hurt) the quest to win the hearts and minds of team members. We need to know what levers we can suggest and advise, and that only comes from knowing what the ramifications will be in the business.

Tabita Andersson: With communications now having a seat at the table in many more companies than ten years ago, what do you think is the most value that the Chief Communications Officer can bring to the C-suite?

Jennifer Temple: I don't know that this is specific to communications, but I think anyone who is at that table needs to be both listening so they can fully absorb what the goals and objectives are, and also be highly inquisitive and ask the "what if" questions. What are we really trying to achieve as a business? What if we don't do this? What are the risks of not acting? I don't know if this is specific to the communications role sitting at the table, but certainly, communicators possess a lot of skills that make us ready for that role because we can think one step ahead. We can predict scenarios. We can imagine what will happen if we don't make a move or if we do make a move. We're constantly scouring for headlines of companies that either didn't go far enough or went too far, and so, in that room, at that moment, we're often the ones with the readiness around bringing those issues to the table. It doesn't have to be us, but because we're so diversified in the way we see the world, and we're inquisitive, we're learners, we're great with words, and we're typically ready and willing to be the provocative one, I think it's a great chair for us to be in.

Tabita Andersson: How do you think that role has changed in the last five or ten years?

Jennifer Temple: CEOs recognise and appreciate the value and significance of communicators more than they ever have. I see this in my own CEO and his decision to make me a direct report. When he first got the job, there was someone who was running all of marketing and communications, much like I do today, but they didn't report to the CEO. So, when our current CEO, who was a first-time CEO, came in, he appreciated having a counselor and partner in me as a direct report to help him win the hearts and minds of our team members. Our business had been through a lot of splits and mergers; we had spun off from HP Inc., we'd become our own company, and we'd spun off some of the other ancillary businesses. He recognised that the health of our culture was a place where a Chief Communications Officer needed to really dig in and help him. He also recognised that he wasn't externally known, so he needed help building his personal brand and establishing his voice as the voice of the company. He was the first technologist to run HPE before Carly Fiorina, and that was something he takes very seriously as the steward of this iconic Silicon Valley brand.

To get back to your question about how the role has changed, CEOs now appreciate that there is a real need to communicate with their publics consistently and transparently and to lean into tough conversations. We should not only speak when the going is good but also be willing to lean in and unpack some of the things that surround us, whether they are business challenges or environmental challenges. That's why I think the CEO–CCO relationship is stronger than ever in most companies, and I'm certainly proud to work in an organisation where that's true.

The other thing that's evolved is the understanding and appreciation of internal employee communications. It used to be that external communications got all the glory because it was what you could read in the newspapers or see more visibly and tangibly, but the importance and significance of internal communications has increased dramatically. Culture work, I believe, has really shifted and is now a strategic function in most companies, and again, that's something I'm really proud of at our own company here at HPE.

Tabita Andersson: Let's explore your role and the not-so-common combined role of communications and marketing. Since you mentioned internal communications, I assume you oversee everything related to communications and marketing. Could you please detail that for us?

Jennifer Temple: Sure, in my combined world, I have five direct reports who lead different aspects of communications and marketing. I have a head of global communications, which includes employee communications, as well as everything external, thought leadership, executive communications, financial communications, PR, industry analyst relations, and social media. I have a corporate marketing leader who leads brand, events, sponsorships, and customer advocacy, which is the outreach we do with customers to get their opinions and reflections on how we can be a better partner. Then, I have product marketing, which is exactly what it sounds like; it's where we are marketing the products and helping our sellers sell, which includes supporting all of our product launches and the way we show up at our big marquee customer events with the latest technology and how we partner with strategic alliances to bring improvements to our technology. I have a performance marketing leader who activates everything from our digital advertising to our paid amplification. And finally, I have a field and partner marketing leader who links arms with our sellers in all geographies to market locally. This is super important because a lot of the time, our customers interact with us locally in the geography where they find themselves. I also have a Chief of Staff and an Executive Assistant, and all in all, these leaders make for a really great marketing and communications engine—and they are a fantastic team.

I think of these pillars as swim lanes. One of the things I really like about our structure is that there's a lot of integration between all of these facets because field marketing relies on the narrative from product marketing, so they can carry that into the geographies more successfully. Performance marketing lights up the airwaves with our campaigns, which include content that product and corporate marketing work together on for both paid and earned opportunities. There's connectivity across the whole team, which is what makes it really fun because they're not hard and fast swim lanes that preclude us from the interchange of ideas.

Tabita Andersson: In that combined world, how do you elevate the communications part of your role? In some industries, communications used to be under the leadership of a Chief Marketing Officer, with no seat at the table, so how did you lift up communications alongside marketing?

Jennifer Temple: That's an interesting question because, as I described earlier, when I first joined, it was the exact same experience as you just described, with communications sitting underneath the marketing umbrella. One of the things I'm really proud of now is that you have a communicator by trade running all of marketing and communications. It's a fully integrated and strategic experience, not a subservient function.

In terms of how I lifted it up, it certainly wasn't all down to me, but I think over the last few years since I joined in 2018, we've demonstrated that none of us can have the impact we want without partnering across the lines. Everything we've done together has resulted in big wins for the company, so the business has insisted on those lines continuing to cross and integrate. For example, every time we've planned and executed our large HPE Discover partner and customer conferences, teams from across the function have to get involved; it's field marketing, sales enablement, product market, and positioning, it's narrative, it's paid amplification, it's earned media by inviting press and reports. We can't run HPE Discover without all of these teams working in an integrated way and being tightly linked.

This even stretches over to our investor relations team, who, for example, ran an AI Day for investors and analysts to educate both the buy and sell side on what we are doing in the AI space. The program needed a narrative, a vision, a CEO talk track, and event planning because we wanted to give the analysts and attendees a tour of one of our factories where we make high-performance computing products. The event needed a bit of swagger; it needed event expertise, it needed thought leadership, and it needed a story. It needed all of these teams to come together; you couldn't make it successful if you just turned to one siloed piece of the function.

I hope those examples paint the picture of how we elevated communications as a function because of our willingness to partner, reach across lines, and create one seamless experience for the audience. Now, we are no longer seen as one siloed function but one that is connected, which I think is a big win for the business and pretty rare, to your point.

Tabita Andersson: We've talked about the structure of the function and some of the activities you do. How do you measure the outcome of those tactics? This is another area where we have made such immense strides forward in the last ten years, from counting clips to having metrics today that we can gain insights from to inform decisions. What are some of the changes you have seen, and where are you landing right now in terms of metrics, measurements, and data for communications?

Jennifer Temple: That is such a great question, and to be honest, this is one that I feel will continue to change almost as much as it has changed in the last decade. I wouldn't be surprised if, in the next couple of years, it changes wholesale, which would be for the good because, to your point, we've always struggled with putting a finger on the value of what we're doing.

What I would say is that I've learned, especially in the last several years at this company, that it has to be both qualitative and quantitative. Certainly, we need to have measurements that can point to when we have gone out in the field and into the market with specific messages. How have they landed? What have customers said about them? We need to be able to tally and count things up in a quantitative way, but I also think qualitatively interviewing some of our audiences. We do this every other year now because we found that there wasn't as much change occurring every year, which is good because that means things are settling. So, every other year, we do a robust reputation audit where we talk to policymakers, we interview both buy-side and sell-side analysts, we get feedback from media and industry analysts, we do quantitative surveys of IT decision-makers and their bosses, so both CIOs and CEOs, and we then merge the quantitative and qualitative data to give us a sense of how people are interacting with our brand and what they associate us with.

I think the measurements that we deploy now are a nice, healthy mix of data you need to show brand, reputation, and pipeline. Of course, we need to show how much we net out for every dollar we spend in marketing and communications, which is helpful because our sellers can then feel confident that we are spending and in the right places and contributing to the pipeline in a meaningful way.

Tabita Andersson: Do you think that new tools and technologies such as AI and Gen AI will help us drive better insights?

Jennifer Temple: I definitely do. We use AI today in our performance analytics. That was the place where it was easiest to gain some early efficiencies, eliminate some of the rote manual counting, and have AI improve the output. My performance marketing team is also running our analytics team and has been responsible for implementing AI in this way, which I think has been really good.

Also, AI will help us eventually free up time. Not only will it make the data richer and give us greater insights and help measurements, but I can see it freeing up the people who were doing this work, so you can deploy them to the more creative aspects of marketing.

To me, AI is a two-for-one because we'll get better data, we'll be able to act better based on that data, and then we'll also be able to redeploy resources into some of the activities that require that human touch.

Tabita Andersson: Absolutely. In terms of content generation, we're also seeing so many new developments; the tools are constantly improving in terms of text to image, image to video, and so on, which is exciting for our profession because it will be able to help us improve and enhance storytelling.

Jennifer Temple: I heard some really great stories when I went to Davos in January, so it's not my story, but it did excite me about the possibilities for the future. One of the companies there talked about how they use AI for everyone who would be a recipient of their annual report. Normally, they would print it and stick it in the mail, but when it landed on people's desks, they never opened it. Instead, this company asked everyone who would be a recipient of the annual report to crowdsource the ability to let them make their own front cover using AI. They had a set of templates that they somehow made available to anyone who would be mailed their annual report, and they would ask the recipients to do what they wanted with it. You could put your own face on it, for example, and I thought that was a great way of not only saving the expense of printing and mailing but also a new way of interacting with your shareholders and stakeholders.

Thinking about AI in different ways, such as this, is very exciting!

Tabita Andersson: That's a really interesting idea. Basically, user-generated content by AI. I can see that being applied in all sorts of ways.

Let's pivot to another topic. You've been in communications your entire career; what are some of the mistakes that you see communications professionals make?

Chapter 6 | Jennifer Temple

Jennifer Temple: When I left Wells Fargo to come here, this was my first CCO role. I was running a number of business line communications teams at Wells Fargo; I ran our wealth brokerage, retirement and consumer lending teams, so I had a number of different jobs within my six-year stint. That was a big job, but I had never been the CCO. Before I left Wells Fargo, I asked for a one-on-one with the CEO because I wanted his advice. I said I'm going to go to my first CCO job; what would you tell me to do? He said to keep being the person in the room who challenges me because a lot of people will tell me what I want to hear, but you never did that. You were always the provocative one who would say, "I don't know if this is going to work," or, "What if we did it this way?" Or "Have we thought through these different possibilities?" It was a great reminder to me to never lose confidence and never under-appreciate that the CEO and your executive leaders, who are your partners, are expecting you to bring your very best advice and counsel. They might not always heed it, but they certainly want to hear you give it. And CCOs and communicators, in general, can fall into the trap of just being great executors. When we're tasked with something, we know we can do it well. It can be easy to just do it because we know we can make it excellent. We need to remember to take a step back first and ask if this is even the right thing for us to do. Is this the right tactic for the right moment at the right time? Should we think again?

I'm not sure it's a mistake, but it's a good reminder that we should ensure we're delivering on the promise of what people are truly expecting of us, which is to safeguard our organisation's reputation.

Tabita Andersson: Yes, I've heard the same in several conversations. It's not always about service delivery, but stopping and thinking, which is where we can add additional value.

Jennifer Temple: Exactly, and it can be hard because, like others, I grew up and had so much of my experience, nearly half my career, in agencies. There's something really valuable about learning client service, and I do actually think I'm a better communicator, a better business professional, and a better leader because of my agency experience, but that client service mentality sometimes can keep you in the box of wanting to please the client when actually your job is to bring the very best out of the client, the brand, and the opportunity. That might not initially feel like you're pleasing your client, but you're doing what's right and maintaining a balance of how you're trying to move things forward. It's a delicate balance. We have to be careful that we don't listen to our own inner voice when we know that it deserves to be said externally.

Tabita Andersson: Do you think that's also important in crisis situations? We've recently faced some real crisis situations, such as the unprecedented pandemic, where communications played a key role. Do you think that being a trusted advisor, standing up, asking questions, and being inquisitive is important when it comes to crisis communications?

Jennifer Temple: Absolutely. No question about it. It's probably the most important time to be willing to say what needs to be said, even if it's difficult… to have the courage of your convictions, and to remind your CEO and others of their convictions. Sometimes it is intimidating to feel like you're going to be standing up for something, or having to respond in a moment of vulnerability, to remind others about what's guided them. This is where we, as CCOs, can add real value as whisperers, advisors, and coaches, and that's probably the most important part of a crisis.

The other thing I'm famous for telling my team is that in a crisis, you want to have all the scenario plans that you could possibly have thought through at the ready, and you then have to be prepared to throw them all out the door. You want to have thought about any possible wrinkles or skepticism or ways something could go sideways, and then, inevitably, there will be something that you didn't anticipate that will call for a different set of circumstances or reactions. Then, you have to be nimble to be able to flex, but it's that preparedness matched with the willingness to throw things out of the window when the circumstances call for it. That makes for a good communicator in a crisis.

Tabita Andersson: That's also one way we can really prove the value of communications, in that crisis situation, where quite often people don't know where to turn when something happens, so they come to communications!

Jennifer Temple: That's very true, and sometimes, if that's the way we engender goodwill that then transcends the crisis. I've had a lot of my team members grow in importance or gain a seat at the table that they didn't have because they've weathered a crisis with a business partner, and then afterward, in a non-crisis situation, the same business partner will turn to them and say, "Hey, I'm thinking about launching this product. What risks do you see with it, or how do you think I can poke holes in this plan?" But it's only after they weathered that storm alongside the business partner that they're given the invitation to think more broadly. Sometimes, those storms not only serve the interests right there at that moment, but they also help lead to a really productive relationship afterward.

Tabita Andersson: There's also the other side of the crisis in terms of protecting the brand and reputation, which is also crucial for CCOs and communications teams. Would you mind sharing a bit about what you do for HPE to protect your brand and reputation?

Jennifer Temple: To me, I've always thought of protection as living up to your values and your mission throughout the ups and downs. Ensure that people really understand and appreciate who you are, so you show up consistently as an organisation. The best way I've seen to protect a brand is to have a clear declaration of what you stand for. One of the most meaningful exercises I've been through in my seven years here was to create the company's first-ever culture blueprint, which we literally held up in front of all 60,000 team members. Here are the beliefs that we hold as an entity and the behaviors that underpin those beliefs, so everyone can see their work through the lens of what HPE stands for. We believe in accelerating what's next. We believe in bold moves. We believe in the power of yes, we can. We believe in being a force for good.

It's been great to have these tenets that everyone could understand as declarations of how we do our work. We can then shine a spotlight on the behaviors that underpin those tenets when we see someone being curious and going the extra mile for a customer, which we can then celebrate. Protecting the brand comes first from declaring what the brand stands for so that in moments of conflict, crisis, or industry dynamics, you can stay true to who you are.

In addition, it's about determining when your brand needs to take a stand and when it doesn't, because there are times when it's okay to be quiet. Even during the time of crisis around COVID, I used to tell my team if we have something helpful to say, we should say it, but if we don't, we should be quiet because there are other people out there with advice and information about vaccines and about what the government will do next, and those voices need to be heard. If we're talking too much, then our constituents will not be able to hear the real voices. So, "be helpful or be quiet" is a tenet that I've used many times.

Tabita Andersson: Do you think it's becoming more complicated now to provide advice in the situations we find ourselves? Or is it because the situations themselves are getting more complex?

Jennifer Temple: There is no question that the situations we face today are getting more complex, and that's because they're changing. We've all dealt with complicated leaders, complicated environments, and complicated economics, but so many changes now on a daily basis, so it's getting harder for brands, companies, and leaders to figure out what the most important thing is that we should react to or address.

I don't believe that changes my advice. Even if we weren't living in this hugely dynamic, ever-changing, evolving time, my advice would stay the same. Be true to what you stand for, where you personally can contribute to the conversation as a brand or as a leader. Be helpful in that moment where your brand or leadership is needed, and then be quiet when there are other voices that need to be heard. Continue to uphold the values you're committed to because our current environment is ever-evolving, and I think that gives you all the more reason to stay true to those tenets.

Tabita Andersson: We've touched on protecting the brand, so let's pivot to talk about building a successful reputation. HPE is a large organisation with a global brand, a long history, a great legacy, and a futuristic outlook. How do you best build the reputation you want for a brand like HPE?

Jennifer Temple: That's a great question, and I don't know that I have all the answers, which is what makes this whole job very fun! Every year and at every opportunity, we have to interact with the various audiences that hold us in such high regard and have high expectations of us, which makes it an ever-changing and ever-evolving task to ensure the reputational health of our company. There are a couple of key things, however, that I look at.

Number one, we're a technology company, so we need to be bold. We need to be innovative. The world around us needs to see us solving some of the most complex challenges because we're continually evolving the technologies that can be deployed to meet those challenges. In order to have a healthy brand this time next year or this time five years from now, we have to be seen as modern, current, relevant, and innovative. Equally important is that we have customers who tell us if our technology is every bit as good as any of our competitors and if our pricing is similar, whether they will pick us because we uphold the values we have. Being able to be declarative about culture, purpose, and mission while at the same time innovating and showing the world what's possible with your technology is a great combination. For us, reputation is having the technology, heritage, and expectation that we will always be innovators while also being true to the character and culture of the company.

Number two, we have to have great talent. A lot of how we protect our reputation is by showing people who want to come work here what an exciting, amazing place this is. Our employee value proposition is very much part of our reputation advantage, and keeping people here and seeing that they can continue to have long careers here, reinventing themselves along the way. Talent is constantly on my mind for that reason. So, innovation, culture, and the quest for having the very best talent and making this a wonderful place to work are what I'm spending most of my time thinking about.

Tabita Andersson: You mention talent. What would you look for in upcoming professionals for your brand, communications, and marketing teams? What are some of the skills and attributes you look for?

Jennifer Temple: On the one hand, there are always the hard skills. Our CEO likes to say that everybody needs to have a minor degree in Artificial Intelligence. I think continuing to invest in talent that can help us see the possibilities of AI as a marketing and communications function and as a brand, and the pace of change in that area is massive, so having people here that can help us see around the corners, make suggestions and get things out of pilot mode and into mass adoption will be very helpful for the future of our team and profession. From a hard-skill perspective, I think continued investment in AI and digital expertise will be really important.

On the other hand, I also believe having soft skills is equally as important because, to me, it's a strategic skill to be able to ask the "what if" questions, to ferret out the stories, to get people to become more willing and comfortable with the relationship with our organisation, to share and bring us to the table early and often. Soft skills are important when you are looking for talent. Ask questions about how they set up and structure their interactions with stakeholders. How do they continually re-evaluate whether their interactions are healthy? What mechanisms do they put in place to make sure they have shared goals and objectives? It's a relationship business at the end of the day, and to me, that's the most important skill for the talent that works with us.

Tabita Andersson: Do you have any particular nuggets of advice that you would like to add?

Jennifer Temple: Something we didn't cover in detail is the CCO's relationship with the CEO and how important it is. I believe that it takes some intention to build that great relationship, and you have to be intentional to ensure it's a healthy one. It's not just about having frequent one-to-ones; it's setting up a regular rhythm with the executive communicator who's writing the CEO's voice; it's having a really robust relationship with the CEO's Chief of Staff and with their Executive Assistant. Having a symbiotic, shared relationship with the CEO is a very important part of the CCO role. That's also something I've really enjoyed about my chapter here at HPE so far.

Tabita Andersson: We have not touched on how other executives in the C-suite can most effectively collaborate with you as the Chief Marketing and Communications Officer. What's your advice for them?

Jennifer Temple: That's a great question, and honestly, it's about bringing us in early and often into conversations about business decisions. It's not just coming to us when you've decided to do something, and now you need communications to execute and amplify, but having a conversation about the decision, what risks are associated with the decision, and what aspects could be considered unhelpful to all or some constituents. Having those debates and discussions about product roadmaps and potential differentiation in the marketplace before a decision is even made is very helpful.

I try to spend time every day with a business leader, a head of sales, or even our CEO so that we, as communicators and marketers, can understand the heartbeat of the business and contribute counsel to decisions. Early, often, and frequent engagement lets us be active, open learners about their business challenges so we can provide the very best recommendations and advice.

Tabita Andersson: That's great advice. To finish our conversation, what is the one thing that you would like to be remembered for in your role?

Jennifer Temple: Giving the next generation of communicators the confidence they can, and will be, a really big voice for change and impact. I would love to be known as the leader who sets the next leaders up for great success and brilliance.

CHAPTER 7

Nicola Green

Chief Communications and Corporate Affairs Officer Virgin Media O2

Nicola Green is the **Chief Communications and Corporate Affairs Officer** for **Virgin Media O2**, the joint venture between Liberty Global and Telefonica, and one of the UK's largest businesses. Virgin Media and O2 are two of the UK's most iconic brands, serving 45.8 million broadband, mobile, phone, and home subscribers, and employing 16,000 people. The brands have come together to give the UK more choice and better value—good news for customers, communities, and businesses all over the country.

For more information about Virgin Media O2, visit virginmediao2.co.uk.

Nicola's LinkedIn profile: linkedin.com/in/nicolag/

Tabita Andersson: The role of a Chief Communications Officer can sometimes be difficult to describe, even for someone who's been in a communications role for a long time. Nicola, how would you explain the role to your grandmother?

Nicola Green: I still don't think my mum, let alone my grandmother, really understands what I do! I would explain the role by saying I manage the reputation of the business I work for, and that's important because people want to buy from companies they like, trust, and believe are successful. For example, we all know it's important for celebrities to manage their reputation with press and online, and it's no different for organisations.

My team and I act as guardians of the organisation and its name.

Tabita Andersson: That's a good description. What value do you think a Chief Communications and Corporate Affairs Officer, someone who looks at an organisation's reputation at the highest level, brings to the company?

Nicola Green: I think we play two critical roles. The first is about managing reputation on a daily basis, and the second is about bringing the outside in. In our role, we speak to a lot of stakeholders, whether that's the press or political figures, and we bring a huge amount of insight back into the organisation to help with critical decision-making.

The higher the role is in the organisational structure, the better able we are to contribute. This is how we can influence from the outset, rather than after a decision has been made. Often the right thing to do is to advise leaders not to do something at all. However, if you're further down the line in the decision-making process, all you're able to do is mop up afterwards, which is not using Corporate Affairs to its best advantage.

Tabita Andersson: Being brought in early is coming up in several conversations I've had, and that's also a good point to make for how other executives can most successfully work with communications.

Nicola Green: Yes, absolutely. We've all been in situations where well-intentioned people are desperate to make decisions or press ahead with ideas. If we can take time to help influence, shape a plan, or perhaps even take it in a slightly different direction to enhance the impact, then we bring value together.

Tabita Andersson: What other advice would you give to executives or other stakeholders within an organisation on how to best work with their communications partners?

Nicola Green: I think trust is so important between stakeholders, and to develop trusted relationships, you have to invest time. I've worked in environments where we haven't been able to build the necessary relationships because of a lack of prioritization or an underappreciation of the importance of comms, and everyone needs to realize that it's essential.

I have worked with CEOs who haven't initially considered the value of communications until a crisis arrives, but as soon as they invest the time and space, they are convinced!

I would add a point around open-mindedness and being willing to take on advice and feedback from perhaps more junior comms professionals. To do this job well, we have to give advice honestly and openly. Sometimes, that can be really hard to hear. But comms done badly has big organisational consequences so counsel needs to be listened to. It's essential that everyone invests time and builds trust so that those honest conversations are possible.

Tabita Andersson: Do you think this has become more important over the last five or ten years as opinions become more polarized, reputations become more challenged, and, with the advent of fake news, there's a more urgent need to shape the narrative differently?

Nicola Green: Yes, definitely. We live in a very uncertain world where things happen that we never imagined would, and we have to navigate that in a very exposing world, thanks to tech and social media use. For example, I never thought we'd be in a situation where Diversity, Equity and Inclusion (DE&I) is a global priority that has been considered to have gone too far. We're now seeing organisations rolling back on their commitments when we've been pushing so hard for diverse and wide talent pools to enhance organisational culture and effectiveness. It's fascinating and often shocking how quickly public agendas can shift.

I think COVID was a massive opportunity for corporate affairs professionals to demonstrate their worth. How do we engage workforces that all of a sudden were working remotely? How do we manage some of the crises that emerged during COVID-19?

Post-COVID, the world has shifted again and we are tackling bigger issues than ever before, so our role has become even more critical.

Tabita Andersson: That's a good segway into talking about crisis communications because this is often an area where we can help provide value as a profession. It seems we're dealing with more crisis situations now than perhaps ten years ago. What type of changes have you seen in terms of crisis communications? You mentioned the pandemic. That was a massive crisis we couldn't foresee, but we've also had other situations recently, such as DEI, which is a crisis for some organisations but perhaps not so much for others. What do you think has changed regarding how we handle crisis communications?

Nicola Green: The main change is how quickly information spreads. A few years ago, I dealt with a 24-hour network outage just as social media had become a mainstream communication channel. Our Twitter feed just blew up and we couldn't control it. As a corporate affairs team, it meant we had to manage our customers directly on Twitter at the same time as feeding information to the press and other stakeholders. We noticed how members of the press were relying on what was happening in social feeds and how they could access real-life experiences in a way they'd never been able to before.

This is now commonplace, but the point is that the pace of crisis has sped up. We have to react much faster and deal with situations much quicker. Today, we often know if there is a problem on our networks before being alerted by internal teams, because our customers experience it first, and comment on social media, which is flagged to us immediately. This means that we, as a team, have to be on call 24/7, and respond quicker than we ever have before. That creates a significant strain.

Today, I have a crisis team that works for 12 hours maximum before handing over to a second group. That can be hard in itself because we all love working on crisis comms, but we have to ensure we have fresh minds that can make the right decisions.

Tabita Andersson: How is your team set up to deal with crisis situations and best manage communications when things happen?

Nicola Green: We have a crisis playbook, which isn't always useful in the moment because you haven't got time to read a big document when the crisis is happening. But we use it to practice and scenario-plan what to do when a crisis happens. Regularly practicing what to do in these situations ensures that everyone is clear on their roles and responsibilities and how we all work together for a seamless resolution.

We also link up well with the rest of the organisation. We've been very clear that we can't just work in our own little world, but bring in the right expertise from across the organisation to help us to recover in the best way. For example, I have one team member whose responsibility it is to liaise with the website team. They have built a good working relationship between them on a day-to-day basis so that when the time comes and we're in crisis mode, they can handle what needs to be done quickly and efficiently.

Another thing we do is build out the risk register with the relevant teams. Preparing for the worst possible scenario sets you up in the best way.

Tabita Andersson: That's good advice. Thank you for sharing the examples. Let's continue to talk about your team, its structure, and how that has changed over the last three years or so.

Nicola Green: I have recently merged public affairs and external communications as a trial because I can see the value in aligning public affairs campaigning with our proactive external communications efforts. My other divisions are internal communications, ESG, and a strategy-and-planning team that leads content, channels, and events. I've set up my team with a discipline focus and with a strategy and planning team that offers their specialist expertise across the team.

I'm a big believer in joined-up communications. What I mean by that is thinking about what we do in a campaign way. What I don't want to see us do is have separate external, internal, and ESG communications plans when we launch a new product, for example. I want to see cross-team working to drive campaigns in a joined-up way. In doing that, I believe we're more effective and more efficient, and the results have improved dramatically; it's been a real step-change from how we managed campaigns in the past.

There are many different ways to structure your communications team, and I think I have quite a big remit compared with some of my peers who look after internal or external communications, but not both. Regardless of reporting line though, I advocate behaving like one team. We work together as one team and have one voice when we work with the various stakeholders across the organisation. This one-team approach has made a massive difference to our delivery, our results, and our impact.

Tabita Andersson: Thinking about that one team, one voice ethos, is that now your philosophy for building your communications team, and how do you attract talent to your team to help you on that path?

Nicola Green: I try to create an environment where people feel empowered to grow and develop. I always tell people our team is a hotel, not a prison. They should feel motivated to be here and free to leave, and people have come back to my team over the years. One of my current direct reports came to me as a graduate, stayed in the team for two years, then went off into public affairs and the agency world, before returning a few years later.

Very early in my career, I had a boss who threw me in at the deep end and gave me a lot of big projects to work on, and I flourished from that experience. I took on a huge amount of responsibility, and I grew and developed to where I am today. So, I constantly think about how I can do that with the rest of my team and how I can allow them to take on extra responsibility. Many of my team have stepped into temporary roles while we recruit, which has enabled them to gain additional experience without having to go elsewhere. To me, breadth of experience is important, and it leads to greater long-term commitment.

I also believe it's important to have fun together. We spend a lot of time at work, and having a laugh makes it a lot more enjoyable for everybody.

It means we celebrate successes and work together when things are tough or we get things wrong. We're not perfect in any way, shape, or form!

Tabita Andersson: That's exactly when you need trust because we all make mistakes, and sometimes those situations become our best learning experiences. Also, I think having that trust and building great relationships helps the team through the good and the bad times.

What particular skills and backgrounds do you look for when you build your team? What advice would you give to someone who's junior in communications and would like to build a career in our field of work?

Nicola Green: Good, fundamental communication skills are still, ultimately, the most important. It worries me that writing skills are declining, and you have to have solid writing ability to do well in communications. I think it's so important for children to get their basic writing skills nailed at school. Perhaps if less time was spent studying old texts (even though I personally love Shakespeare) and more time on grammar and storytelling, we'd be setting up our young people better. That's my personal view!

Also critical is the right attitude and having an open mindset to grow, learn, and develop. If you have that, then you have what we need to succeed. In addition, creativity and being aware of what's around you are helpful in our roles. Watching TV, reading, and consuming content from different sources is key because it sparks ideas.

Another important attribute is the confidence to engage with other people and particularly senior stakeholders, because you have to be able to advise and influence, and that can be challenging at times.

One of the things I don't think we do well as an industry is attracting the right talent. I'm a big believer in degree apprenticeships rather than just degrees, because I think having the experience of learning on the job and in an office environment is really important in our line of work.

For communications professionals, my advice is to go and get work experience, either in an agency or in an in-house team, and demonstrate that you have the right attitude and appetite for learning. That will stand you in really good stead to succeed in this world. You need to think about what will give you your extra edge, as well as ensuring you have the basics like good communication skills, being able to write well, and being a people-person.

Developing emotional intelligence over the course of your career is so important. We recently underwent an IQ and EQ assessment as an Executive Leadership team and my EQ was way over the normal scale—I think that's one of my superpowers! Being able to judge how what I'm saying will influence and impact the person I'm talking to helps us to be more effective. I imagine IQ levels are consistently high across most Board tables, but perhaps the emotional side is where we can contribute real value-add.

Tabita Andersson: I can relate to that; we often hear a lot about the numbers and technical details around the table, and sometimes it can feel a bit lonely being the voice that reminds people about how decisions make people feel and bring that different emotional perspective to the conversation, which I believe it's so often needed for balance.

You mentioned earlier about one of your bosses throwing you in at the deep end and how that was a great learning experience. I'm curious to find out more about your career path; how did you start in communications, and what has your path so far looked like?

Nicola Green: I was one of those weird kids who knew what I wanted to do when I was doing my A-levels, which was a real blessing. I used to read Jackie magazine when growing up, and once, in the sixth-form study room, I remember reading the back page of one of their issues, and they had a feature about career choices. This particular issue featured someone who worked in PR, and as I read that article, I thought, well, that's what I want to do. Having that focus allowed me to be very driven, so I did a lot of work experience in PR agencies local to home.

I didn't get the grades I expected at A-level, and so I took a year out to re-think. At one point, I was convinced that I'd go back and re-do my A-levels, but I managed to secure a role at PowerGen, which had a link with Nottingham University. As I worked in their corporate communications team, I ended up going to university on a monthly basis to complete a range of different business and marketing courses, and from there, I re-applied straight to university, but rather than doing English and History, which was my original choice, I changed to do a more vocational course and ended up at Leeds University doing marketing, communications, and a PR course. While I was studying, I spent every holiday gaining PR work experience from all sorts of places, including Boots, Yorkshire Electric, and at different PR agencies. There wasn't a time when I wasn't doing some sort of PR if I wasn't studying, and I was then lucky to get a graduate trainee placement at Burson Marsteller.

Burson is a global PR and communications firm headquartered in New York and London, and it was a good place to start my career. I wanted to do that specific trainee course because they sent you to New York, where they had the Burson Marsteller University. I don't know if they still do it, but I really wanted the opportunity to work in NYC and cut my teeth in their consumer department. I ended up doing work for various Unilever brands, everything from Hills Pet Nutrition, slimming formula for dogs to margarine and hair care products, which gave me a really good overview of what it's like to work for consumer brands.

One of the clients that Burson had at the same was Dr. Pepper. Sadly, their brand manager fell ill at one point, and they asked if I would go in and cover her role in-house. This was the time when they were owned by Cadbury Schweppes. I said yes and realized after a while that this was exciting work, being in control of one brand. In an agency, I always felt one step removed.

After that placement, I went back to Burson and very quickly realized that I wanted to go in-house and luckily, by complete fluke I have to admit, I managed to get a role in Orange [a mobile network operator and Internet service provider that launched in the UK in the 1990s and was bought by France Telecom in 2000]. It was a fantastic opportunity to build a brand and be disruptive in the market; to do things that were different to what has been done before. That's where I met the great boss I mentioned before, who generously gave me so many opportunities. We still have a very strong relationship, and we spoke earlier this week. We have a reverse mentorship relationship now too, where I mentor her on some things, and she mentors me on other things, so it works really well.

I was then approached by O2, and as my boss at Orange had left to have a baby, I thought it might be a good opportunity to again go and build a new brand using my experience from Orange. As you can tell, I really enjoy building brands and turning them into a household name.

I joined as head of consumer PR and slowly worked my way up to Chief Communications Officer. During my tenure, I've been given opportunities to experience other disciplines as well, which has made me much better at what I do, and that has been phenomenal.

In my early years, I launched the iPhone into the UK market and was involved in the re-launch of the Millennium Dome to The O2 arena, which is still providing value to the business today, which is amazing. As my experience of big projects grew, I inherited and built new teams, until eventually I was managing external communications and PR, then internal communications, public affairs, and then ESG.

When the merger with Virgin Media happened in 2021, I had to interview for the Corporate Affairs job for the combined entity, and went through a rigorous process in order to secure the job as Chief Communications Officer which sits on the executive committee. I was already a part of the executive committee at O2, and I feel very passionately about that being where the role belongs.

It's been a really interesting career path, and even though I've been at the same organisation for a very long time, I've never stopped learning. That's the experience I want to give everybody in my team—an opportunity to continue learning and add extra strings to their bows. If an organisation is going to invest in you and give you new opportunities, then I think you're in a very powerful place, and you can learn just as much from staying in one organisation than you do from moving around.

Tabita Andersson: Absolutely, and with the pace of change within organisations speeding up, we also get more opportunities to learn and grow. If we go back, say, 20 years ago, organisations were typically quite stable for longer periods of time, but now the pace of change is so fast, even within organisations, so even if you're staying in the same place, it's not the same organisation in five years' time because so much happens all the time. You launch new programs; there are restructures, things happen macro-economically, there are mergers, and organisations always move forward; they don't just stay stale and stagnant, so I agree the opportunities for learning as you go are the same.

What advice would you give yourself if you could go back to your early days and do something differently?

Nicola Green: I've spent a lot of time overthinking everything that I do and sweating the small stuff. In some ways, it makes me good at what I do because I'm always thinking about whether I've done the right thing or made the right decision. I care so much about everything I do. But there were times when I drove myself to distraction because of the stress that I put myself under, rather than being a bit more confident in what I did. So, I would say to my former self: make sure you get the balance right and don't go too far on overthinking; listen to your gut instinct, be patient, and bigger, better opportunities will come.

Something else I tell everybody, as well as myself, is to never stop learning and always stay curious. Before I joined the executive committee, I completed a Non-Executive Director Financial Times Diploma to boost my knowledge and ensure I could play an important role at board-level. We should never stop learning, otherwise problems arise and opportunities get missed.

Tabita Andersson: Interesting comment about overthinking; that's something I've seen a lot of people do, too, including myself. I wonder if it's a communication professional's habit or if it's a female habit; what do you think?

Nicola Green: Well I know my husband doesn't overthink in the same way, so while I would like to think it's a combination, sadly, I believe it's definitely a female trait, and we need to try and give ourselves the confidence to quiet the mind.

Tabita Andersson: Saying that, I do believe because, in communications, we often have to think one step ahead and outline the various consequences of decisions; it sets us up for being overthinkers, especially if we're already leaning that way.

Your comments about learning are also interesting, as they have come up in several conversations with other Chief Communications Officers. Because we face so many situations that none of us have faced before, such as the pandemic, we still have to advise and guide our organisations through them, and we have to be life-long learners. Is it almost a prerequisite for being a communications leader?

Nicola Green: Absolutely. You only have to reflect on how significantly the role has evolved in the last ten years to appreciate how important it is to keep learning. For example, data and analytics are now fundamental to our success, and that wasn't the case just a few years ago. We had data on what people are buying, but the volume of analytics available at our fingertips today means that, whereas I used to make a lot of decisions based on my instincts and experience, I now use that in combination with data and analytics to make the right communications decisions.

Look at AI, for example. In the past, we didn't have to worry about the implications of deepfakes and digital trust, yet, we need to be ready for it. I don't know if I'm quite ready mind!

Tabita Andersson: Our use of data and analytics has definitely changed dramatically since I started in communications. You were literally just counting how many press releases you were sending out compared to the spectrum of insight we have today. I'd be interested in hearing more about how you use data and how you think that will change going forward.

Nicola Green: Of course, we're using data in the obvious way to monitor everything that's going on, and it gives me quick insights into which audience we're hitting and how decisions and campaigns are landing, which is important to us.

With Artificial Intelligence, I say to my team that we shouldn't be scared of it; we should embrace it because we can't change it. It will come our way! I joined a talk recently where the key outtake was that you can't humanize AI as much as needed right now, so we're going to have to put a lot of effort into training AI in order to get the right output. Of course, it can write a press release if you want it to, but you can't guarantee its quality. I use it more for sense-checking our work and whether key messages will land. I will ask my team to put their draft press release through a GenAI tool, and ask it to return the top three key messages. If they're not the same as the ones you intended, then the press release isn't right!

So, I think there are ways in which we can make ourselves more effective, such as using AI tools to make sure we get our messages across and simplifying processes. For example, perhaps there's a bot on your website that journalists can use to learn the facts about your business, which saves time for your press team.

Right now, I'm asking my team to go and play with the AI tools that are out there, and it's really interesting to see how they react. One of my team members admitted to me they're worried about their job being replaced. At the time, I thought that this was no different from how my mum, who's a secretary, reacted when spellcheckers were introduced. What we're going through with AI is no different from what they went through; it's just the next re-iteration. So we just have to embrace it, let it take on those jobs we don't want to do, and use our human intelligence to think about how to do things in a different, better, and more effective way. We're only using it on a very basic level at the moment, but with a high level of curiosity to explore the opportunities available to us.

Tabita Andersson: The majority of people I'm talking to at the moment are using it at that level, although I have come across a few communications teams that seem to be super-users who are leading the way, which will be super-interesting to follow. I think your way of using AI to check key messaging is clever and not something I've seen elsewhere. It seems that everyone is on their own journey with AI, so it's going to be very interesting when we start to pull together all these use cases as a profession and see how we can all grow and learn from each other. That will be an interesting next step once we get out of trialing, piloting, and figuring out what the best uses are.

Do you see any other trends coming that will impact our communications jobs in the next five or so years?

Nicola Green: Perhaps how we deal with managing the increasing demands of multiple stakeholders within an increasingly complex operating landscape. This is a real skill we're having to build, considering how interlinked our stakeholders are and the voice of the customer being more powerful than ever.

Someone recently posed a very interesting question to me: are influencers really influencing? My response to that was that I don't know, but customers, for sure, are now influencers, and perhaps we should change the label because it's actually just the voice of the customer that's so important. Do you really need to have a badge that says "influencer" in order to influence purchase decisions? Or do people just want to trust the general population, or their friends, or their families? I wonder whether that will be an interesting development for our stakeholder groups and how we work with them in the future.

Tabita Andersson: The influencer generation is certainly interesting from a communications perspective. Just a few months ago, my team was talking about how the younger generation consumes content and what their buying habits are, so we set up some conversations to dig in a bit further, and I thought those conversations were fascinating. Some were saying that they don't buy anything unless they've seen it used on TikTok, and they consume all the buying information they need from those influencers, as well as their friends and peer groups. To me, that's a very different behavior that will be interesting to watch in the future, and it touches on your point about what an influencer really is.

Nicola Green: I think we're going to have to watch those trends because the landscape is changing rapidly. I believe our stakeholders will develop, and buying behavior will change even more so over the next five years, which will be very interesting to watch.

Tabita Andersson: Talking about stakeholders and stakeholder management, how do you and your team manage the different priorities? In communications, we work with a wide range of stakeholders both inside and outside the organisation, and sometimes it can seem that those stakeholders have different or even competing priorities; how do you balance that in your work?

Nicola Green: It comes down to aligning to what we want to achieve as a business, and giving focus to the right things. It's one of the reasons why I believe in joined-up disciplines within the communications team. It means we can cater to more priorities in one campaign than perhaps we could in the past, where we'd have political influencer work happening independently of our proactive comms campaigns, or where we weren't considering the whole range of stakeholders in order to make a clear decision.

I also live by prioritizing where we have a good position to take. Don't fight where you are weak, or where there isn't a business priority. Pick the things that you know are worth leaning in on.

Tabita Andersson: We've touched a couple of times on how you're working closely with your CEO as the trusted advisor on communications and reputation. How do you think that relationship can best work? How do you best work with your CEO to help them become most effective from a reputational perspective?

Nicola Green: I've worked with three very different CEOs across the senior years of my career, and each one has required something slightly different when it comes to communications counsel. I don't think there's one way of doing it across the board. You have to really understand the CEO and what their authentic style is. What do they care about? What do they not care about? If you don't go through that process right at the beginning, you'll struggle to succeed.

I also think it's essential that CEOs are seen and heard, and we have to find a way that's really authentic to them as leaders. There's no point forcing a square peg into a round hole because it won't be good for anybody! What you did for your last CEO isn't necessarily right for your new one. I think that's an important perspective for anyone in this role.

Personally, I try to spend time with them to really understand the issues that matter to them. I always try to guide our conversations to be solutions-focused, and not just highlight problems. I also work hard to build relationships with everybody in the CEO's office. Most CEOs these days have a Chief of Staff; that's another good way of influencing and understanding what they're thinking because, ultimately, we're all working toward the same goals and same challenges, and it's so much easier when you're working together in lockstep. When you work hand in hand with the CEO and have agreed on clear objectives, it becomes easier.

Getting time in my CEO's diary is the hardest thing in the world and now I've put in a regular cadence to ensure I get the time I need. I think you have to come to a bit of an agreement between you because if they don't invest time, then you won't be able to meet your goals!

Tabita Andersson: Do you have any final nuggets of advice or something to add that we haven't covered?

Nicola Green: I'd end by saying that this can be a really exciting and rewarding profession, and I think we need to encourage as many people as possible to be curious about this career and what the role can do.

For anyone already in the job, keep learning, keep innovating. Our profession never stands still and it will look completely different in the next few years, so see it as a journey and stay on the road and ahead of that change curve.

And finally, invest in relationships. You never know when you'll need them. And never lose sight of the power of authentic communications in order to form them.

CHAPTER

8

Stacey Jones
Chief Communicator Honeywell

Stacey Jones is the **Chief Communicator** for **Honeywell,** an integrated operating company serving a broad range of industries and geographies around the world. Aligned with the powerful megatrends of automation, the future of aviation and energy, Honeywell is a trusted partner helping customers solve the world's toughest, most complex challenges with actionable solutions and innovations. The company's current business segments are Aerospace Technologies, Industrial Automation, Building Automation and Energy and Sustainability Solutions, which help make the world smarter and safer as well as more secure and sustainable.

For more information about Honeywell, visit Honeywell.com.

Stacey's LinkedIn profile: linkedin.com/in/stacey-jones-cco/

Tabita Andersson: With over 100,000 employees worldwide and a large remit in terms of industries and areas of focus, can you describe how Honeywell's communications structure is set up?

Stacey Jones: It's a global function and a collaborative place where we work tightly together—"one for all"—as one Honeywell.

This approach was a key objective when I joined the company about a year and a half ago: ensuring fewer silos in how we communicate and more continuity and coordination in how we tell the Honeywell story. To be effective, I believe our story has to come to life through the lens of each business, whether it's aerospace, industrial automation, building automation, or energy.

Shortly after I started, I received a communicator's greatest gift: clarity on our corporate focus and mission, when our CEO announced that we are aligning with three mega-trends in the world. They are not our mega-trends, but they are the most important things that are shaping how our customers do business and the problems they have to solve. We are engineers, so we spend our days deciphering the industry's most complex problems. Honeywell probably touches your life multiple times every day, and you don't know it. For example, when you fly off on holiday somewhere exotic, the plane lands because Honeywell's controls help it touch down safely. It's not necessarily important that everyone knows that, but it's motivational for the people who work here, because we do a lot of things that really matter to people. However, our business became very complex over time, so our CEO took a step back and said, "These are the three mega-trends we are focusing on," and that will help direct and energize our organisation.

Subsequently, he restructured us into four businesses, which also helped us chart a clear course of communications. I'm not saying it wasn't clear before, but it sharpened our ability to prioritize and know what's most important to talk about, and it gave us the option to customize exactly how we tailor that to each area of the business, including thought leadership and executive positioning. It helped with our financial communications and our social program for executive leadership voices. It also helped us shape what awards and rankings we want to apply for, how we communicate client wins, and how we position our thought leadership campaigns, and then amplify those stories. For example, how do we best tell our people when something good is happening in the world and ensure they're aware and feel part of the story?

That focus and mission are now essentially our anchor and framework, and we use various tools and communication channels to bring it to our audiences, our people, our shareholders, customers, partners, and communities. Honeywell is in 80 countries around the world, so it's important to us that we are active in those communities. Often, we do so through a variety of partnerships, from relevant NGOs to local or regional sports teams. If I could walk you over here to look out of my window, you would see the huge Bank of America Stadium, home of the National Football League team the Charlotte Panthers -- and a Honeywell partner. In part, this is important because of the proximity of the location and how important the team is to our city, but we have also found a way to work with the Panthers to change STEM education in the local schools and put our stamp on delivering something that's uniquely in Honeywell's corridor of engineering. We are building the next generation of future shapers.

Tabita Andersson: That's a great example of how to bring a company's mission to life. With the four different business divisions, how have you structured your communications team to be as efficient as possible?

Stacey Jones: We have a mixture of reporting lines, so, for example, the internal communications team is largely an HR function, but there are also internal communications people inside the businesses who have a matrixed reporting structure and work hand-in-glove with our external brand and communications team.

Brand, public affairs, external, crisis, and financial communications report directly to me around the world. Brand is very much part of our team, and we set the brand strategy and standards that are executed across the company. On the external front, having one brand linked to our business strategy and bringing our corporation together is non-negotiable.

No one focuses on who reports to whom day to day because we work as a group that prioritizes getting things done. We all have a boss for a reason, but we focus on the outcomes. While someone has to have the first chair on a project, you often need a big, broad team running the execution. It's legal, finance, HR, investor relations, and so on.

Tabita Andersson: The combination of communications and brand is something I've seen increase over the last few years, becoming much more closely connected and working together as one team. In the past, the functions often worked in silos, with brand sitting in marketing and communications in a separate function. What benefits have you seen from having a closely knit brand and communications team?

Stacey Jones: The way I think about it is that business strategy drives the brand strategy, which drives the corporate narrative. That narrative and brand are then expressed through many channels, one of which is customer marketing. That's essential, right? The ways you express yourself, set standards and the look and feel of the house are crucial for bringing customers into the house. We worked closely with customer marketing on a messaging exercise aimed at taking our top-of-the-house messages and differentiators and expressing them for their business, be it aerospace or building automation. That way, we have a coordinated but customized message across the organisation. At the time, a number of people told me that it was something they hadn't done before, and it was exciting and motivating for the teams to work together and dig in across internal communications, external communications, brand, and marketing. It was very much a team sport.

Right now, with the upcoming separation of our divisions, the brand piece is especially exciting. We need to create a new brand for at least two of the businesses, because Honeywell will remain. Our brand has tremendous value. We just completed a new brand health tracker, and I was initially surprised at how good things looked; then, after digging deeper, I can see places where we can do better. I'm not declaring victory and turning the lights off, but I feel really good about our brand. Our brand positioning is: the future is what we make it. The advocacy scores, even if you don't use our products or services, are over the top, which is amazing.

For our customers, this means we'll have a new brand for our Solstice Advance Materials business, and the Honeywell brand equity will be associated with our Honeywell Aerospace business, which also has a long history of success. At the same time, we will be creating and launching two distinct brands for new Honeywell and Honeywell Aerospace that leverage the value of our legacy, reputation, and credibility, while supporting future growth with their respective differentiated narratives.

Tabita Andersson: That's an interesting direction because if you look at GE, for example, that went through the same separation process recently, they decided to keep the GE brand as the main master brand across all three new companies to protect the equity they've built. With you going in the direction of creating a new brand for your separate businesses, how do you think you'll be able to protect and capitalize on the equity of the Honeywell brand while building the new brand?

Stacey Jones: It's something we'll have to craft along the way. I don't have a silver bullet answer here! I believe that our 100+ years of history of trust, loyalty, and advocacy will set us on a good course in terms of momentum. There will be a lot of work to achieve exactly what you just articulated.

Protecting the brand is what we do intuitively every day as communicators and professionals, but when you're going through a separation like we are now, it's under the microscope. The brand has an additional meaning to all our audiences as we tell the story and take everyone along on the journey of where we're going in the future. I was just talking over the weekend with my colleague in internal communications, and she was saying you've got to keep telling people our key messages. That's so right. You can't just tell people once; with everything else going on in the world, we have to find ways to keep people's attention and give them what's most relevant to them.

Certainly, within our journey, there will be a "what's in it for me"-type question from people, which is natural. To answer that successfully, our leadership has been vocal about transparency; as soon as we are able to communicate something to our people, we do so. Our CEO has numerous sessions where he takes questions and answers absolutely everything he can. And if we get a question that we'll only be able to answer in the future, it's captured and answered later on. That type of personal connection and interaction has been really important for our people. They see our leaders stand up, look them in the eye, and say, "This is our plan, and this is everything I can tell you today." That is higher-touch brand protection. If you don't have your people as your foremost brand advocates, the rest of the stuff breaks down.

For us, it's business as usual right now, making sure that our customers know we're focused on delivering. We're heads down on the day-to-day work because that will keep the trust, keep the momentum going, and continue our growth. For example, we've made multiple acquisitions in the last year, which we have to integrate, so there are a lot of moving parts, and we have to make sure that we focus on executing the day-to-day rather than getting carried away with what's way down the road. That's something I talk about with the team a lot, and so far so good, but it's important we have those regular discussions and ensure everyone's on the same page.

Tabita Andersson: What's your opinion on the importance of the communications function when we work through these situations? Can we help more now than perhaps a decade ago, when it was much more about controlling the message and being strict in terms of what we say? You mention your CEO being open and authentic. Is that something we've seen change over the last decade?

Stacey Jones: That's a really smart question. I think it depends on the industry, the company, and the people. I can say that, having been through the IPO at Accenture, which was a while back. People are everything in the professional services industry, and right now, people are everything here, too. You can't make a product or deliver a service without people. Professional services was a pioneer in prioritizing how to engage people, but I'm struggling a bit to answer your question about looking back ten years, because it's such a different frame of reference. However, I believe our CEO would have been equally as transparent—that's just who he is and how he approaches communications. I think part of it is leadership and the authenticity a leader naturally brings.

Throughout my career, I've done a lot of CEO positioning work, and several years back, I listened to a presentation by the editor of The Economist at the time, who was speaking to a small group of us at the World Economic Forum in Davos. The advice was: "I don't care if you have the smoothest style, it's the authenticity that you bring to a conversation, and how I feel about what you're telling me. If I feel like it's a corporate message, or you're trying to convince me about something based on talking points, it won't be successful." I've remembered that throughout my career. It's given me a lot of confidence that some of the things media coaches focus on are less important than the overall package of a leader. It matters more that people believe the leader is speaking from the heart and speaking the truth, not just standing there pretending to be transparent, but actually being transparent. That's perhaps not exactly what you asked for, but that's my view.

Also, a little earlier, we mentioned trust, which is so important to build with customers, employees, investors, and other stakeholders, and it takes time. First, you need to be able to articulate your vision, but then people will watch you. Are you delivering it? Are you consistent? What do you do day by day? I came from a role where I'd been for 20+ years and where I built enormous trust with my colleagues and my team, to the point where many of them are dear, dear friends today and not a week goes by that we don't talk or connect or have a laugh about something.

Coming into a new role, one of the things I quickly realized when I sat down at my new desk was that it would take time to build trust, and that's not abnormal or bad. When you've been in a role or company for periods of time, you might take it for granted, but it's one of the most important things for every leader, particularly communicators. The advice we're often giving is trust-based. Every recommendation we make and every outcome we measure either builds trust or erodes it.

Tabita Andersson: You mentioned your time at Accenture earlier. Can you describe your career path and how you ended up in communications?

Stacey Jones: I went to a liberal arts college, and it was well-known for writing, which is what I love doing. I was an English major specializing in 16th-century poetry, and I really enjoyed the full college experience. I was involved in a lot of activities, from student government to varsity athletics to Greek life, you name it! Then, when I graduated, I didn't know what to do.

My parents were both in education, so they had no real idea about how to counsel me on broader careers. I thought a lot about what my degree had prepared me to do. The answer: I can think critically, and I can write. So that led me to apply for a position as a journalist in the nearest big town, Columbus, Ohio. I had a friend from college who asked me to come live with her there, as she was in medical school, which was a huge bonus.

I had no idea what I was getting into when I started as a journalist. I tried to quit after two weeks. I ended up in a newsroom full of J-school grads from The Ohio State University, who all had very different training. They spoke a language I didn't know, but they couldn't have been nicer. It was more about me feeling that I couldn't do it. One day, the editor asked one of them to take me out to lunch and tell me to "hang in there," and that was some of the best advice I've ever received. I did just that for a couple of years, and I learned a ton by osmosis, given the close-knit newsroom environment.

During my reporting days, I met a terrific woman who was a PR director for the town that I was assigned to cover. She helped me understand the issues I was covering and the history behind the issues, and she'd answer any question, but I never felt like she was trying to spin a story. I'm sure she had an agenda, but her delivery and her transparency are things that I continue to look back and think, "Wow, that's a successful PR person." I knew that's what I wanted to do. Plus, she had her own office and wasn't covering board meetings until two in the morning or getting called out to report on fires. I knew that was the career I wanted. She influenced me because I saw someone I respected in action, and it set me on a specific course. I eventually moved to Chicago and worked as an editor, but I was constantly looking for that first job at a PR agency, which I finally got. The rest has been being in the right place at the right time and continuing to develop my skills.

Tabita Andersson: Do you have any non-communications experience or skills that you think have helped you in your career?

Stacey Jones: I don't know if I'd be so generous to say it's non-comms experience because I think being a journalist gave me a leg up to understand the news media. However, I sat directly in front of the copy desk, so I knew that when a news release came in, they would mark through the fluff and the extraneous details, and I learned how many spaces the headline needed. That really taught me how to think like a journalist and how to be additive and not irritate them unnecessarily. I've sat in their chair. You're not always going to have the same agenda as journalists, but being one definitely shaped the way I approach things, and it's given me a realism that I can bring to conversations as an in-house counselor.

Tabita Andersson: What advice would you give to someone junior in their communications career regarding how to best plan their career?

Stacey Jones: My son just graduated from college, and he is starting his career in communications, so that's a very appropriate question! I would say: Get your hands on everything you can. Try things, put your hand up, and be the person who gives it a shot. Listen to conversations, join the calls, and learn as much as you can. Early in your career, you will do a lot of work that you may not think is fun; perhaps you're just clipping and reading news stories, and it does not feel that important. But ask the question to understand "why" you're clipping the stories and "why" you're sending something to a client. Don't just do the task; understand the context and work hard to get the insight. Connect the dots, and you can grow fast in this industry. But you won't grow fast if you begrudge being asked to do things that may seem transactional but are truly essential to the bigger picture in what you're providing the client, regardless of whether it's an in-house client or an agency client.

Working in an agency is a wonderful way to get hands-on experience and do a variety of things. This is particularly true at smaller agencies, because they will throw you right in at the deep end, and there is naturally less hierarchy.

Something else I'd like to add is the importance of figuring out which communications and brand specialties you enjoy the most and least. It's like a deck of cards, and you need to choose which cards you like and which ones are not as interesting to you. But getting your hands on everything early on will empower you to narrow things down. Getting some broad experience and "trying the glove on" before you declare you want to go deep can save you a couple of years of recovery if you end up somewhere you don't want to be … because time goes fast!

Tabita Andersson: It does indeed! What kind of skills and talents do you look for when searching for a new communications leader or independent contributor to your team?

Stacey Jones: I interviewed someone yesterday who was near entry-level, and I knew from my team that her skills were all checked out in terms of capabilities and college work, so I focused on the fit within the organisation, the cultural fit and what she was looking for. Could she carry a conversation in a poised way for 30 minutes? Yes, she could. Did she take the initiative to answer my questions above and beyond what I expected? Yes, she did. She brought a PowerPoint deck and showed me who she was. I intentionally left the conversation open-ended because I wanted to see where she would take it and how she would lead in a situation where, clearly, she was far from the senior person in the room. She had the stage; how would she use that stage? I evaluated her interest, her executive presence, her aptitude, and her hustle factor. It all went really well, and when we got to the end of the interview, I said I'm so excited to welcome you to our team. She said, but you didn't ask me any real interview questions, and I was so worried. I replied: I did, but maybe not the ones you were expecting, because I trust my team to evaluate your skills and capabilities. I really wanted to get to know you as a person, as a professional, and how you show up and present. I wanted to give you a chance to ask me questions and understand what I stand for, what the company stands for, what kind of culture we have, and how that fits with you. If you have the right motivation and skill set to start with, you can learn almost everything.

I look for hungry, lifelong learners, people who want to try new things, and people who have strong skills but are not satisfied. I look for people who want to grow and develop, and I think you can read that in conversations with people: how they think about their next steps, what they've done, and how they talk about it.

Tabita Andersson: Being curious and having an appetite for learning have come up in quite a few conversations, so that seems to be a golden thread. In addition, in communications, you have to be prepared for it not being a traditional nine-to-five job. Something can crop up any time of the day or week, so having a proactive, curious attitude is helpful because you don't know when you might receive a phone call from the media at eight o'clock at night, with a deadline two hours later and you just can't say "sorry, I'm clocking off so can't deal with it right now!"

Stacey Jones: That was one skill I learned as a reporter. I can't control when the fire is happening, I can't control when the Board meeting is taking place, so you either embrace that fluidity and thrive on the unknown and unexpected, or you may need to find a different area of communications that's more predictable.

That's a choice you can also make at different points in life. Right now, I'm at a point in my life where my sons are out of the house. When they were much younger, I consciously opted for a different role, and my boss gave me more flexibility. I still worked full-time, but it was a different rhythm, and I wasn't called on to do crisis communications at the time or the hot-breaking issues or C-level positioning at the level I'm doing now. It was more focused on ESG and CSR when the company was evolving and putting programs in place to develop capabilities. It was hard, deep-thinking work—but more scheduled, and that made a big difference in my life. My sons would say I still travelled a lot, and things were crazy, but I can tell you that it was much more predictable than other times. I would encourage people to understand where they are in their lives. You may not want to run the same way in the next five years as you've just run the past five years, but be honest with yourself. I have an incredible mentor who told me to look in the mirror; that's the person you have to square it with, and she was quite right. But I will add that it was not easy.

Tabita Andersson: We've mentioned crisis communications a couple of times, so let's dig into that a bit more, as it can be a good place to prove the value of communications. Once you have been through a crisis successfully, you typically build trust and develop better relationships inside an organisation. How do you deal with crisis communications at all levels, both from an executive level as well as organisation-wide? Sometimes, we have particular crisis situations in a region or a division, and sometimes, we have to manage a large crisis like the COVID pandemic.

Stacey Jones: Yes, and during the pandemic, I ran all internal and external communications. The company was looking after 700,000+ people at the time, so it was literally 24/7. Italy would open up, and you'd get a note out, and then one county in the United States would shut down, and you'd have to get another note out. It was like whack-a-mole on a large scale, and it was probably the most extreme experience anyone in communications could have, because it was a global pandemic at a company with a huge global presence. The reason it was hard for us to manage was that you didn't know where the end was. It was a sustained crisis. Crises, by definition, typically have beginnings and ends and reputational overhangs, but this was different. Managing your own capacity in those situations is critical. Then, put your mask on and take care of the team. You can't have everyone going at full speed 24/7, every day. We orchestrated that by setting up a team of 100+ communications people across the world, so we could cover any place at any given time, seven days a week. If someone was not on, they were told to go off, not show up, take a break and take care of themselves and their family. It wasn't just the people at work we were managing; we were also in lockdown, taking care of loved ones and homeschooling with kids. It was pretty much everything you could imagine going wrong at once, both personally and professionally.

That taught me what a crisis really meant. Then you have to compare that with, say, cyber-attacks that we've all managed through in different countries at different times of day. You need to recognise if you are someone who's comfortable running to the fire. If you are, you probably would like to be part of the crisis team. Interestingly, during the pandemic, not everyone in our newly extended team came with deep crisis experience, and one of the most gratifying outcomes was the people who said they never thought they could do this, and they really liked it, saying, "Thank you for giving me the opportunity." There were also a few people who said, "Thank you, this has been great, and I never want to do this ever again!" But suddenly, we had this little black box of people across the global organisation who were crisis experts opening the aperture to teach others. It was a stark contrast with the days when people did not know what issues and crisis teams were. Of course, if you do it right, no one sees it because the crisis is averted.

There was a bit of an odd equation in communications at the time, where some teams were churning out proactive content, tweets, articles, memos, and videos. The socialization of crisis communications during the pandemic raised the appreciation of the function and how it's essential to lifting the outcomes of an organisation to some degree. While it's often not seen, crisis comms is a cross-functional effort, and you have a broad peer group. This is true when we look at the impacts of geopolitical movements on our organisation. These are not crises—just something you deal with in countries around the world on a regular basis. But you can't do it alone. This is very much a team sport, and I believe we can bring a few great things to the table, including knowing what an issue is, knowing what a crisis is, modulating your own approach, being the rock during the crisis, and keeping other people calm. We have the context for how a crisis is going to play out, so we can tell people that the sky's not falling if it's not, and that can go a long way to getting everyone's best input and having productive conversations vs. emotionally led conversations, which often are not productive.

Tabita Andersson: I agree. As communicators, we see a lot of knee-jerk reactions. Sometimes, half the job is just staying calm and focusing on what we can do, what the next steps are and being the advisor in the room.

This leads me to ask about the Chief Communications Officer role. What do you think are the key attributes of a successful CCO, and what work can they do most effectively as part of the executive leadership team?

Stacey Jones: It goes without saying that the CCO role should be of an advisor. What that actually means varies from issue to issue and company to company.

Reading the room and understanding where your advice can be most additive is important vs. feeling compelled to always say something or speak first. Often, it's not the person who says the most but the person who's steady and forms relationships, who perhaps can even have the conversation outside of the room to reinforce something, who's most successful. Again, it depends on the organisation. If you're in a room with people who have been through a situation three times at the same company, it's smarter to listen and then figure out how you can add to the conversation.

Over the years, I've found it's valuable, in a conversation, to bring data that other people won't have access to. Or bring the perspective of news media, where the trends are unfolding, which can often provide context that's important to the broader conversation. This way, you will not be saying anything redundant, even if you haven't been through it three times at the same company.

Being relatively new in my current role, I'm working with people who have had tremendous experience doing things that maybe I'm doing for the first time, so I try to bring something they wouldn't know. Often, that's an outside-in point of view that I can offer and match in the conversation with things they know, so the group around the table has an additional perspective to blend with their deep industry knowledge.

Tabita Andersson: In those situations, how do you think other executives or C-level peers can work more effectively with the communications function? What advice would you give your peers about how to become more effective together?

Stacey Jones: I don't mean to take this as an easy out, but there are a lot of variances on that, so I'll try to find beliefs that have a commonality. Literally, just asking, "Do you have anything to add?" is an easy one; it's a simple question. The answer might be no, but being consulted is important. We've all seen the RACI (responsible, accountable, consulted, and informed), and everyone's going to find themselves at various points on that RACI, depending on the issue.

Another is being curious to ask, "What else? What am I missing?" Those are always great questions, and the more open-ended they are, the more information will be contributed by everyone around the table, not just the CCO. For me, that can be powerful.

Also, the more you understand what a function does, the more you can call on them to marshal what they can uniquely bring. It is a result of working together over time: as you mature as a cross-functional team and work together over time, it becomes easier because you know everyone is helpful.

Tabita Andersson: That relates to something that has come up in my conversations about communicators building better commercial awareness. As a communications function, if colleagues have grown up doing only communications, they may not have an awareness of the wider business. You mentioned building an understanding of what other functions do, and thankfully, we don't have to be corporate finance experts, but knowing what they do and how they fit can really help with conversations.

Stacey Jones: That's a great point. I tend to refer to it as business acumen, and it's often what separates mid-careers from more senior people. It's something you develop over time. Just the other day, someone on my team was speaking to one of our Chief Commercial Officers about a campaign and referenced two or three very technical industry terms. You could see the executive was listening because they knew she got them; she really understood. That was impressive, and it was one of those connection points where business and brand came together to be most effective. So, I think you just made a very wise statement.

Tabita Andersson: Something else I've heard is to bring communications in early in a decision. Don't leave communications to the end to be an afterthought, but bring us in early so we understand the decision and give advice accordingly about consequences and impact. Would you agree with that?

Stacey Jones: I've had good experiences with that, so it wasn't on my shortlist of things that need to improve. For me, there is a risk of bringing in communications too early because you end up grinding hours on calls before decisions are ready to be made. I believe there's a tipping point where the use of resources is balanced with timing, so it's not too early or too late, but the right time for communications to be additive. The downside of that is that you end up not contributing, so it might be better to withdraw until the time is right. And it's okay to say we'll be back when everyone is ready, because we need to manage resources and the optics of contributing in a valuable way.

Tabita Andersson: We haven't covered how to best work with your CEO. What advice would you give to a CEO on how to get the most out of their communications person?

Stacey Jones: That goes back to the conversation we had about understanding the business strategy, because everything I bring to my CEO has to be connected to the business strategy. It has to support his goal, which our CEO has been very clear about. It's all about growing the business; there's no mysticism about what we're doing here. If something happens, it has to fit within our strategy; it can't be a one-off.

Planning is important, but overplanning is bad because who has time for that at the CEO level? You have to find the balance so you're leveraging their time correctly. Have a conversation about how much time they can spend on certain activities. Do they need to be more visible right now, or are we going through a quieter period? How does that align with how we're going to amplify the brand right now? Explaining, in the context of the business strategy, why you're recommending something is crucial, in my opinion.

The CEO will have many advisors, and you're one of them. I believe it's important to listen to both external and internal voices, be aware of the bigger picture, and not get too caught up in your own agenda. Everything sits on a bigger stage, and it's all in service of the strategy that the CEO you're working with is driving. Sometimes they will say that they don't want to do something you are recommending, or they have other ideas. We need to be flexible and think that perhaps I wouldn't have thought of that, but it fits very well into the strategy.

It is paramount to be able to build the story, momentum, and brand and also prepare for any hurdles that might come at any moment. Know your leader. Know how to use their time economically and effectively, especially for preparation work. Not every leader wants to prepare the same way with the same detail, so just knowing the rhythm of what they find most useful is part of the success of working together.

Tabita Andersson: Is there anything else you would like to add?

Stacey Jones: I'm at the point in my career where I feel like I'm still learning every day, but at the same time, I feel grateful as I look at the talent in future generations. I'm extremely fortunate to have a job where I don't have to look at the clock and say, boy, I wish my day were over. If future talent can have that same excitement and that same sense of reward, they know they've picked the right profession. I would recommend it to anyone, knowing it's not for everyone. For those who choose it and love it, it will be a truly rewarding way to spend their work life. But always balance that with what you want your bigger life to be, because both are equally important to the whole human being.

CHAPTER

9

Amalia Kontesi

Chief Communications and Marketing Officer
NATO Innovation Fund

Amalia Kontesi is the **Chief Communications and Marketing Officer** for the **NATO Innovation Fund,** a venture capital fund backed by 24 NATO Allies, deploying €1 billion+ in deep tech. The organisation invests independently and empowers deep tech founders to address challenges in defense, security, and resilience. Backed by 24 nations, NIF provides deep tech dual-use entrepreneurs with adoption pathways to both commercial and government markets.

For more information about NIF, visit nif.fund.

Amalia's LinkedIn profile: `linkedin.com/in/amaliakontesi/`

Tabita Andersson: To set the scene, please give us an overview of the NATO Innovation Fund (NIF) and your current role as Chief Communications and Marketing Officer.

Amalia Kontesi: NIF is a venture capital fund that invests in dual-use deep tech technologies. With deep tech, we mean technologies backed by hard science; with dual-use, we mean technologies that have applications in both defense and security, as well as industrial resilience. The fund was initiated by NATO a couple of years ago and is the first multi-sovereign venture capital in the world. That means that our investors are NATO nations, and, as we like to think about it, ultimately, our stakeholders are the citizens of these nations. We have a mandate to make really good investments, both to meet our commercial goals and to deliver the capabilities of the countries backing us. We have a very strong mission to help the technologies we're backing get adopted by governments or large industry players within the Alliance.

I joined NIF almost a year ago to manage the fund's Marketing and Communications. It was the first time I took on a role where I had full oversight of the department, and because it's such a new fund with a strong, well-known brand, it was an incredibly appealing challenge. On the one hand, we have to build a new brand, but then you also have to account for, respect, and protect the brand that's already attached to the fund itself, as well as the mission that needs to be aligned and the role it's been built to serve. That all makes the communications and marketing role poignant.

With a fund like ours, it's not just about commercial growth or the adoption of technologies; it's also about how we can help set the bar for critical conversations that can help create an ecosystem with other funds. Together, we can pour more financing toward patient capital, defense, security, and resilience technologies, which are our bread and butter. This is a big aspect of the communications role, which goes beyond what an average fund communications and marketing role would entail.

Tabita Andersson: What are your role's key objectives and mission, and what type of stakeholders do you typically work with?

Amalia Kontesi: It's a unique setup with a very diverse set of stakeholders. The most important internal stakeholders for us are the fund's partners and our Board.

A big part of what I do is to make it easy for the people who make the investments, or set and execute the strategy, to do their jobs. Sometimes that's preparing for and helping prevent a potential reputational crisis; sometimes it's about how we can best position ourselves to get the best deals in the market. Nothing matters if we can't work with the best innovators, and if we can't help bring them to scale and can't help connect them to governments or organisations, to ensuring that we have a reputation as a really good investor to work with, who will support the company throughout its life cycle and will create pathways for adoption across the nations where we operate, is a very important mandate.

This involves building the general brand, which we can affect via good executive communications and the kind of thought leadership we engage in. For example, we're very mindful that we need to push for certain policies that we believe will be critical to the startups that we support, so we're sharing a lot of research on the broader state of the market, not necessarily about us, but on how the venture capital sector is evolving.

Other important stakeholders for us are the startups we fund. So, a big part of my role is about how we can be thoughtful and supportive of our startups, which are all at different levels of development, thinking through their own communications and marketing strategies. Some are at an early stage, so they are trying to answer organisational questions such as whether to build a team in-house, hire an agency, or do both. For some others, the conversation is about an upcoming big product launch, looking for more financing down the line, or how to gain a certain customer in a certain country, which means they may need advice on how to think about doing campaigns in a different nation for the first time.

Finally—and very importantly—we also take the fact that we are backed by nations very seriously. We want to make sure that, to the extent we can with our small team, we have a presence at conferences and in the press in those nations so that people have a direct understanding of what their contributions are going toward. We want to be very transparent to that audience as well.

In summary, it's a very wide role in terms of stakeholders, audiences, and the engagement we need to build, which makes it super-interesting.

Tabita Andersson: You touched on brand building, and I'd like to dig into that a bit more because your challenge is interesting. On the one hand, you have a legacy brand, but you need to build a reputation as an innovation fund, which has a very different connotation and perception. How do you go about doing that, and what are some of the channels you use?

Amalia Kontesi: You have to start with a tremendous amount of respect for the legacy brand because there's a massive opportunity to work off such a brand. Doing so involves a lot of coordination with colleagues with roles like mine within NATO to ensure that whatever we do is consistent with their strategy and objectives. At no point do we want to deviate in a way that could be problematic for the legacy brand, so that's a very important consideration.

At the same time, we've been blessed with a lot of leeway in building our reputation. I think that's possible for us because we have a very specific mandate as venture capitalists. Many of our audiences know NATO very well, but have never thought of it as a source for independent venture capital funding. So, as long as we are aligned on the broader messaging and strategy, we then look at what we do that we're very good at and what makes us different within the VC industry that we can use to position ourselves uniquely. We offer capital for 15 years, while most VCs have a shorter time frame, enabling us to support our companies for a long time, which is particularly helpful in deep tech because research can take years within that industry. This means that the timelines with which many of those companies work are quite challenging. It's a real differentiator for us, and that's a good example of how we leverage our legacy brand.

Another example is our adoption capability. Because we're backed by nations, we have a unique opportunity with our adoption team, which is led by someone with extensive experience in the military and civil service, to have conversations and map the needs on the ground by governments and companies so we can go into conversations saying, "In this country, we know there's a need for this type of technology; we have this type of technology and can connect you." This is another big differentiator for us.

Using the legacy brand to build a new brand is more about what it gives us to make us unique and positioning us within the VC ecosystem in a way that elevates us and the legacy brand itself.

Tabita Andersson: How do you balance that when it comes to protecting the brand? I assume you have to position yourself as independent from the legacy brand.

Amalia Kontesi: Yes, we are independent, and we were founded and set up so that we could move at the pace that our industry needs to be successful. However, we're very honest about who we are and our association. If you look at our website, it's very clear that our mission is to advance defense, security, and resilience for the Alliance, so there's a clear alignment there, and everything we do ultimately leads toward that.

From a communications perspective, the most important aspect of protecting our brand is that we often get a lot of questions about commenting on geopolitics. If you work for another investor or VC and comment on geopolitics, it will be associated with that investor's point of view. If you have a clear association with one of the largest Alliances in the world, you have to be very careful about what you say because you don't want to end up intervening in really important, critical geopolitical negotiations by accident because you opined on something as an investor; however, it was perceived as an official position. On the one hand, it's great that we get the opportunities to be in the press, and I believe in always supporting journalists when and how I can. I'm also always honest and up-front with them about what we can comment on. This is one of the biggest challenges at the moment.

Tabita Andersson: That's interesting because it aligns with the same principle that other commercial organisations use. It's important to understand what an organisation can and can't, or wants and doesn't want to comment on, from a reputational perspective, because there may be voices out there that need to be heard. We don't want to add to the noise; we want to make sure the correct voices are heard.

Let's pivot to talk about your background and career path. I'm curious to understand how you progressed to your current role and where you started.

Amalia Kontesi: Fortune and fortitude! I started my career in communications consulting, and I spent about four or five years in agencies after graduating from my master's degree. First, I worked for PR agencies—an incredibly fast-paced environment. I always joke that agency years are like dog years! You learn so much because you work so much, and it's diverse and intense. The requirement in the broader consulting world is perfection. Anything less than perfection is a problem for you and your team because it's a long supply chain of deliverables, which you only really understand as you become more senior.

Working in an agency gave me broad exposure to corporate communications, financial communications, public affairs, and executive crisis work. I was quite fortunate to immediately land in a place I enjoyed. I had done my master's in Public Administration, focusing on communications and economic development, and I wanted to find a role that would allow me to use that academic background. Again, I was fortunate because one of my clients was JPMorganChase when I worked in the agency world. Years after I worked as part of the team supporting them, I interviewed for a role at the firm's Corporate Responsibility team. I got the job, which changed my life because it was exactly what I wanted to do. It's rare in your career to land where you do exactly what you want to do, and doing so with passion and dedication. I spent nearly six incredibly happy years at JPMorganChase. I ended up holding multiple roles within the communications team, covering almost all activities within the firm's philanthropic organisation and finally taking on sustainability and ESG work. That also took me from being an individual contributor to a manager, with incredible opportunities for mentorship from senior leaders within the firm who knew what they were doing and had the patience to show me. It was a rare moment of being in the right place at the right time. I then transitioned to a role at Google, my first time having a pure EMEA (Europe, Middle East, and Africa)-focused role.

It's vastly different to work at the headquarters of a company vis-à-vis specific markets. Transitioning to an EMEA-focused role at Google, I had to learn how to negotiate on behalf of a market. As the EMEA region contains many different countries with many different priorities and needs, wearing the EMEA hat was very useful and prepared me well for my current job, which also requires me to think about many different cultures, countries, and geopolitical challenges. After two years at Google, I got a phone call about a VC that had been in stealth mode for some time and needed someone to run communications who had experience with government, finance, and tech. At the time, I remember hanging up thinking this wasn't real because a NATO-backed VC seemed like such a different idea from anything else I'd ever heard of, and here I am two years later, which is why I said good fortune! Ultimately, someone played matchmaker, and the firm was looking for someone with a specific background. Over the years, you specialize in something in your career, or certain markets, which helps tailor the things that come to you based on your skillset and areas of interest. Ultimately, it was good fortune and a good match that worked well!

Tabita Andersson: That's a wonderful story, and when you tell it, it sounds like you truly love your job and what you do!

Amalia Kontesi: Yes, I am grateful to be at the right place at the right time. I'm sure there will be other moments in my career where I'm in a job that doesn't quite click. That's just how things work. But it's good fortune when you can do something that challenges you intellectually, with a mission you feel you can support with a good conscience, and people whose company you enjoy.

Tabita Andersson: That is such a poignant and fundamental statement. What are some of the parts of your job that you enjoy the most?

Amalia Kontesi: The answer to that differs for every communications person. I love media relations. Many colleagues say it's their worst nightmare, but I grew up avidly reading newspapers. My first internship was as a journalist before I started working full time, so I genuinely love journalism. When you love something, it loves you back. I've never had a conversation with a reporter where I wanted to hide the ball; if anything, I always feel I'm there to help them better understand the sector, market, or the perspective of the organisation I'm representing. I believe journalists feel that. They feel like they're speaking with someone who respects what they do and acknowledges that what they do is important. So, media relations is something I particularly enjoy.

I also enjoy the strategic planning, the brainstorming, and the more creative side of the work, when you can throw ideas on the table and see what clicks with you, your team and the rest of your stakeholders.

And there's something really rewarding about seeing an executive you've been supporting for a while start to shine. For example, because I was at JPMorganChase for a longer period of time, some people were young directors when I joined, and by the time I left, they were leading departments as managing directors. To have had relationships last for five or six years, working with them hand in hand, helped train them, and taken feedback from them in terms of what was helpful or not, then see them be able to go on stage, or live TV, or be able to motivate their teams, building their executive presence and communications skills over time is very rewarding. I take a lot of pride in that, and those relationships are for life.

Tabita Andersson: Absolutely! Based on your career path, what advice would you give younger communications professionals who want to make communications their career?

Amalia Kontesi: I'll answer that with the best advice I've ever received, because it's advice I got when I was very young, perhaps one or two years into my career. At this point, all you need to be is a safe pair of hands. I thought that was an incredibly helpful piece of advice because we work in such a fast-paced environment, so you will gain trust if you deliver work that's on time and doesn't have a multitude of typos when your manager needs it!

The other thing I'd say is to find mentors early on who are not so senior to you that they don't understand where you're at. That was another good fortune of mine in my early career, as I had mentors who were about ten years older than me, which meant it wasn't like they'd been the Chief Communications Officer for decades and had no idea what I was going through. It meant they could guide me, get me out of the weeds when needed, and push me in the right direction.

I would also advise anyone to keep those relationships going after they leave a job. I make a point of reaching out to everyone who's mentored me as often as possible. I still think I owe them my career. It's a very small world, and relationships matter. Last, but not least, you have to know what you're good at and build your own brand because we're in an industry where you get paid to have an opinion. Very often, what happens, and I understand and have been in that position, is that if people disagree with you and they're a lot more senior than you, you either end up having very heated conversations, or you don't stand your ground. None of those options is a good recipe for success. The right thing to do is to be clear about your recommendations, but then, if the decision goes in a different direction, work within the decision to make sure you protect the people and the brand as well as possible.

Regardless, your job is to form an opinion and personal brand as early as possible because no good communications person will, in good conscience, say they're good at their job because they managed to get 50 press clippings for an announcement. We know that doesn't matter. Good leaders know it doesn't matter because one positive press clipping in the New York Times can be better for the business than thousands of other press clippings. So, that's not the goal.

But to be someone your executives will trust in good times and tough times takes a lot of time and discipline, both in terms of how emotional we can get and how we should contain our initial reactions to things. I think that's my third and most important piece of advice.

Tabita Andersson: Those are great pieces of advice! As we're talking about the role of a Chief Communications Officer, what changes have you seen to the role and our profession over the last five or ten years?

Amalia Kontesi: Every year, we seem to face changes at a faster pace than the previous year! It was all about social media and having a strong and engaging digital presence when I started. It's still about having a digital presence in many aspects of the work, but what that means and how we can capitalize on social media has evolved. It's the same with media relations because we no longer only talk about newspapers, TV, or radio. We have to think about several other channels—news fluencers, podcasts, tiktokers, and more. It's become an incredibly busy landscape, and getting your message across requires many more touchpoints across several different bubbles.

As communications professionals, we should be very aware of this, but we should also remember that not all people are relevant to the entire organisation. Being able to keep your head straight when making decisions is key. A podcast can be really cool, but it might not be quite the right fit for my organisation. Or, I'd love to have my executive live with a certain TikTok influencer, but on certain occasions, it could do more harm than good.

I think the profession is being impacted by the lack of trust in the media. It's not that people don't trust traditional media; I just think there's a massive amount of mistrust and information that we're exposed to, which makes doing our job much harder. When you think about who you're trying to convince, if people are not easy to convince through any channel, that makes the job difficult. Something that has changed negatively on the media relations side is that, on both sides, people are less willing to go out and meet in person or pick up the phone and speak to each other, and that's just a function of how the world is evolving.

The number of people who won't meet up and only want contact over a specific story they are about to file is growing. Relationships do matter, and they matter not because you become friends and someone will do you a favor, but because to truly be helpful to the media, you have to understand what they are interested in, what their editors are looking for, and what types of reporting they are planning on doing in the coming months. How can you do your job if you don't understand the general pressure that newsrooms are under right now? They're down on people, and salaries are kept very tight, so the person you're emailing is a real human being dealing with those pressures. You need to have that personal relationship with them to understand their situation and to value and treat them with the respect required. We must ask ourselves how we can help the reporter on the other end of the line do their job, not how to get a story pitch out to 100 people quickly.

That relates to another observation that not all communications people understand the incredible need to be a subject matter expert on the company or topic they represent. You need to be a useful call to make for a reporter, colleague, or external stakeholder, which means you need to know what you're talking about well enough. I think this is another change that has occurred in recent years—probably because we're so spent on trying to monitor the number of channels that are emerging, the amount of information that's coming out, the amount of likes something gets, if the message is penetrating or not, when there are massive spikes in news cycles, and so on. All of this takes so much energy, but there is a long game we need to continue playing to do our jobs well.

Tabita Andersson: Those are good observations. You mention being a subject matter expert. Is that also important from an internal perspective, as you are building relationships at the highest level within an organisation? In addition, can we improve commercial awareness or business acumen as a profession?

Amalia Kontesi: That will get you respect from your colleagues—and therefore, a license to operate internally. First of all, spending the time to get to know someone's work will get them to like you, and that, I believe, is the absolute bare minimum. It is nice when someone says they'd like to know how you spend your day, talk about what's important to them, and how you can best support them. Second, time during the workday is very tight, so it is very unlikely that you'll be in a meeting and something will come up, and they will go: "Oh, let me just translate that into layman's terms for the communications person to understand it." You could ask that question—and I'm a big believer in asking questions when you don't understand what's being said—but the more up to speed you are, the more you can follow along at the pace of delivery, the better off you are because you will be able to ask the right questions. The more informed you are, the better the questions you'll ask. Third, as a communications professional, you have an opportunity to walk into a room and try to look for the blind spots when launching a product or making a new investment, regardless of what it is that we're doing. That is very important internally for your ability to do your job, maintain respect, collaborate with senior executives, respect their time, and be as useful as possible when things go wrong.

Tabita Andersson: And things always go wrong at some point, which brings me to working in crises. How can CCOs and their teams step up and take a leading role to help guide an organisation through a crisis? We seem to get more of them, and the pace at which we have to react is sometimes shorter. What is your experience of crisis communications in general, and how can it show the value of communications to an organisation?

Amalia Kontesi: My contrarian point of view is that nobody has ever received kudos for managing successful crisis communications because people won't see or feel anything if you are successful. It's one of the most unrewarding aspects of the role, but also incredibly important.

I believe there are two aspects to crisis communications. One is the kind of crisis that you can predict. For example, if you know you will have a leadership change, you can prepare your communications. It won't happen in one moment, so you can prepare for a departure and then announce an arrival.

For these, you should have standing plans, know who needs to be in the room to make decisions early on, and be able to go into the room and be the voice of reason when everybody else is panicking. The team appreciates that in the long term.

The other aspect is working through those crises that we can't predict. For example, we were all in the room during the early days of COVID when we had no idea what we were dealing with. Nobody did! I remember trying to decide whether to cancel an event just before the lockdowns started. It was going to be a high-level event, and we were all just sitting there staring at each other, wondering what the best course of action would be. The best thing to do in those situations, in my experience, is to bring enough perspective into the room so that you have as good an understanding as possible of all the ways the situation could go. For example, making sure government relations are in the room because if we go all warm, fuzzy, and excited about something, they're the ones that will tell us to wait because something is being discussed at the highest level of government, so your plan might backfire or cause problems. And have a lawyer in the room because they can tell you about the different implications something might have. Having a diverse perspective in the room when you're trying to make decisions and understanding what the business wants from it is important, so you can look at all the potential roadblocks before making a recommendation.

The other thing is that I thought reacting quickly in a crisis was important. I now believe that's not always the right answer. I used to believe that we have to go live with a response as fast as something happens, but in some situations, things change all the time, and you don't have perfect information, so taking your time is good.

In our profession, we built a habit over an extended period, thinking that any brand or organisation has to opine on everything, but sometimes you just don't have the tools. You don't know enough to opine on everything, so we have to figure out how to opine enough, or early enough, authentically, or prevent another crisis? And understand why to stay silent on something else. These are the decisions that are shifting my mind right now. I now start out thinking more case-specific. You have to have a holding statement, but sometimes you have to be honest and say you don't have an answer for something.

Tabita Andersson: I agree. On that note, saying nothing can also be taken as an opinion today, which we didn't see a few years ago. Nobody thought twice if you didn't have an opinion, but now, you have to balance the fact that if you don't say something, people still perceive that as an opinion. It's becoming trickier to balance and manage communications.

You make a really good point about stopping and thinking before reacting. Quite often, we are under pressure to do something, so it can feel hard to take that moment and be mindful.

Amalia Kontesi: Our team is diverse, and we have people with science backgrounds, with finance backgrounds, and with military backgrounds, and they often say "move slow to move fast" to each other. There's a lot of truth in that. Sometimes you know you have to move constantly, but doing it carefully is what you need. Of course, there are some things that you obviously have to jump in on quickly, but jumping ahead when you shouldn't is as problematic as staying silent when you should speak up.

Tabita Andersson: Do you have any final pieces of advice that you would like to add?

Amalia Kontesi: I'd like to reiterate that I've always enjoyed having really good mentors. I think most of my advice for people is rephrasing what my mentors have said to me.

One of my greatest mentors always said that the PR person should never be the news. That's always bad, and I've resisted that. Although we live in an era where you have to do a lot of personal branding, it's still good advice. The more you can use your people in the organisation to do the appropriate work as spokespeople for the organisation, the better the organisation and you will be.

I don't know if the following is communications advice specifically, I think it's just good general advice, but if you have people whom you trust, frequently asking them what your blind spots are, is helpful. Nobody loves negative feedback, and the more senior you are, it doesn't mean you suddenly love negative feedback. Still, if you have people you trust, you can put them in a position to tell you what you could be doing better or tell you if there's something you're constantly doing wrong but you don't see yourself, that's helpful. It has helped me shape my career as much as encouragement and help.

Something else that has served me very well, that I don't see many people do, is that I've always had other things I care about that I take pride in that are not my work in communications. Personally, I do a lot of theatre, which doesn't have to be what other people do. I have friends who are marathon runners, and they take a lot of pride in that. I just think having something that grounds you, that you can take pride in, and look back with joy on when you've had a bad day at work, especially as you get more senior and the pats on the back or someone telling you well done today, are much rarer and always never come, but you will hear when you've done a bad job! It's very important to construct a life that checks and balances you when you don't have people around who will do that for you.

CHAPTER 10

Heather Campbell
Chief Communications and D&I Officer Eurostar

Heather Campbell is the **Chief Communications and D&I Officer** for **Eurostar,** the only high-speed rail service that directly connects the UK to mainland Europe. Celebrating over 30 years of service and having carried millions of passengers, Eurostar offers connections to a range of destinations, including Paris, Brussels, Amsterdam, and Cologne.

For more information about Eurostar, visit eurostar.com.

Heather's LinkedIn profile: linkedin.com/in/heather-campbell-a9751949/

Tabita Andersson: Let's start by talking about your background, career path, and experience. How did you get to where you are today as the Chief Communications and D&I Officer for Eurostar?

Heather Campbell: I started my career as a journalist, which is similar to a lot of people who work in communications. I studied English and American literature at university, and I loved writing, so my natural progression was into journalism. When I started, I worked predominantly in women's feature magazines at a time when magazines were beginning to struggle, so it wasn't the most sustainable career choice, but I enjoyed connecting with people, writing, and thinking about stories, people, and themes. At that point, internal communications started to become a profession, and I was given the opportunity to join an agency that specialized in internal publications and magazines, which was great timing because I went into that profession just as it was beginning to blossom into something strategic and companies were beginning to think about needing to be a bit more proactive in engaging their people. It's a big part of how people feel about working for a company. The millennial generation was demanding about wanting to know more, holding the business accountable, and asking questions directly. It's less about the management telling staff what to do and more about how we can turn the work experience into a collaborative effort.

I worked in an agency for four years, during which time I progressed from writing employee publications to becoming more strategic. I had the opportunity to work with lots of different types of companies, from big blue chips and multinationals to very small charities and educational institutions. It was a great grounding to see behind the doors of businesses.

During that time, I saw the industry begin to take the profession seriously, and I started to see more businesses having dedicated internal communications people at a more senior level, sometimes even at the board and executive level, as you get quite frequently now. That was the start of my corporate communications career, and I began to add external communications experience to my skills.

After a while in the agency industry, I had the opportunity to go and work at London Gatwick Airport when I moved down south to Kent, and it was my first time working in-house, directly with the executive team and CEO, gaining experience at a senior level, advising, and not just doing the tactical activities. While I was there, an opportunity presented itself to join the media team for a six-month assignment, and I said yes because I'm very open to learning. As I started out as a journalist, I had some understanding of the media landscape, but it was a real baptism of fire because your first press office role, especially for an airport, is super intense. However, I really enjoyed it, and I think the complementary skills in internal communications of being mindful about how a story lands with people and knowing how to shape the narrative and messaging put me in good standing to deal with the media. I ended up staying in media relations for quite a long time, and throughout my career, I have flipped between the two, internal and external communications, quite frequently. I've become a real advocate for hybrid roles, and it is what ultimately shapes you to become a really good head of communications and Chief Communications Officer.

After spending four years at the airport, I took a year out traveling, and when I came back, I ended up doing an interim internal communications role at Ernst & Young, which was a much larger international business. I worked in the EMEA (Europe, Middle East, and Africa) internal communications team and regularly dealt with 12 different markets, thinking about how campaigns can transcend different cultures and how messages land in different markets. That was super interesting with really interesting people to work with and a people culture.

I was then tempted back to Gatwick for a project role to work on their pension scheme. It was a change management and communications role with lots of union engagement and involvement. The topic was difficult and very emotive, and it involved working closely with the Working Council.

This is where the strategic and advisory role of internal communications comes in; it was less about being in the room with the unions and more about advising the executive team before they stepped into the room with the unions and then being there to help them chew over options and the best way to communicate with employees about what was going on. From an external side, I worked on campaigns to grow the airport, which meant a lot of community communications, working with stakeholders, public lobbying in the media with politicians on the airport's runway campaign, which was an expansion campaign in competition with London Heathrow Airport. Eventually, I moved into a head of communications role where I looked after the press office, internal communications, our website, social media channels, and digital communications.

Just before COVID, I got the opportunity to move to the railway industry in the role of head of media for GTR (Govia Thameslink Railway), where I helped set up the company narrative, sort out a new way of working, professionalizing the press releases and I conducted a lot of executive media training, presentation training, and engagement. As this was just as COVID struck, I also ended up doing a lot of crisis communications. When I worked at the airport, we had to do a lot of crisis communications, dealing with anything from security risks to a drone attack, weather issues and then COVID. So, when I moved to GTR, it was a continuation of crisis communications. We had to keep the railways going as the country went into lockdown, and then closely follow the guidelines that were coming out from the government. After COVID, we then experienced a lot of industrial action here in the UK, and the railways went into nearly two years of continuous strikes. All the public communications around these challenges were very challenging; it was a long, sustained period of saying the same thing over and over again, which was difficult.

After three years with GTR, the Eurostar opportunity came up. This was the first time they had put a communications role into the executive team. Eurostar was a new company after merging with another organisation on the continent, had a new brand, was more ambitious, and was a much bigger business, so it was important to have a senior communications role. Many businesses are now doing the same, and there are many good reasons for doing so.

In the CCO role, I look after reputation, media relations, external communications, and internal communications across the three countries where we have staff. Interestingly, the role also looks after diversity, equity, and inclusion, which was a new area for me. The reason it sits with communications is that the corporate communications function has such strong relationships across the business. It knows all the different departments, and it's a strategic function, not tactical. DEI is extremely well placed there.

Tabita Andersson: That's a great career journey! A few things stand out in your experiences. Firstly, the connection between internal and external communications, which is something you have gained along the way. How important is that?

Heather Campbell: For anyone who wants to become a senior person in corporate communications, it's super important to have experience across both disciplines. In some ways, the skills are different, but the core competencies are similar. It's about understanding people and how they like to receive information. It's about turning information into something interesting, whether that's for a journalist or for someone in a business who's working on the frontline with customers or in a depot. Sometimes, you see businesses think about internal and external communications as two separate things, but I see them as two sides of the same coin. It's super-efficient if you have a hybrid team that can think about a story in terms of the medium and also in terms of what's going to work for colleagues and how to connect with what's happening in marketing. That also makes for an interesting role to work on if you're a communications person. I'm a big advocate for moving people within the team to give them that experience and give people growth opportunities. If you work in a business that has to do a lot of reactive communications and crisis communications, you potentially then have ten communications experts rather than five press experts, for example!

It also makes the profession more interesting because there are so many more opportunities for growth, and it's definitely what helped me get into my more senior roles.

Tabita Andersson: What advice would you give to a more junior communications person who's looking to advance their career?

Heather Campbell: Say yes to as many opportunities as possible! If you work in internal communications, for example, perhaps try to be part of the on-call press team or get involved in something that's going out both internally and externally, trying to work on both sides. Try out as much as you can and see what you like and enjoy doing. Don't be scared to flip between areas and get wide experience.

Something else is to think about corporate communications strategically, not just tactically. I always say to my team that we're not a support function; we're not people who just push stuff out; we're part of a strategic business. All of our objectives help the business succeed, and we're the gatekeepers of that success. You have to get really good at asking questions about people's objectives, what they want people to come away thinking and feeling, not just about the tactics and pushing stuff out because we're told to do something. You have to challenge what's being said and planned. Being able to influence people, being comfortable with challenging people, and asking good questions is crucial, and it's quite a hard skill to learn. When you start your career, being the challenger can be scary, so I think practicing that skill and working with your senior people to ensure it's part of your development plan is important.

Tabita Andersson: How can you best make the switch from supporting functions to being a trusted advisor? At the end of the day, that's what every communications person wants, but sometimes, that can be hard. How can we help the younger generation do this well?

Heather Campbell: Especially when you start your career, I think you have to take the opportunities that present themselves in the big moments to show your skillset and knowledge. Especially if your company is going through a time of change or there's a difficult thing to communicate. Take the time to really think through what your advice would be to someone senior, and take the opportunity to be brave and challenge a bit and show that you're not scared to show your worth and your skill set.

The other thing is that you constantly have to be your own PR person in your team. Within the first year, get out around the business and tell people what you do so that others understand what you're there to do, what they can help you with, and what you don't do. Being very clear about your role and being able to say no in a nice way is important. PR people are sometimes the worst at doing their own PR! Much of what we do is unseen, so you have to tell people about what's going on in the background, all the stories you've stopped, and all the things you have done to try and balance coverage. Those are the activities that people don't see, so you have to talk about them to help people understand.

Tabita Andersson: Is that one of the ways we can prove value above and beyond metrics? We've become quite data-driven, and of course, we have to have our KPIs (key performance indicators) and our metrics, but there's so much value in providing advice that you can't put a number on.

Heather Campbell: It's about building strong, open relationships, which takes time. To be a good communicator, you have to understand how the people you work with function. You have to spend time to get to know them, not just at a work level but from the perspective of what's important to them personally, what things scare them about going to do a media interview or speaking in front of a large audience, because they have to trust you, and they have to be vulnerable with you so you can help them most effectively.

The biggest compliments I've ever had are when people say: "I feel like you're inside my head when you write or when you create something for me." For that to happen, I have to spend quality time with them and make a real effort to get to know them through regular check-ins. Sometimes, that means making mistakes and getting things wrong along the way to find out what works. It can be a scary process, but aside from KPIs and hard metrics, which are still tricky in communications, it's about how you make people feel at the end of the day and whether they trust you. That's something you can't measure; it's always tricky.

Tabita Andersson: Let's discuss metrics and measurement. What metrics are you using to evaluate external communications?

Heather Campbell: The data you can get is fine, but you want to get into the details about whether you are hitting the right audiences or landing the messages in the right places. Ultimately, you want to know if what you are doing is going to affect your business objectives and if you are getting through to the right people.

For example, at Eurostar, we want to know if we are reaching the people who regularly travel with us or future potential customers, because although it's lovely to get coverage in a high-profile location, are those readers the people who are really going to make a difference to our business? It's great that people like the brand, and our reputation is good, but does it add to our commercial objectives? You have to be quite granular about what business objectives you need to support from a commercial point of view, but you also have to be honest about what communications can achieve on its own because there are certain things we just can't do. We can't make people convert to buy something or start a journey, but I can educate them about the experience. Then, measure back the messages that have landed that sentiment, checking if we've hit the right target audiences.

It's even harder to measure internal communications because it's hard to tell if people are engaged with the message just from click-throughs or other statistics. From an internal point of view, I believe it's more about the informal things you can do, like getting direct feedback through focus groups or having a network around the business that can test messages and provide feedback on how they work or not. At Eurostar, we have a frontline communications group that helps us deliver communications in the correct way for specific parts of the business, but also to provide feedback on things to say if something doesn't make sense to someone working in a depot or if something doesn't resonate in a certain language. It's hard to measure, but ultimately, it's about having a good gut feel about how things will land. If you have an employee engagement survey, there can be a strong link with what you're trying to achieve in internal communications, so you want to work as closely as you can with your HR team or whoever does that survey to make sure your internal communications objectives are aligned with your engagement objectives.

Tabita Andersson: You've just mentioned HR as one of the key stakeholders for communications. Who are some of the other stakeholders you work with?

Heather Campbell: It's almost everyone around the business! HR, specifically for internal communications, is absolutely key. For external communications, it's the commercial side of the business, the marketing team, particularly social media and brand.

Being commercially driven is important to help with your PR objectives. If you have customer-facing colleagues, it's important to keep your finger on the pulse. That's also important because a big part of our role is to assess risks and advise on those, saying: "Well, if you make that decision, this will impact our reputation."

It's a bit of a catch-all, but you have to connect the dots between all the different departments, and I think communications is in a unique position to do that.

Tabita Andersson: You mentioned earlier that you are in a good position because your CEO already recognised before you joined that there was an opportunity for someone to come and build a reputation. What is your advice to a CEO or another C-level executive who hasn't quite arrived at that point and is still wondering what the value of communications is and why they should have a CCO working at that level?

Heather Campbell: It's a real missing link because it's a role that can really help support the CEO and executive team. It's like having a right-hand person in the room as your sense check on everything. As the famous quote from Warren Buffett goes: "It takes 20 years to build a reputation and five minutes to ruin it." Why wouldn't you have someone in the room who's an expert on reputation and hear their advice in exactly the same way as you would commercially, operationally, strategically, and legally? It's another skill set, so why wouldn't you have that?

There are so many things we can turn our hands to and help the executive team with, such as presenting to the board, shareholders, regulators, governments, and colleagues. Whoever it is that you need to communicate your plans to, this is where communications can help engage with that audience and tell your story in the way you want it to be told.

Having a CCO around the table is incredibly important. I've noticed that in the last five or six years, even at a Board level, there are now often people whose background and core skills are corporate communications, reputation management, and corporate affairs. It's really shifted. Especially after COVID, leaders now recognise the value even more.

Tabita Andersson: I agree. All of a sudden, there was a light shining on the function and on what we could do because everyone came to communications asking what to do next! It gave us a good opportunity to highlight our value, particularly for internal communications.

How do you work with the wider executive team across the C-suite?

Heather Campbell: I'm sure it works differently in every business. Here, we have regular weekly meetings, but personally, I like to have conversations with each of the C-suite individuals on a monthly basis. For me, it's much about trust and relationships, so having regular check-ins, seeing what's challenging them in their world, what things they need help with, what you can advise on if you see risk coming their way, it's all important to build the relationship.

Formally, being in the room in person with people and regularly meeting with the senior teams is also important because being visible and available around the business is critical. I always encourage my teams to get out there and get into the business, not just sit in the office.

If the organisation doesn't have a chief communications officer, it's more about making sure you have regular time with the CEO and asking questions. Don't be scared to ask for 1:1 time with your CEO and the executive team, get in front of people, and understand what's going on for them in their areas and for them as people in their roles.

Tabita Andersson: What advice would you give to someone who's stepping up into a CCO role at the C-level for the first time, who needs to become a business leader as well as a functional leader?

Heather Campbell: That's exactly it. With the promotion, you shift from being purely focused on your discipline to being a member of the leadership of the business. It's a big jump because suddenly, you're in the most senior room, needing to have an opinion on many things outside of communications; you're in the CEO team, so you're the owner of the strategy of the business. It's a super interesting role, but you have to shift from being tactical to being more strategic. Also, suddenly you have a more visible leadership profile in the business, so you have to take the advice you would normally give out to other people. Get out and be visible, speak to people and role model the values of the business. Be ready to answer lots of different types of questions and hear lots of different types of concerns. It's a different responsibility.

In my role here at Eurostar, I went from advising the CEO on how to present our business objectives for the year ahead in a presentation or video to being the person presenting it live or in a video. It's an interesting dynamic because you're so used to being behind the camera rather than out in front of the audience. Also, people view you very differently, and that's a big responsibility.

Tabita Andersson: What skills do you look for in communications people? I believe that, especially when you look for more senior communications leaders, you need people who have commercial awareness alongside the typical communication skills; would you agree?

Heather Campbell: Yes, absolutely, and that's true regardless of whether you work in a commercial business, a charity, a public body, a government, or a membership organisation. As a senior communications person, you need to get your head around strategy and what objectives the business is trying to achieve, so your communications can mirror those and show the worth of communications in relation to the organisational objectives.

What I see when people come into the profession is that they start with the tactics. They start with their written skills, content, engagement, and events, and that means they can't always understand the links between what they're doing and the overall strategy.

Tabita Andersson: What are some of the other skills great communications professionals need to have?

Heather Campbell: Being able to influence people, have good conversations and ask good questions to get to the root of something when needed can be quite intense because you may feel like you have to grill people to get to the actual objective. Being able to ask questions and then advise and influence is crucial.

I do think you need to like to talk and get to know people, have a genuine interest in people, and build relationships, which is key. Being curious and able to think creatively is also useful, as it allows you to come up with new ideas and enjoy the creative process. On the external communications side, in particular, you need to be calm and stay thinking. You have to be able to deal with pressure, have resilience about you, and have the ability to take a step back and stay calm before you jump to a decision. It's definitely something that can be learned, but as a core skill set, I'd always look for someone who's fairly calm and who doesn't feel like they need to rush to make a decision or say something. Someone who likes to think before they decide what to do and doesn't mind talking it over. There are so many choices you can make; it's not black and white. It's very good to have a reflective course and be comfortable with that.

You often find that you can be pressured by others to say something or do something immediately, especially in a crisis, and that's often when the most mistakes are made. Being calm, being good with people, being able to influence and ask questions, and being curious are great attributes.

It's also important to be open to learning and adapting, and not to be too precious about your work because it's a collaborative process. You will receive feedback, and you have to learn not to take it personally. Have a small ego!

The other thing is to learn how to be challenging in a positive way. You have to be able to say no, that's not the right thing, and stand up for what you think is right at the moment. A lot of people find that difficult because they're often just told what to do. Sometimes, you have to be able to say that what's about to happen will not help you achieve objectives, or it can be damaging to the business. You have to find that confidence and find your voice.

Tabita Andersson: You speak fondly about your job; what do you enjoy the most about being a Chief Communications Officer?

Heather Campbell: It's getting to know people and their roles. I've always worked in a very fast-paced operational business that deals with lots of different types of people because they're generally traveling somewhere, whether that's airports or railways and that's what I love. I love the quirky things that happen, the commitment of people, and the opportunity to help them shine.

I also enjoy seeing people go from being fairly junior to becoming confident in their space. This could be through public speaking or doing high-profile interviews in the media. That's personally very satisfying. I've worked with several people throughout my career and seen them move from middle management roles where they don't need media handling experience to be on a primetime news slot and handling it exceptionally well.

Tabita Andersson: We haven't covered what external factors influence how we lead communications. What are some of the factors you see that have a big impact on what you do?

Heather Campbell: There are so many! When you work in a multinational company, one of the factors you have to take into consideration is politics. Last year, there were general elections in all the countries we work in, and that can affect how people in the business feel, but it also affects your customers.

Another aspect is understanding how changing government agendas could impact your business. You have to work very closely with your public affairs team because they're the ones getting to know the new people who might be coming into a government or who might be influencing the agenda. Nowadays, the mood of the nation, especially around certain topics, can vary so much, and we need to keep our fingers on the pulse.

There are so many things that come up now that wouldn't have cropped up ten years ago, especially in my diversity, equity, and inclusion role. In a communications role, it's important to understand the emotions behind these topics and be mindful of how that impacts your tone, voice, and general communications. Your employees, for example, all have unique backgrounds, experiences, and cultures, which you need to accommodate.

As I work in the transport industry, I know that there are also many external things that can happen. We have many partners that have a role in our business operations, infrastructure, suppliers, etc., which means there are so many people involved in what we do, and another role for communications is to have a good idea of who those people are and involve them in communications, sharing information on a regular basis. For us, there are a lot of things that happen on a frequent basis, whether that's peak times of the year, summer holidays, Christmas traveling, or industrial action.

With all these external factors impacting our work, you have to be very adaptable as a communications professional, and I believe you also have to enjoy that.

Tabita Andersson: There's also the multi-country, multicultural aspect of communications. How do you manage that across your regions?

Heather Campbell: We manage communications centrally, but my team is based across different countries. Some of our team is based in Brussels, some in Paris, and some in London. We also have a frontline communications group, which is made up of representatives from all around the operation. Although we're a small company, we are incredibly diverse. We've got nearly 40 different nationalities, which is a real challenge and opportunity for internal communications.

It's also a challenge externally because you're talking to media in different countries, so having experts in the team who can speak the relevant language and who can sense-check the tone of how messages are going to come across is useful. There are a lot of things you could say that people might interpret in different ways, so having a solid group of people who can check messaging because they have an on-the-ground view is very important.

We translate as much as we can into French, Dutch, and sometimes German. It's really important for people to have the choice, and it's quite a challenge when you do a webcast or presentation. We've experimented with having interpretation services or having people dialing into different events with different languages, and it's hard to find the right balance. Ultimately, we need to give people a choice of how they consume our communications.

That is also a growing trend overall. There is less push and much more about people opting in and selecting what they need themselves. It's something we see outside of work, especially with the growth of social media platforms. Communications used to be more direct and less tailored, but now that people have a choice, they are also becoming savvier in how they consume information, which means we have to work harder to get the right information to the right people that hits the message we want to convey.

Tabita Andersson: In terms of trends, how do you think technology is changing the profession?

Heather Campbell: I think it's massively changed it. Firstly, because it can make you more selective about what you want to see, and secondly, people have become overwhelmed with information. That makes it even harder in corporate communications to get people to engage with us.

Artificial intelligence (AI) is also interesting. Some of the more junior members of my team and those who use technology skills in their everyday lives are at the front, leading, while those of us who are more senior or less familiar with the latest technologies can learn from our junior colleagues. There are some good opportunities for letting technology help us ease the workload so we can focus on using our strategic and advisory skill sets and letting AI do some of the tactical things for us. But it's something the profession really has to grasp and get ahead of, because you can see the argument about what impact it will have on communications roles and for those who are more skeptical about letting AI do it all! If anyone new to the profession brings AI skills, they will really stand out.

Tabita Andersson: In addition to AI skills, what skills do you think we'll need in the function in the next three to five years?

Heather Campbell: For internal communications in particular, I think it's less about skills around channels and more about engagement. In general, employees are more demanding, more skeptical, and have a lot more questions because they want to understand things. Having the skills to understand what people will engage with is more important than ever.

In addition, we all have to be more resilient because it's a tough world, and there are a lot of big things happening around the world. We have to have our fingers on the pulse and truly understand the bigger issues at play more than ever.

With everything moving so much faster than before, another skill that's becoming crucial is crisis communication. Reputation issues are becoming much more nuanced, certainly in the diversity and inclusion space. Just one post on social media these days can cause a huge reputational storm, so to be able to manage that both externally and internally and advise a business on how to navigate a crisis or how to work out what's significant or not is a great skill to develop.

In crisis communications, it's a great skill to try to be at the forefront of an issue rather than having to catch it afterward!

Tabita Andersson: Do you believe our skills are transferable between industries?

Heather Campbell: Yes. When I started in communications, you had to choose your industry and become an expert. Today, communication skills are totally transferable, even between non-profit and non-commercial organisations, where they could sometimes utilize people who have worked in hard commercial areas and in government. I also believe in the reverse, having people come in who have not had a super commercial role but who have excellent people skills and who can create campaigns that are much more in tune with what the target audiences are feeling and experiencing.

Tabita Andersson: Do you have any advice to share for CEOs on how to best work with their CCO?

Heather Campbell: Think of the role as a personal advisor, not as tactical output. You'll get a much better outcome if you engage early and discuss strategy. Get together regularly to discuss what you want to achieve, not tell them what you want, how you want it and when you want it. That will not deliver the best outcome!

Something else I would add, more generally, is to diversify around the table inside communications teams. Mixing experiences, cultures, etc., will make the team more successful today than ever for a multicultural company. Some of the best ideas I've heard have often come from people with different backgrounds!

Tabita Andersson: If you had to pick something that you're going to be known and remembered for as a Chief Communications and DE&I Officer, what would that be?

Heather Campbell: Helping people feel like they've succeeded in their own careers. Whether that's someone I've helped train or someone I've helped develop, having a lasting legacy from helping people be successful in communications is what gives me great satisfaction in my role.

Also, to have made an impact on diversity and inclusion, which is an area where communications can really help. Getting it right can mean you have a real possibility to change someone's life.

We're in a profession where we can have a real impact, and that's what I would like us to be remembered for.

CHAPTER 11

Ryan Curtis-Johnson
Chief Communications Officer Valuable 500

Ryan Curtis-Johnson is the **Chief Communications Officer** for **The Valuable 500,** a global organisation of over 500 partners and companies working together to end disability exclusion. Unified to accelerate inclusion for the one in five people living with a disability, the non-profit organisation transforms business systems to transform society. By engaging with the world's most influential business leaders and brands, the Valuable 500 has a market cap of over $23 trillion, combined revenues of over $8 trillion, and employs a staggering 22 million people worldwide.

For more information about the Valuable 500, visit thevaluable500.com.

Ryan's LinkedIn profile: linkedin.com/in/ryan-curtis-johnson-b2233330/

Tabita Andersson: As the Valuable 500 is not a very recognised brand, would you mind giving us a bit of color on what non-profit organisation has been set up to achieve and what the background story is?

Ryan Curtis-Johnson: I'm the Chief Communications Officer at the Valuable 500, the largest global CEO network, second only to the United Nations. All 521 CEOs in our network have committed to ending disability exclusion in business.

Why 500? The story is that our founder wanted to end the CEO silence about disabilities, so she set the goal and started the campaign. Over the years, we've expanded, and we now have a two-year strategy based on what we call synchronized collective actions. If I were going to give a visual description of the strategy, it would be that of a murmuration of birds or fish in the sea; they're all moving in the same direction, but you can be at different parts of that journey, but all heading to the same destination or working toward the same goals. Our three synchronized collective actions are Leadership, that is, trying to get CEOs to be more aware and confident about disability through storytelling. Secondly, we run a mentoring program called Generation Valuable, which is at an individual senior executive level. The individual in the program must be a senior executive either with a disability or with lived experience of disability, and the program aims to educate and provide insight and a personal approach to understanding disabilities in the workplace. We see it as a reverse mentoring program. Thirdly, we have reporting getting businesses to review their own reports such as sustainability or annual reports to make sure we are including disability within those. We believe that unless you have the data, how can you measure how well you're doing—but you also have to ensure you're not abusing the data; it's not just gathering data for the sake of it, but the important part is what you do with that data, we have provided 5 KPIs for our companies to align with where possible within their organisations. The last pillar of our strategy is authentic representation in advertising, internal and external collateral. For many years in advertising, photos of people with disability were not of real, authentic people with disabilities. Sometimes, it was asking a model to sit in a wheelchair or asking someone to pretend to be a person with a disability. Talking about authentic representation, we cover visible and non-visible disabilities.

We believe we can see systemic change based on these three synchronized collective actions.

Tabita Andersson: Why is communications and reputation so important to the Valuable 500 as a non-profit organisation?

Ryan Curtis-Johnson: I've been at the Valuable 500 for three years now, and prior to that, I saw a lot of ignorance when it comes to understanding accessibility in communications. We've all written and produced things in our careers. Can I say that I made sure every single campaign I ever created was accessible? No, I can't say that, and I think many companies and brands were in the same situation. There is an ignorance out there about the value and importance of accessibility that many are not aware of unless it affects them. But there are many people who do think about it, creative teams, for example, who consider it part of their work, but often it's not considered, or when challenged, we don't have a budget to make changes. So, we utilize the fact that CEOS are the ultimate leaders who can make real systemic change within an organisation. Communicating that message is important to us.

Another aspect is to highlight and communicate the good that is happening within organisations. We see a lot of fear. Organisations are doing lots of great stuff, but don't want to talk about it publicly because they're nervous about getting it wrong or saying the wrong things. And we get it; there are many factors you need to consider when it comes to ableist language, accessibility, and making sure everyone can consume your content, whether that's reading, looking at something, or at least getting an audio description of what it looks like. From a moral perspective, why wouldn't we want everyone to consume whatever content we produce?

Tabita Andersson: How about the CEOs who support you? What do you think they see as the benefit of belonging to the network?

Ryan Curtis-Johnson: I can't speak on behalf of any of the CEOs we deal with, but I think the moral side is important. We know this is the right thing to do for people, our community, and society. Some of the individuals in our network may have experience with disability, whether it's lived experience through their own personal stories or family members.

If we look at the data, we have an aging population with 17% now registered disabled. If we then take into consideration neurodivergency, that number would grow dramatically. At the same time, there's a lack of self-disclosing within organisations with older generations that may have worked through because they regarded having a disability as a weakness, so they wouldn't feel comfortable with self-disclosing. On the other side, we have a younger generation coming through the workforce, the future workforce, who are so morally compassed and who will not work for an organisation unless they believe that they have a purpose and are authentic. What businesses realize when they try to align with this generational shift is that it's not good enough not to be doing something, and it's not right, which is all part of the transition. Many companies that I talk to have made accessibility part of their everyday work now; it's part of their DNA, which is how it should be, but it takes time. Changing systems, processes, and policy takes time, but we see that change. A great strength for organisations that are part of the Valuable 500 is that we can effect change together and lobby for what we believe is a great opportunity. We believe what's right for business is right for society.

Tabita Andersson: How do you go about building the type of reputation that you want and need as a non-profit organisation with your specific target audiences, stakeholders, and the wider community?

Ryan Curtis-Johnson: What we say is apolitical. We don't get involved in political activities or campaigns, so we must be careful with our messaging. We are also extremely careful because we work with some very large organisations that we can't talk about. On the other hand, we also try to utilize the fact that they are bigger than we are to help deliver and share the messages. Building reputation, for us, is about speaking with our partners and companies in the network, involving them, and creating joint case studies or articles showcasing the great work they are doing in disability inclusion.

Tabita Andersson: How do you structure communications? Are you a one-man band, or do you have a team to help?

Ryan Curtis-Johnson: We have a team of three people. We have a head of communications and a social media manager, and then it's me. We do all of our communications together, so everything is integrated. For example, we carry the same messages in our mailings, as in press releases, and our features on the website. We also guest-compose articles for various publications and then utilize social media to amplify our messages.

Tabita Andersson: Communications is sometimes a hidden job, done behind the scenes, that many people don't quite understand. How would you explain your role to someone who has no idea what our profession does?

Ryan Curtis-Johnson: It's about staying calm and collected and making sure you're fully aware of how to best either approach or how to best communicate a scenario, a situation, or a positioning on something. It can sound very bizarre to explain it that way, but communications is not something you can turn on and off. It's not a nine-to-five job. I believe you constantly need to be on alert because you just don't know what's going to occur.

In our case, because we're a global organisation, parts of the world are only just waking up when we're going to bed, so there's an element of managing those timelines, too.

For me, the real beauty is being able to promote why disability inclusion is so important. I'm neurodivergent myself, and I have two children who are also neurodivergent, so it's not just because this is the right thing to do, but it personally affects me, and it affects my children. Wouldn't it be wonderful to know that the story, or the legacy we leave behind, is something that changed the workforce or the working environment for the better, for good?

Tabita Andersson: You've touched a little on your background; how did you become Chief Communications Officer? What was your career path?

Ryan Curtis-Johnson: I feel like I've done a full circle now, but it's probably not the most normal career path. My first role when I left college was working in a school as a special educational assistant—I don't like to use the word special needs—and I was working with two children who needed support within a mainstream school environment. One of them had Down syndrome, and the other had autism. It was my first experience of understanding how, societally, we don't really encourage these individuals to have a voice or to be completely incorporated into our environment. I used to discover really simple things, like when we walked down the corridor together, and I'd be asked how they both were. I would be perplexed and say I don't know; why are you asking me? I would then flip the question back to them and educate that person. In that role, it was also important to help the children build life skills; helping them be able to have conversations was key, not only to bring out their personalities but also to give them the confidence to access the world, which isn't very accessible if you look at it in the grand scheme of things.

Prior to working in the school, I was a dancer, and after a year and a half there, I went back to being a dancer. I performed for a good few years and became a choreographer working in the entertainment industry. It's such a fast-paced industry, which is something that suits me, but it's also so intense that it's not something I can do in the long term, so I steered sideways into artist management and PR, promoting artists, and then fell into communications working for an agency for ten years, leading all of their PR, marketing, and social media as an internal role. Personally, I've always worked better in internal roles rather than on the agency side with lots of different clients. After ten years in the agency, COVID arrived, and I think that period changed many of us and made us reassess and realign. I had to homeschool two children, for example. Going through something like that really changes your perspective on what you do. I realized I was doing something that didn't feel right for me morally anymore, in the sense of what good I was doing and what change I was affecting. The role of Director of Communications here at the Valuable 500 came up, and I applied. I was then promoted to Chief Communications Officer 18 months ago.

I feel like I've done a full circle because I was going back to doing something that I was passionate about and meaningful.

Tabita Andersson: That's an amazing story; thank you for sharing. What skills have you picked up in your non-communications roles, such as dancing, that you think have been useful in your current role?

Ryan Curtis-Johnson: With regard to dancing, it's the intensity. If you're working on a project and you have three dances you need to learn, and you're going to be performing live, it's intense to try and nail it before it comes to performance day. The intensity of that situation is trying to find ways of remembering, writing it down, and being creative in finding ways of getting it to stick. It's also the mental stage of preparing yourself during those processes and those elements of intensity. Those experiences really prepare you for crisis contingency work and for staying calm. In the entertainment industry, for example, you can't always guarantee an artist will turn up on time or what state they may be in. The job involved a lot of reassurance and risk mitigation, being the face before the artist turned up, and staying calm when everyone else was panicking. That ability to stay calm in an intense environment is something I've carried through. Communicators, and anyone who works in communications, will often experience last-minute drops and last-minute changes, so we have a real ability to adapt and be the calm within the storm because we're able to think, hang on a second, just give me time to go away and come up with a solution. It's then like our minds work in that mindset to have a calming influence in quite critical moments.

Another example is when you produce and host events. We've all had clients who ask about registrations and panic when the list isn't full, and there are only three weeks to go. We understand that people like to register late because we've learned the ebbs and flows of how things work. We're not fortune tellers, but we can reassure everyone that quite often, it's a case of waiting, and things will work out.

I think this is something we, as communicators, don't receive full appreciation for. We work hard to be known as trusted; people around us trust our judgment, but they're seldom forthcoming about saying that they totally trust us, and they still need reassurance.

We wear many hats when it comes to being communicators. Adapting to those hats and roles is one of the best skills I've developed. I also think having people skills is important in communications, and I think it's tricky for the younger generation because of the way they've grown up with social media and devices. They haven't just picked up the phone with someone or networked in a room with 50 people they don't know, having entered on their own. It's never nice; I don't think anyone thrives in those moments, but for me, having the ability to use the performing side in those situations has helped me because I can conjure up confidence rather than just put on a front. If I can perform in front of 1.2 million people, I'm sure I can perform in front of 50.

Tabita Andersson: You mentioned how the younger generation is doing things differently. How do you think we, as communicators and content experts, can help our organisations adapt to different ways of consuming content?

Ryan Curtis-Johnson: We can challenge how our organisations are doing things, and because of the trust that individuals within senior roles in the organisation have in us, that challenge often gets heard. I think challenging is often seen as a negative, and it shouldn't be; it's a positive.

When we talk about the younger generation, we often use it as a negative, but there is so much we can learn from them. I wish I had lived with the values they live by. Their sense of work is not everything; they want a work-life balance, whereas my generation I've worked in has worked all hours. If you weren't seen to be on, you felt like you couldn't progress or go further. There were never enough hours in the day. That doesn't mean I was disorganized; it was just how I worked, so in some ways, we have to understand that the world is no longer the same as it was. What we need to do is to know what we get in return if we change. For most people with senior roles, there's always the question about the return: how does something affect the bottom line? As much as we don't want to put figures on people, it's how a business works, and business is business at the end of the day.

Tabita Andersson: Do you think communications should sit at the top table, and how can we elevate the role better? We've done a good job during the last ten years, but there's still more to do.

Ryan Curtis-Johnson: More communicators should be at the board level, in my opinion. It's needed to support and drive a business forward. For example, when you hear of something that's perhaps leaked or not landed well with colleagues, it's often because an organisation doesn't have an internal communications person in the right place. Hence, they weren't able to advise or provide support.

I agree with you. We've seen progression, but there is still nervousness within the C-suite and around the board table, so the message is still not getting through; it's not cascading to the right people. Perhaps one roadblock is that we may not be looking at how content and messages are best delivered. Is it fully accessible, done robustly and clearly, or is it a long-winded bit of written content? Are we being creative? There's always room for improvement, which will help with the C-level conversations.

There's so much more we can do here. I grew up in the industry, it was all about the numbers, getting coverage, and the Advertising Value Equivalency (AVE) figures. I know some regions in the world still use it, but for us, it's a bit like a swear word! So, we've come a long way in how to measure what we do.

I do a lot of work in apprenticeships for PR and communications, and I've been writing the standards for the past eight years or so because I've always encouraged everyone to give something back, whatever it is, skills-wise. What's really interesting to see is that there are many of the apprentices that I deal with and their managers who are about the numbers. If there's anything I've learned in communications, it's that it's not about the quantity but the quality. One well-placed piece could be better than 50 pieces that have been copied and pasted into a platform or a wire that has been sprayed everywhere. Yes, it gives you great numbers, but you also pay for it, so it doesn't feel authentic; it doesn't feel real. You've just paid someone to reshare it.

I always ask my team how we can rip up the rule book a bit and be more creative. We see that more with communications, through podcasts and video content, and bringing that creativity into our everyday communications. It's not all about writing anymore; we have to bring the creative element to cut through the noise because we have social media that moves at a faster pace, so we have to be more innovative in how we deliver our messages.

Tabita Andersson: On the other side of the coin, we have the advent of fake news, so it's not just cutting through the noise; it's also about what's real and trustworthy.

Ryan Curtis-Johnson: Yes, there's fake news, but there are also influencers, or people with high profiles, or accounts with many followers, so that their one post, if not crafted well, can be quite damaging and adds to the cancel culture. We've experienced that here. If you give something too much time and give it too much air, you're only adding more fuel to the fire. You have to be sensitive and careful in the way you handle these situations. This is exactly where I believe you have to be less reactive, calmer, and more collected, and say, let's give it 48 hours. We're going to keep an eye on it, but let's give it 48 hours before we react. That procedure used to be to respond on the spot and shut it down quickly, but I don't think that works anymore because people have more confidence and power than they used to when it comes to communications.

Tabita Andersson: Part of that is also about educating our colleagues internally. Quite often, you can get a crowd internally being immediately upset or angry about one single negative post when what we need is patience. Building that knowledge about when to react, and an understanding of why staying calm is important in those situations.

Ryan Curtis-Johnson: That's also why it's so important to communicate internally before you go external, and I think this is where there's a need for speed. There's never enough time because you have to prepare everything that needs to go out externally. Still, it's important to balance the fact that people like to work set hours, and they don't like to get emails outside of working hours, so we have to be flexible and accommodating in how we communicate. At the same time, we can't be too overly sensitive because if it's something we need to communicate, sometimes we just have to go out with it, even if it's outside of working hours, because we want to ensure colleagues have sight of it before it goes out externally.

Tabita Andersson: Aligning internal and external communications is so valuable, and we see this done much better now than in the past. Is that your experience, too?

Ryan Curtis-Johnson: Yes, 100%! My rule is always internal first, then external. In my role, we also have to do that with the companies we work with, so communications with them as partners is aligned with what we're saying internally. This is another place where you build a trusted reputation because you're not seen going rogue or off-piste!

Of course, you can't always get it right, and hindsight is beautiful. Sometimes, you don't get the chance to do it right or to follow the process, so we have to adapt at times. I've learned that it's good to have the process there, but it shouldn't be the only way to do something. We need to be able to flex to achieve what we need to accomplish.

Tabita Andersson: We've touched on data, metrics, and measurements a couple of times. This is something that we, as a profession, have really improved over the years. I remember back when AMEC launched the Barcelona Principles, and we were so excited because, at that time, those reporting frameworks were groundbreaking in PR; we'd never measured our work in that way before. Rolling forward to today, we have an array of data and metrics at our fingertips. How do you think this will continue to change and improve in the future, and how do you think we can make the most of it? We might have moved away from using AVE numbers, but sometimes, we can still get caught up in, say, the number of clippings.

Ryan Curtis-Johnson: It's tricky, and this is just my opinion; we're spoilt for choice now, with so much data to use, and it's easy to fall into the trap of using big numbers because they look better. I see this quite a bit with the apprentices I deal with, who sometimes look at how impressive numbers are and use a certain number because the impressions were higher, or the viewership was lower, or a publication only has 30,000 subscribers compared to another one. Of course, it's tricky also because it's never consistent, but I think we need to be confident in what we're doing. For a long time, communications was based on metrics and numbers, and I get it; we were the department that cost money to hire, but there was no commercial gain back from it. I always used to say to the leaders I've worked with that it takes several good pieces of coverage to give you a good reputation, but just one bad piece to give you a bad reputation, and it could be gone for good because it's hard to come back from it. So, it's much better to understand and look at whether something is good or risky for the business before it goes out.

The commercial gain is something we don't always get an understanding of. I've struggled in most organisations I've worked in to get people to ask the question: How did you hear about us? For example, I'd get the receptionist at the agency to ask on behalf of the whole agency and then just jot down in a document because all I needed for the board was that one person had said, I saw your article in a publication and that's why I got in touch, or I saw your advert on an award, or your logo at a conference or event, that would be all I needed because the board was often challenging us about what we bring to the business. I've been through several acquisitions, credit crunches, and recessions, and when you've been through all of that, you always have to show your worth as a department because it's always questioned.

I remember the days when I used to pay a company to send me press clippings in the post, and I would laminate them and put them in the reception because my CEO at the time loved to see them on the walls. We used to send them to all the different offices, and if they were not displayed, I'd be really annoyed because I'd spent time laminating the coverage, and I knew the CEO loved to see it when he walked through the doors of those offices. It was an important way of visibly showing what we do.

We've now come to a point where we're not physically seeing that evidence anymore; it's much harder for us to show the benefits of what we do. When social media arrived, it helped us show that we didn't need to spend so much on advertising if we used organic traffic correctly. What is the sad part, and I know you haven't asked me this question, but when you go through all analytics, the fact is that it's so much harder now to get a story placed with certain publications, and it's much more pay-to-play. I don't like the bargaining about paying for having a press release published. For us, we're a charity, so we don't have a big budget. Also, if you think something is a good story, why do I need to pay? You've just told me you think this is a really good story and would fit into your publication, so surely you can use it as I'm gifting it to you. You don't even have to do any paperwork; you can simply have it!

Another sad part of the industry now is that due to the fast pace, it's not as easy to build a rapport with reporters and journalists because they don't have time. I might come from an old school of PR, and we used to be able to go for lunch and sit down to plan your year with a publication, talking about the feature list. Then, you would add a diary reminder and connect when appropriate. It's so much harder now when we can't do that, and there's so much more rejection. When I deal with apprentices, they get much more rejection than when I started. Don't get me wrong, people would put the phone down on me, but those were occasional situations; today, junior communications professionals experience relentless rejection when they send a press release. There's no response, you send it again several times, chase them on social media, try their phone number, and get nothing. It's a hard slog.

Tabita Andersson: You're right, also, the way we pitch has changed completely. Today, you can't even get a number for many journalists, so there's no way of picking up the phone even if you want to.

Ryan Curtis-Johnson: Exactly! Then you end up feeling like you're just going into someone's mailbox or a general news desk mailbox, and you pray that you wrote a good subject line and that the message is short and sweet, and they will reach out for further details.

It's so much harder now, and that's what makes me sad. Primarily, when you work with local publications, because that's what I found at the agency: you had to pay, say, £25 to get your press release published. And I understood it because these local papers needed to start making money. After all, it wasn't affordable to do free publications anymore. But then they would miss out on some terrific local stories that could encourage the next generation of our workforce into jobs. We used the local press to show the great opportunities that the organisations in the local area would offer, and that's so much trickier now.

Tabita Andersson: I'd like to circle back to talking about data and metrics. We covered the external side quite a bit, but I'm also curious about the internal side. It used to be the poor cousin, and then the pandemic came, and all of a sudden, internal communications became the star of the show. How has this helped propel the profession, and what's your experience of the progression of internal communications?

Ryan Curtis-Johnson: As an internal workforce, people want to know more information. That's exciting, and that's how it should be; however, there's still an element of balance within organisations and knowing how much to share internally. It's about cementing colleagues' understanding of something that's happened or sharing information about some companies or brand partners doing wonderful things. We're all on the same mission, and we're all playing a part in it collectively internally.

Tabita Andersson: On that note, do you think communications can help an organisation build a good culture or impact its culture?

Ryan Curtis-Johnson: It does, and it's really important, although you're never going to get it right because what one person likes is very different from what someone else likes, so it's hard to meet everyone's expectations. In, addition, if you give too much information, you build an expectation, and people will want to know everything. Unfortunately, that isn't how business works because there are certain fundamentals that you just don't share. Again, getting that balance right is difficult, and no one is getting it right all the time. You just have to be flexible, and you need to do both push and pull communications. Sometimes, it's really good to give lots of information; in times of recession, for example, or when there are external impacts that are affecting an organisation or just affecting the world, that's when we need to double down and give more. Then, when there's nothing happening, it's just good to turn it down a bit. It's like your heating; we don't always want it scorching hot, so it's more about keeping it on a base level and understanding when we need to dial up and down.

Tabita Andersson: Do you think people come to work today with an increased attitude of being entitled to know more just because society as a whole is a lot more open, something that social media, for example, has enabled?

Ryan Curtis-Johnson: Yes and no. I think the difference is that information is so much more accessible. Gone are the days when you couldn't go and dig for more information or find a forum. I always feel sorry for those who have products to sell because there is always one negative review somewhere that gets cascaded and given much more attention than the positive reviews. Our tricky scenario is that it's so much easier to find information, and because of that, workforces are so much more informed. That could be about the industry, a political situation, or something that's happening in society. Because of that, by the time you've communicated something, they've already read it somewhere else, so that's when you get the sense of entitlement. It's hard to get the balance right because, in some ways, we'd need someone to be working 24/7 to be able to meet all expectations and demands and be prepared before anyone has started work to make sure the communication is in their inbox before they've seen something else on the way, on the commute, or the news. We must be honest and transparent about not being able to work at the same pace as the world runs because the world never sleeps; when one part wakes up, the other one goes to sleep.

Tabita Andersson: What do you think are some of the trends that are coming that we should take advantage of as communicators, such as AI?

Ryan Curtis-Johnson: When we look at AI, many communicators have thought it would take over their roles and jobs so that we wouldn't be needed. There's always the fear that comes with adapting to new technologies. It's about being adaptable; communications have changed over the years, and we've adapted. How we live and our society is very different from how it was many years ago, and it's the same with these new technologies. They're not always a hindrance.

Do I believe that you could get them to do all our work and write press releases for us? Absolutely not! But could we utilize the tools to save us researching time, proofreading time, or correlating data to make it more digestible—yes, absolutely—and that's where we should use it? Not to do the great work or replace the skills we have because we've built those over the years, and it's not necessarily a skill set that can be taught. AI is a system that gets fed into based on all the work many of us have done over the years, and it can do it at a faster speed, but that doesn't mean it's accurate. I don't think you can just say we've used it, and this is how it went. For me, I use it as a benchmarking tool or to research topics, to check what's already out there, and then fact-check to make sure I've got it right.

Tabita Andersson: Is there anything you'd like to add or comment on that we haven't covered so far?

Ryan Curtis-Johnson: For those promoted to a Chief Communications Officer role for the first time, I would like to say that we're dealing with humans, and we mustn't forget the human side. If we can all just be morally aware of the importance of ensuring everyone can access what we're doing, I just constantly remind everyone. Did you think about captions during your town hall with the CEO? Are you improving the internal accessibility of all content? As we grow into more senior roles, let's not forget to make sure that everything we write, do, deliver, share, and put out is accessible to everybody, regardless of whether someone is asking for it or not. We shouldn't have to wait for someone to ask.

CHAPTER 12

Laura Brusca
Chief Communications Officer Forbes

Laura Brusca is the **Chief Communications Officer** for **Forbes,** who champions success by celebrating those who have made it and those who aspire to make it. Forbes convenes and curates the most influential leaders and entrepreneurs who are driving change, transforming business and making a significant impact on the world. The Forbes brand today reaches more than 140 million people worldwide through its trusted journalism, signature LIVE and Forbes Virtual events, custom marketing programs and 49 licensed local editions in 81 countries.

For more information about Forbes, visit forbes.com.

Laura's LinkedIn profile: linkedin.com/in/laurabrusca/

Tabita Andersson: What is it like to be Chief Communications Officer for one of the most iconic media brands in the world?

Laura Brusca: It was such a proud moment for me when I was named Chief Communications Officer. I've been at Forbes for ten years, and I originally came from the agency side, so I started my career in communications in a PR agency. I've always loved journalism and the media world, so working for Forbes was a huge honor. Then, climbing the ladder and eventually having a seat at the table among the highest leadership was a meaningful moment because our brand stands for so much.

Chapter 12 | Laura Brusca

Our brand stands for success, which is a word that resonates with all our audiences globally and is core to the stories that our journalists write, whether it's fall from success, climb to success, or the stories of the people who are aspiring to reach that level of success. Journalism matters so much in the world we live in today because there's so much work that goes into the reporting, investigations, and lists. Now, we're deep into working on a couple of our rankings and lists, such as the Under 30 in Europe and the Billionaire list. The people listed in these rankings take it very seriously, and that's the same on our side; we work hard to ensure they're accurate and reflect the most up-to-date information.

Tabita Andersson: With the advent of fake news and the decline in trust in media that we've seen increasing over the last few years, how do you help combat that in your role as Chief Communications Officer at Forbes?

Laura Brusca: You're right; there's certainly a lot happening that is eroding that trust, and we talk a lot about it in the PR and communications industry. I was on a board call with one of the industry associations the other week. We were all talking about the spread of disinformation and misinformation, how to stop it, when to speak up, and when to stand on the sidelines when conversations are happening that you can't control or information that's spreading that's not true. It's tough nowadays, especially with artificial intelligence and how information is carried through technology. I'm very passionate about promoting the journalist and that journalism that is happening at Forbes, and that's a critical part of how our team thinks and works with our newsroom.

Our communications team works across our entire organisation, covering everything from employee engagement to internal communications, crisis communications and management, and promoting our different business ventures. Whether it's a new initiative, a new licensee, or a new big project, if our technology team is doing something cool, we're there promoting all the work everyone is doing. Our journalism is a critical part, and it's where we make sure that the great exclusives, scoops, and stories get a wider reach than just forbes.com and get out there so they are picked up by social media, and people talk about them. We then track the impact of our journalism as well as the effectiveness of our communications. For example, when a story comes out that resonates on Capitol Hill, it could end up in a source document, like a President's economic report, or a resource that can impact the investigative work that's done to inform bigger decisions and in that way, journalism can help create change, and we see the real outcomes of what we do.

Tabita Andersson: That's interesting to hear because typically, from a pure communications perspective, we'd look at the impact an article has, but you are able to take the next step and see what impact the story has on the world and figure out the outcome and impact of your work. In terms of that outcome, how do you measure that success?

Laura Brusca: I'm a big believer in quality over quantity and getting the right kind of exposure or the right messages out there. It's not about delivering 50 messages; it's about making sure that the three key messages you want to get across are picked up and carried through or that you're getting coverage in the right outlets, which might not be the top tiers. It might be those outlets that understand your story and are able to tell it in the right way. To me, this is a critical part of how we measure success. There are so many things that you can't calculate, and even if we have data, we need to understand what the data means. Some of it is the conversations you're having and the impact you have on your target audience. It's when we talk to a brand, a CMO, or another business leader in an industry that touches yours, and they say: "Oh, I read that story in Forbes," or "I heard about that story; you guys did that great scoop!" That shows real impact, and that's hard for us as communicators to measure. It's not like paid media, where you can tell when something drove a certain number of clicks, which resulted in a certain number of sales, or whatever conversation it is, but we're looking for a wider impact on an audience at the end of the day.

Tabita Andersson: Do you think we're getting better at it? We now have access to a lot more data, but have we improved at analyzing the insights that data gives us and using them to inform our work?

Laura Brusca: I would say yes, but there's still a lot of work to do. One of the reasons for that is that we all wear so many hats. This was something else we covered during the board call with the communications association the other week. When there are so many things happening, it can be hard to take time out to truly dive into the data and analytics, to understand it unless you have a big team with a person who focuses just on that, which not everyone has, or if you have an agency that can digest the data for you. So, I would say yes and no to your question. Sometimes, we just know what the C-suite or top investors want, and sometimes, we need to get closer to the business and understand the true purpose and goals of your company. Understand what provides value for your leadership. For example, it is helping to sell your services through major partnerships by giving them data that can help the partner understand the exposure they're going to get by using your services, or is it to show the reputational changes, sentiment, and how your brand is being perceived in a certain market? There's a lot more work we can do in this area, and that's partly due to the challenge of our roles as communicators and the fact that we have so much to do.

Tabita Andersson: What do you think we can do about that going forward? Perhaps we could take more opportunity to learn what trends like AI are offering us to leapfrog our skills.

Laura Brusca: AI is interesting, and I'm seeing a lot of use cases for it within our profession, especially in terms of how to analyze things. I'm paying a lot of attention to how it's being applied and integrated into tools and reputation tracking, as well as how to spot things. AI will change our industry in the next five years or so, and this conversation will be very different.

In terms of improving how we use data, I believe it's about making it more digestible and not just relying on topline numbers but explaining the numbers and what they mean. I also think there's a deeper partnership with the marketing team that companies can have in terms of merging metrics or audience data with other pieces of the business, which requires everyone to talk to one another a bit more. If someone is seeing an audience trend that is affecting the brand understanding, then the PR metrics could be showing the same effect. For example, there may be conversations happening on social media that could be causing people to not come to your website. There's a lot that we can better partner on across the board inside an organisation.

Tabita Andersson: You touched on working well with the C-suite and connecting what we do with the business strategy and objectives. What advice do you have for how we can do this more effectively? This is a key way for us to show value as Chief Communications Officers.

Laura Brusca: It's all about relationships and trust. If you're a part of a leadership team and your other leaders trust you, then it becomes so much easier for people to be open and transparent with one another and understand what each other needs, which means you'll know when to alert someone vs. when you don't have to.

I'm grateful to work with people whom I've known for a very long time, and we all fully trust each other in a positive way where we can problem-solve together.

The other thing I always say is that I think communicators should work within their function as journalists. We all serve a function of understanding the untold stories within our brand, and we should do the work of investigating, going many layers deep to understand what stories are not being leveled up to you so you can see the opportunities that exist.

When I say journalist, I don't mean reporting back or writing up stories, but I use it as an example of the type of role we play within the organisation. We need to have conversations, understand situations, set up calls and speak to as many people as possible, going down investigative holes, checking sources, etc. You could be talking to your CTO and Chief Digital Officer and uncover an issue or opportunity, and you then need to continue working on that thread, going down to the sources, finding out who's working on what and talking to people at all levels about what they're working on so we can understand not only what they're doing but also what it is that we're doing differently, or the details of how we're building something.

Tabita Andersson: Understanding the company and building solid business acumen are key to our role's success. Would you agree that we, as a profession, need to improve our commercial awareness?

Laura Brusca: Yes, I do. However, it might depend on the size of the company you work for. Although Forbes is a huge brand, we're not necessarily a huge company. We only have about 500 employees, so it's probably easier for me to say that because I'm not working at an organisation with 10,000+ employees or more where there are so many divisions, products, and markets that you need to understand.

I also believe that reporting structure matters. I report directly to my CEO vs. reporting to a CMO or another similar structure. If you're sitting one layer beneath, and you're not necessarily reporting to the top leadership, you don't always get the same insights as everyone else in the leadership team. Being part of that top team benefits me in that I really do understand our business challenges and opportunities, and I can explore those in more detail. For those in larger organisations, I would recommend using your team to play that role. It shouldn't all fall on you as a Chief Communications Officer. Distribute your team so that each person owns certain areas and can have regular calls with the leaders across the business. For example, I have regular weekly calls with my legal team, my HR team, my Chief Digital Officer, the person who runs our business ventures, etc., in addition to my CEO. It's important to have those calls because we can catch up on the latest, and there's always constant change.

Tabita Andersson: We're now seeing the CCO role reporting directly to the CEO on a much wider scale than ten or 15 years ago, which is fantastic and something we should continue to promote. What do you think are some benefits and advantages that an organisation can realize when there's a close connection between the CEO and CCO?

Laura Brusca: As a CCO, when you understand the vision of the top leadership team and can work in lockstep with them, you can perform much better and do your job in an aligned way. I view our employees as our most important stakeholders, and I think it's critical to think about our employees in every part of our communications. Every time we make important decisions, we want our employees to find out from us first before they find out from a news outlet or social media. That's not always possible, for example, if you work in certain public companies or regulated sectors, but I do think it's important that we understand the highest vision, goals, and objectives and how those change over time. We can then build our plan and strategy underneath, knowing it will be fully aligned and supporting the right goals.

Tabita Andersson: What advice would you give to a CEO about how they can work best with their CCO and communications partners?

Laura Brusca: Trust them fully with everything. Understand that they know how to handle information confidentially. This is critical because the problem oftentimes is that we run into crisis and issues management on an almost daily basis. Someone on another call recently said: "I want to work on fireproofing vs. firefighting!" which I loved. The better the relationship between CCO and CEO, the more transparent and trusting you can be, bringing them into the matters that only a handful of people know about and telling them about what's coming early on so they can do their job well. If you don't, what happens is that communications get fumbled, so bring them in early so they can do their job and give advice.

The CCO is your partner. Give them an opportunity to advise you. Thankfully, the leaders I've worked with have been wonderful, trusted partners, and I'm so appreciative to have worked so closely with them. They're on my speed dial, and we text each other regularly, sometimes just to say, "Hey, did you see this?" Being in constant communication is important because sometimes you have to react and respond quickly as a brand, and if you don't have a good, clear and transparent relationship, things can fall apart very quickly.

Tabita Andersson: The subsequent benefit to the business and wider organisation is that the brand will be better protected, you can catch things early and engage better with colleagues.

Laura Brusca: Exactly. That was such a great question, and I really hope some CEOs will read and take note!

Tabita Andersson: As a CCO, what are some of the biggest challenges you face at the moment?

Laura Brusca: The everyday crisis is always having new things popping up. It's the distraction of issues popping up, alarm bells going off, and people are on a deadline or need a response straight away. It takes you away from doing a lot of the high-level strategic work that you often really want to do. It feels like we're always on in the world today, and that's something we have to navigate to be able to come back to a moment of peace. It can be a lot to juggle, and it's my biggest challenge right now.

Another challenge is the changing media environments, and being in the media world, I can really speak to this. The media space has changed in the past five to ten years, and newsrooms are very different from how they once were. When I started out in PR, it was much easier: you'd grab a coffee with a reporter, invite them to an event, and they would have time to show up. Today, reporters are very focused on certain types of stories, and that's all they want to talk about, so unless your story fits into their story, there's no way of getting featured. For us, that means we have to find meaningful ways of not being so reliant solely on media relations but finding opportunities to provide value through other channels, whether it's creating your own platform or your own thought leadership to deliver your message on your own terms.

It could be on LinkedIn, through speaking engagements, live events, or events that you host yourself. I think we have to be more creative in order to see the impact.

Another challenge is that we need to better educate our stakeholders about our role. PR doesn't stand for press release. We're not a press release machine, and press releases don't just turn into instant media results. There has to be a strategy underneath. I've tried to get our organisation away from doing press releases every other day because it doesn't resonate and it doesn't have an impact. I believe it's more important to come up with strategic, high-level pitches when you think something could actually have an impact.

Tabita Andersson: You've mentioned a couple of times that you started off in an agency. Can you share your career path? What made you start in communications, and how did you get started?

Laura Brusca: When I was in college, I thought I wanted to be in advertising, so one summer, I had an advertising internship. At that time, my dad worked for an energy company, and when the internship ended, I still had a few days left for another project, so he asked me to come work in their corporate communications team, so I ended up doing two internships. I didn't enjoy working at the advertising agency as much as I did the corporate communications department. They brought me into projects, I helped create their newsletter, and I interviewed employees. There was so much storytelling that went into the job, and that excited me. Being able to build something and see it come to life was such an incredible opportunity, and I knew then, from that day on, that this was what I wanted to do. During my senior year at college, I called so many alumni to try and learn about their jobs and understand the different forms of communications and PR, and I applied for a ton of different types of internships and graduate programs. Two weeks before my graduation, I found out that I'd been selected for the external communications graduate program at Ruder Finn, which was a three-month program. I accepted, moved in with my grandma and thought I'd see how it works out. Since then, I've never stopped! They gave me such a great start to understand the craft, and I learned everything, from pitching for new business to managing product launches. Two years into my career, I managed a launch in Africa, and it was one of those incredible events that will always have an impact on my life. We launched a pediatric drug for malaria in Tanzania. I got to go to a hospital with a photographer and see children taking the drug, and it gave me goosebumps to know that lives were saved and we were getting exposure to it so that the world would hear about it. That has always been my drive. People wouldn't have heard about the stories we tell unless we tell them.

Tabita Andersson: What a wonderful story! What advice would you give to someone who's junior and wants to build a career in communications?

Laura Brusca: Raise your hand for everything. Don't be shy, be proactive. That's what makes a good PR person. Something else I heard from another very senior communications leader, whom I have great respect for, when he got promoted, they said to him that he's not the best writer, not the best this or that, but you have a very good gut instinct, and that's what we trust. You get a good gut instinct by getting experience. Some of it is natural, but my advice for anyone is to go get that experience. Learn from your failures and mistakes, don't let those mistakes get the best of you, and continue to raise your hand and put yourself out there.

Tabita Andersson: What skills and attributes do you look for when you need a new communicator for your team?

Laura Brusca: We always look for a good personality fit, so for us, that means we look for people who can juggle a lot at once, who can pivot and be proactive, and at the same time be self-sustaining. With that, I mean someone who can find a project that's going to help meet our mission and who can continue to maintain and manage those projects while at the same time coming up with new ideas and throwing the ideas out there. We want people to be proactive and have a positive attitude toward the work we do.

Tabita Andersson: Would you say it's more about the attitude than the skills?

Laura Brusca: I think you must have some sort of foundation, for example, having done a level of pitching and understanding how media relations work. I love hiring people from agencies because I feel that one year in an agency teaches you so much. It's the best crash course because of its competitive nature and how it drives people.

I speak to a lot of people who are trying to get into the industry, and I often say it's better to start small than not at all. You may not have the top internship or the top experience, but start small and get any experience you can under your belt. It could be a volunteer project or anything that helps you gain the experience you need to get to the role you want.

Tabita Andersson: At the other end of the scale, what advice would you give to someone who's just stepped into the role as a CCO for the first time?

Laura Brusca: It depends on whether you're new to the organisation or if you've been there a while, but I would say get to know the top leadership well and build trust and relationships. Also, look to your team and give them opportunities like you've been given. I think it's so important to continue to raise people up and let them ride the tide with you, passing around the opportunities. So, really look to your team, find ways that you can support them in their career journeys, and at the same time, build relationships and trust with the people who are going to be your core partners moving forward.

Tabita Andersson: Do you think there are skills that you need to have as a CCO today that weren't as prevalent five or ten years ago or will be more needed in the future?

Laura Brusca: Definitely! Understanding AI and how it works, even at an elementary level, is crucial today. When my friends were trying out ChatGPT in the early days when it was still in a demo version or beta, I kept telling my team about it and how it was going to change everything.

The more you can be the smartest person in the room and understand when new technologies come around, the stronger you'll be as a person. AI is one of my side projects. When I have time, I try to experiment, understand how it works and learn about it, whether it's reading reports or seeing how other people are using it.

Technology changes have definitely changed how we work in communications. Social media, for example, is much different than it was just five years ago. We've all seen how social media has become such a critical part of our ability to better listen to our audiences.

Tabita Andersson: With that also comes the ability to keep calm. So much on social media is easy to get worked up about, so being able to keep calm is a big part of what we do. Would you agree?

Laura Brusca: Yes, 100%. It's so important to stay calm, keep a level head, put the situation back into perspective, and tell people not to jump into a conversation. Our job is to remind everyone that—depending on the situation, of course—small things will often go away on their own. We are going to monitor it, but we don't always need to do something; everyone just needs to stay calm.

Also, if people are getting worked up about something, it's our job to focus on how we're doing to solve it. Is this a real issue? Should we be concerned about it? Should we communicate or not? I think this is something that a lot of us have to deal with now that we never really had to do because social media was a different world. People acted differently on social media. Today, people can act wild and just say anything!

Also, on some platforms you can no longer report misinformation anymore which I think is interesting. That happened a few years ago and that's why it's sometimes a little tricky to navigate content on those platforms. It's also why some people are shifting away from those platforms. Even a platform like LinkedIn now carry some of those more testy conversations, but overall tends to be a bit more grown up.

Tabita Andersson: As a result, have you started to see a shift away from some of the traditional social media platforms to some of the newer ones?

Laura Brusca: I think it depends on where in the world you're based. I have seen some people get off social media completely and just cut from their lives entirely. But not large-scale migrations away from the traditional platforms.

Tabita Andersson: If we go back a few years, we were often asked as an organisation to comment on what's happening in the world around us. Do you think we are dialing back on that trend? And how do you think we can help guide our organisation on whether to comment or not?

Laura Brusca: I think you're right. Naturally, we do a lot of employee communications when things happen, but as a brand, we want to take a neutral stance on certain things. We talk about checking in and caring for people and making sure we're connected when something happens, whether it's wildfires or geopolitical situations. I think it's getting trickier for a lot of organisations to work out what they say or what they don't say. Unfortunately, we've recently seen a lot of organisations pulling back from DEI messaging, for example. I also think some brands probably have felt like they were criticized after saying something but then getting into worse trouble for not saying anything at all!

A lot of the time, people just want to say, "no comment," or they don't want to respond to anything when they get into those points. As communicators, it's our job to recommend to people why they should say something or when they shouldn't say something, with a focus on the importance of speaking up from time to time or not at all. This is where our real challenge is. We need to be able to read the room, push back where needed, understand when to say something and when to not say something, and sit on the sidelines.

Tabita Andersson: Do you think those decisions are easier or more difficult when you're a strong, iconic brand like Forbes? You have such clear editorial guidelines for your journalists, which are good principles to guide decisions. Do you think that makes your job easier?

Laura Brusca: Yes and no. Because we work with a newsroom, the other challenge we have is when to say something internally. I always say that anything internal should be instantly considered public in any company at any time. Every single time you say anything, it should be considered public or external. Also, you're never going to please everyone. Sometimes, the language isn't what employees wanted to hear, or maybe you didn't go far enough, or maybe they didn't want to hear anything at all, or it didn't feel authentic to them. It's a hard space to navigate and especially when you're a big brand like us, we have to take it seriously and balance when we speak and what we say.

Tabita Andersson: You mention employee communications; how do you think internal communications can help build a culture within an organisation and engage colleagues?

Laura Brusca: The more you can connect employees to your purpose, the more you can bring them into the why; why do you show up, and why do you work at Forbes? The more you can give them the purpose and meaning behind what they do, the more fulfilled people feel when they do their work, even on hard days. Having a purpose is very important for all employees, and it has to resonate across the board.

Another aspect of using internal communications to build culture, I believe, is to understand the needs of your employees. Do they need to feel more recognised for their work? Do they need to feel more connected with our values? Do they need to feel like they have an outlet to speak up or say something when needed? Part of that understanding, I believe, comes from using your communications team as a sounding board. Quite often, someone isn't going to tell you everything because you're a leader, or they won't say it while you're in the room, so use your team to know what people are really feeling and not be immune to their answers but trying to understand them is core to building a good culture.

Tabita Andersson: What would you like to be known for as a Chief Communications Officer?

Laura Brusca: I want to be known as a problem solver—someone who doesn't just say okay to everything that's happening as if I can't do anything about it but who is a strategic partner to people and helps them solve their problems for the business.

One thing I pride myself on the most is being a connector between people. I try to help solve problems by making connections.

Tabita Andersson: I often say that connecting the dots is a big part of what we do because we have such a unique perspective. We work across the entire organisation, which very few people inside an organisation have the privilege to do, and that's something I find exciting.

Laura Brusca: Yes, I feel like we're so lucky that we get to know so much about what's happening. Then you realize that not everyone knows that, and I have to remind my team about that sometimes. Not everyone on the technology or product teams, for example, has access to the same amount of information, and it's important to bring everyone along.

Tabita Andersson: What do you think we can do as a profession to promote and amplify the role? Most communicators are very passionate about the role and enjoy working in it, so what can we do better?

Laura Brusca: It's an interesting challenge. Not to compare ourselves to Chief Marketing Officers, but when you see the CMO community come together, they are so bonded. They all know each other. They all help each other. They are a group, and they hang out together. I don't think we have that same bond as Chief Communications Officers with other CCOs. It's one of the reasons why I like being on boards and getting to know other people in communications. The more we talk to each other, the more we realize that we have shared experiences and problems. The more we can come together as a group to meet regularly and have honest conversations, the more we can elevate ourselves. When you see people helping each other out and elevating each other, they also elevate the industry. CMOs, for example, often get recognition while we're often the "behind-the-scenes people." And sometimes we do things that we can't talk about. My CEO sometimes says she wishes she could call me out for something I've done, but it's confidential, so we can't talk about it. You take the verbal 1:1 praise, but I think it makes it harder to get recognition as an industry.

Tabita Andersson: That is so true, and that's what we need to do. We need to lift the lid and help people understand how much we, as communications people, do that is purely behind the scenes. Someone the other day said the best crisis communications is when no one knows there was a crisis!

Let's pivot to another topic. What is your opinion on the difference in communications between different industries? Do you think there is a difference between B2B (business to business) and B2C (business to consumer), for example?

Laura Brusca: Apart from the fact that certain industries have bigger resources and bigger teams, I think there are a lot of similarities, and we are all facing very similar challenges. That's what I hear when I connect to more people within our profession. We're all experiencing the same challenges, so how do we solve those?

Tabita Andersson: What other advice do you have for other CCOs?

Laura Brusca: One of the things I worked on last year was my public speaking skills. Oftentimes, the CCO is the person who puts everyone else up on stage, but it's important to also build your own brand, to be out there and practice what you preach! I hated public speaking, and now I feel more comfortable, but it took me throwing myself on stage doing classes, putting myself out there and seeing the experiences of the audience to get more confident. When you're speaking in front of 500 people, and there's applause or a like reaction, you can better understand what other speakers go through when you're putting them on stage on behalf of your business.

My advice is to face your fears and whatever is holding you back, and if it's connected to what you're telling other people to do, try to understand their experience better so you can deliver better in your job.

Sometimes, I also think women can suffer from impostor syndrome. We might be wondering whether we're really ready for something or whether we're the right person for a job or role, and the more we gain in confidence, the more we can trust our gut and instincts, and the more successful we can be.

CHAPTER 13

Amy Lawson
Chief Communications, Brand, and Corporate Affairs Officer Sage

Amy Lawson is the **Chief Communications, Brand, and Corporate Affairs Officer** for **Sage,** the leader in accounting, financial, HR, and payroll technology for small and mid-sized businesses (SMBs). Sage exists to knock down barriers so everyone can thrive, starting with the millions of small- and mid-sized businesses served by the company, its partners, and accountants. Customers trust the finance, HR, and payroll software to make work and money flow. By digitizing business processes and relationships with customers, suppliers, employees, banks, and governments, the digital network connects SMBs, removing friction and delivering insights. Knocking down barriers also means the company uses its time, technology, and experience to tackle digital inequality, economic inequality, and the climate crisis.

For more information about Sage, visit sage.com.

Amy's LinkedIn profile: linkedin.com/in/amy-lawson-76b95716/

Tabita Andersson: What can Chief Communications Officers do better to prove the value of communications at the highest level within an organisation?

Amy Lawson: The world of business has become much more rounded in terms of its stakeholder focus. Corporations and organisations have learned that they need a license to operate from all stakeholders, meaning shareholders, customers, employees, and the communities in which they operate. This has helped elevate the role of Communications and Corporate Affairs because the only way to navigate that right is with the help of excellent judgment and strategy advice.

The pandemic was an opportunity for cultural topics to rise to the agenda, and it helped businesses see that they needed support in navigating through uncertain times.

However, we won't stay at the top table unless we do a couple of things. Firstly, being deeply ingrained with the commercial objectives of the business. Communications professionals have to understand what's driving the business they're in. Somebody once said to me that good communication is not about messaging and activation; it's about capital allocation. When you are working in the proper senior Chief Communications Officer role, you are influencing the way the business makes and spends money, which is exactly where we should be. Getting deeply commercial and getting close to the business is very important.

Secondly, don't lose sight of the business strategy. This is something that was deeply ingrained in me when I started in a PR agency and in my early career. Earning the place at the top table is one thing, but if we're seen as tactical-, delivery-, or execution-focused, we will lose the seat because I believe we have to show every day that what we're doing is not just about activation, it's about the strategic future of the business.

Tabita Andersson: As communications professionals, what can we do to improve commercial awareness? Should we do it earlier in our careers or later?

Amy Lawson: It's easier to do early on in your career because what sometimes happens with people in our profession is that you can become very senior without being very commercial. In that case, you will not be able to elevate the profession within your organisation. It's, unfortunately, easy to become very senior as a communications professional without understanding the levers inside a business. At that point, it might be too embarrassing to ask someone to explain management accounts, the strategic objectives, or the budget for the business.

I give advice all the time to people in my team to go find an up-and-coming, friendly finance person or a brilliant salesperson who will let you shadow them and sit down to find out exactly what they do and how they interpret the data they see. It's one of my favorite things to say to the team! Go and sit down with the management accounts from last year and get someone who's bright in the finance team to explain to you what it all means and what the drivers are.

Spending time with customers is something else we all can and should do. It's sometimes easier to do so earlier in your career, although I believe we should be doing it throughout because it helps us understand the environment we're operating in and how it works.

Tabita Andersson: That also aligns with how we work with our peers in the C-suite. How can we do so more effectively to elevate the profession?

Amy Lawson: We're unique as a profession in a lot of ways. I feel we have the license to roam everywhere, which is fantastic because you should be able to go out and spot opportunities and risks everywhere in the business. We know those can come from anywhere, and that's the good bit; the responsibility it places on you is to build relationships everywhere. I always have regular one-on-ones with all my C-suite peers because I need to understand what's going on in their function and how much communications and corporate affairs are supporting what they are trying to achieve. I need to understand where there are risks that we may not be seeing, so it's important that we establish those peer relationships and nurture them properly.

Tabita Andersson: What advice would you give to the Chief Executive Officer about how to best work with their CCO and the communications function?

Amy Lawson: I would split the function and the individual. It's important that there's a trusted relationship between the individuals, but be mindful that you don't become a quasi-Chief of Staff or personal adviser. I believe it's important you establish yourself as having a unique role. Often, you're the only person in that team whose job it is to say to the CEO that their idea is not great, or something didn't go down very well, or wasn't particularly effective. It's a unique role from that perspective. You have to have a trusted relationship where they trust that you are absolutely dedicated to the same objective as they are, so if you're giving tough, challenging feedback, they know where it comes from. At the same time, you must be careful that you don't become the CEO's publicist. It's an important distinction for the individual in a CCO role.

My advice for the CEO to work best with their communications function is to give them problems to solve. Don't give them strategies and tactics because that's what you pay them to do. You will get a much better outcome if you go to your communications team with challenges and rely on them to come up with solutions.

The same is true for anyone who works with the wider communications team. Give them a challenge that you need to solve because you need someone who thinks, feels, or does something different. Show them the outcome you want, but rely on them as experts in their craft. If they're any good, they will want to suggest the strategy, not just deliver a bunch of tactics.

Tabita Andersson: How would you describe the role to someone who doesn't know what you do and perhaps is bemused by what communications is within a company?

Amy Lawson: I always say that I'm here to help the company explain what it's there to do. I'm here to help the company tell stories that its customers, employees, shareholders, and communities want to hear. Hopefully, I spend most of my time telling positive stories, but sometimes, we have to use storytelling as a technique to explain when things go wrong as well.

Tabita Andersson: Building on that, when things go wrong, or when there's a crisis, it's often also when we can prove our value. What's your experience of crisis communications and the role we play in managing those scenarios?

Amy Lawson: Often, one of the only good things that can come out of a crisis is that organisations understand the value of a multi-stakeholder view, the calm judgment and counsel under pressure, and how vulnerable an organisation's reputation can be when it comes under scrutiny.

My experiences in this role have been quite varied. I started in a PR agency and then went to Channel Four News at a time when journalism and media were under fire because of the Leveson Inquiry and phone hacking. After that, I worked in the Government, where it often feels like you're in constant defense mode; it's a constant crisis. I then joined Sage, where I'd say we've had two or three significant crisis situations, and I think those are moments where communications teams really prove their worth.

They're good moments to remind everybody what we do. Done well, a lot of the time, people don't even notice the value of communications because we don't measure or evaluate all the things that don't appear or the reputational crises that don't unfold because we've prevented them. This means we have to do a good job of explaining those risks to the business so they understand.

Tabita Andersson: You talked about your career path and some of the various roles you've had. What advice would you give yourself if you could go back and redo your career?

Amy Lawson: I didn't design this career path. You can only connect the dots when you look back; you can't really design it from the start. I've been in a lot of environments where I felt quite different from the people I'm working with. Channel Four News is a good example of how I felt intellectually inferior to the razor-sharp intellects in that newsroom, and that was really intimidating to start with. Over time, I began to spot things that others didn't because my experience is very different, and I articulate and understand things in a way that's different from many of my colleagues. The advice I wish I'd learned sooner is that being different and bringing a different perspective is a real strength if you understand and know how to harness it.

I would encourage myself to be bolder because when you're a communications person, and maybe because we're not chartered in the same way as other professions, it's easy to have a slight inferiority complex in our roles. I would say my gut and my judgment have usually served me very well, so I would go back and say be even more confident, demanding, and assertive when you have a gut feeling about something, because I believe it would have gotten me to outcomes faster.

Tabita Andersson: That's great advice! Further to that point, what are some of the skills we need as CCOs that weren't so prevalent if you go back five or ten years?

Amy Lawson: One skill is to truly understand our audience. That was true before, but I think there were fewer places where the audiences were, and now we have to deeply understand everything from social platforms to how people communicate, how they organize, where they are, and how they buy. It takes a deeper understanding of our audiences than in the past. For example, the lines between marketing and our role have blurred slightly in terms of understanding social media forums and other platforms where the audience lives.

While we need to understand what we did in the past, we have to get better at interpreting and gathering insights. That can be difficult because there will always be a degree of what we do that's judgment-based, but you must arm yourself with as much data and insight as you can. My role encompasses both brand and corporate affairs, and my observation is that the brand and marketing side of the house is much better at gathering and working with insights than the communications side of the house. I'm trying to bridge the gap between the two so that we are more insight-driven in communications and then a bit more willing to take risks based on judgment in the brand team.

Tabita Andersson: Metrics and measurements for communications are things we've improved a lot over the last ten or 15 years. We have data points now that we didn't have access to before. What do you think we can continue to improve, and how can we use the data to better inform decisions?

Amy Lawson: We must be less resistant to the idea that what we do is measurable and what we do relates to commercial targets. I've seen communications teams say we're not here to deliver the commercials, and I don't think we should be held on the line for generating leads or delivering sales targets because that misses the point of what we do. At the same time, we shouldn't be resistant to the idea that we contribute and play a part in the broader surroundings in which our business stakeholders live and operate. We need to get better at having data and being able to use that data to make a case and make an argument.

I've seen people walk in with all the data there is, but don't think about how it makes sense, and I've seen people go in with just opinions and conjecture. The problem with that is that you always have to look around the table and think about who you are influencing. For some stakeholders that you need to influence, opinions won't be enough, or data won't be enough. The combination is critical.

Tabita Andersson: How can we improve? Do you think we need more education, or is it just that we don't have access to the right data points?

Amy Lawson: It's about collaboration and working with parts of the business that have data points. You have to get past organisational silos. Almost every organisation that I've worked in has had teams wanting to generate their own data, whereas it's much more compelling to look at your colleagues and other teams and look at the econometrics behind running a campaign and see what happened with web traffic, or sales, or whatever it might be. To do that, we must collaborate rather than always wanting to walk into the room with our own bag of data. We can have a much more compelling discussion with the business if you have a story that other people can get on board with.

Understanding social media metrics is also very important because our audiences are so fragmented. They exist in so many different places now, so we have to understand their entire footprint. My team, for example, is working on a LinkedIn newsletter, and what's brilliant about it is that we're working with the marketing team on how it will fit with their other campaigns, data points, and content. Collaboration is key to making this a success, so we're using the right content that is relevant to the customer audiences we're trying to reach.

Tabita Andersson: We've touched on the number and volume of stakeholders we have, not just target audiences but other stakeholders, too. How do you balance working with such different audiences, inside and outside of a business?

Amy Lawson: This is a massive strength of communications teams because most other teams within an organisation have a primary audience or stakeholder, a key person they need to address. Whereas communications teams are very adept at saying, hang on, if we're saying something over here, what's this audience over there going to hear? Across every area of the business, my CEO rejects this idea that we can't find solutions that serve all stakeholders, or that there are always winners and losers. That is the job; that's what we must do. We need to find a way to understand the trade-offs. Of course, there will be trade-offs, but overall, we should be able to look ourselves in the eye and say, as an organisation, we have shown up for all stakeholders.

For us, it's not implying that we can create a perfect world; it's about having a deep understanding of all those audiences so we can explain the choices we make. For example, if we tell our colleagues that the overall pay increase will be 4%, although we live with inflation at 11%, and they then see that we're giving customers a 10% increase on their subscriptions, and they can see what we pay in dividends to shareholders, as communicators we have to be able to clearly explain the choices we make as a business. Often, the job is to know what the reactions will be of the various stakeholders and advise on how to navigate through those. That is the key career strength of most communications teams.

Tabita Andersson: I agree. In addition, over the last few years, we've been asked more and more to comment on societal changes or external events. In my opinion, those requests are declining, and we may be heading for a more neutral position again. What's your opinion on how we can help an organisation navigate that environment?

Amy Lawson: It's the same thing, in the sense that we'll never have all the answers; these things are complex. Your job is not to make it easy for the organisation, but it is to make sure you have understood and surfaced all the tensions that are at play so you can help the business prioritize and navigate through them.

For example, one of the things we do is to have a topic matrix that helps us work through whether something is an issue that we should comment on or not. It's essentially a two-by-two box that guides us. Sometimes, we do something and say nothing; sometimes, we do something and say something, and then reverse flip. We work through a series of questions that help us understand if it's important to our stakeholders, if we can make a difference, if we speak out, if it is material to our business, and if it materially impacts any of our stakeholders adversely if we speak out. Essentially, the questions help us go through a process, and the benefit is that they help lead the business to clarify its thinking and make a good decision. The other benefit is that you can then explain to your stakeholders why you haven't spoken out on a topic. This process has been very helpful to us because we can clearly state when we're going to speak out about something because it might be happening in a region where we have colleagues, customers, or partners, but we're not going to speak out on a topic where we don't have stakeholders in a particular region and where we don't believe our voice is additive to the overall discourse.

Tabita Andersson: With the increasing amount of fake news and distrust around us, what do you think we can do as a communications team to help our stakeholders and organisations navigate that environment going forward?

Amy Lawson: Sage has a very strong brand trust. The brand has been around for around 40 years. We are FTSE 100, and we regard that as a precious asset because we're essentially asking small businesses in all our markets to trust us with their most important data so they can run their businesses. In a world of AI, trust becomes even more critical. It's, therefore, important to us that we work in a way that builds trust and doesn't erode or dilute it.

Trusted sources of information are going to become even more important as we navigate through this period of intense change. I talked earlier about how everything is fragmented. I think there may be some really trusted sources that will start to emerge, which will help us as communications professionals, because if we maintain good relationships with those sources and know how to use them, that will help us connect with our audiences. It's going to be messy and difficult for a while, but, in the end, we might emerge in a place where there are some trusted places to go, and it's our job to make sure they are fully appraised of the facts and tell the story in as clear a way as possible.

Tabita Andersson: You mentioned AI as a hot topic, and it's the same for us as a function. How do you think we can take advantage of AI, and how do you think it will change in the future?

Amy Lawson: Put simply, there are two parts to our jobs. There's content creation, and there's judgment, advice, and decision-making. The content creation and campaign planning part is made for AI. I'm trying with my team to remove the stigma around using AI and telling them it's okay to use AI to help with general tasks. However, you have ultimate accountability and responsibility for the quality of that work, so you need to make sure you're the human who's certifying and validating the work. Your judgment is still going to be critical in everything you're doing, so you can't abdicate responsibility for something.

We also have a responsibility to be clear about where AI can help and where it can't. To give you an example, my team, like most, sends a note to the organisation in the morning with all our press cuttings, showing where our business was talked about that morning. Right now, this is a manual process. A human being sits down, scans the cuttings, writes the note, and sends it to the organisation. For me, the first part of that process should absolutely be AI-generated, but a human needs to read the cuttings and validate them. Someone needs to check if they're correct and if they're described accurately in the note before sending. The quality of the content is key, and we need a person to check it.

There is a secondary reason for this, too. I need my team to read about Sage every single morning for their own professional development, skills, and understanding of the business. That's the part I think we won't lose yet because we still need to develop the craft, our own experiences, and expertise.

Tabita Andersson: That's a great observation. Have you seen any other applications of AI that we can build on in the future, apart from content generation?

Amy Lawson: My team has been using a tool that helps you have a debate or an argument online, using AI, which helps flesh out all the edges of a discussion or a debate. Using the tool as a thought partner to check and test messaging is a really good use of AI for communications teams. Everyone is using Generative AI for the first draft, which is fine, but using it to pick holes in arguments, find weaknesses, and test yourself is super good.

Developing mini-LLMs within communications teams is also going to become very useful. Leading up to that, we're making sure we have all our content in one place on our internal platforms so we can ask it to, for example, give us 200 words from the CEO on a particular topic in the voice of a LinkedIn post, and include an audio clip of him talking about it. That's the end game, which I think will be fantastic!

Tabita Andersson: Absolutely, that would be super useful. What are some of the other trends you see for our profession, outside of AI, that are going to increase over the next couple of years?

Amy Lawson: One of the things we're focusing on is how we pull together our disciplines and see how far we can push it. We have public affairs, PR, marketing, and social media all coming together around topics. The truth is, 20 years ago, you could create a big PR story and get a few good days out of that one story, but that doesn't happen anymore because of the fragmentation of audiences. You can't dominate any longer; it's much harder to cut through the noise. However, you can line up all your different channels and hit audiences with the same message in lots of different places. That's the way to cut through. We're being much more collaborative in terms of how we get the disciplines to work together.

We're also seeing a trend of being smarter about paid media and advertorials because we're seeing the influence of traditional media diminishing, so the mixture of paid and earned media channels is becoming more important. In the past, this was something PR and communications teams were dismissive of, but the reality is that those sources are becoming more critical and trusted, so we're looking into paid sources more and figuring out how we can best use them all together.

Tabita Andersson: How about internal communications? How do you think employee communications can contribute to building a great culture within an organisation?

Amy Lawson: The key word is contribute. We need to be clear that communications is just one part of the mix. We don't own the engagement score; we don't own the culture of the organisation, but we see communications as not just top-down but also employee-to-employee. One of the key things for us is understanding our employees as rounded people. If you're not going to go home and read 3,000 words on a global news topic, you're not going to read 3,000 words on an internal learning and development topic or cyber security training. We need to challenge ourselves to use all the techniques that grab our attention in the real world, so we don't show up with an intranet that feels like it's from 2005! That's a big driver and how we can contribute to the culture because it shows our colleagues that when we say we want them to innovate, we want everyone to innovate all the time, whatever role they're in.

Tabita Andersson: What are some of the other things internal communications can contribute to? As a profession, it used to be a bit hidden. External communications sometimes get spotlighted more because of the media coverage, which is highly visible, hitting the headlines. What are some of the ways that internal communications can contribute just as much to the business strategy and objectives?

Amy Lawson: This goes back to being commercial and understanding what's driving the business, deeply understanding how we help the different communities within our organisation. This includes understanding how to rally a sales team in the final week of the year and what messages they need to hear, which might be different from what it takes to rally the HR team around a particular project or what it takes to get the business through a transformation. Positioning ourselves at the top of the value chain, asking what leaders are trying to achieve, and then bringing us in at the right time is critical. The best internal communications teams don't see themselves as a delivery arm. They say no a lot, and they are very clear about what's important and what's not. They should be regarded as top-tier treatment rather than just execution or activation.

The most important aspect for communications professionals overall is that you always return to what the business is trying to achieve and are adamant with people when they try to start a conversation with you about the tactics. This is the biggest difference I've seen in communications teams that make it to the top of the organisation vs. the ones that don't. They don't get the business to start the conversation with tactical execution. They have business conversations.

When I started my career and started leading people, my advice was always not to go straight to talking about the press release, the campaign, or the crisis. Have a business conversation first; understand the mindset, the pressures, and the objectives of the person you're talking to. If you spend five minutes at the end talking about communications, that's fine because those five minutes will be much more impactful if you've understood clearly what the person is trying to do. We need to keep pushing for those conversations. We should tell those leaders who aren't sure about communications being at the top table that they will get a much better communications function if they bring me in early and talk about everything because I'll be able to spot the risks and opportunities, and then you'll get a plan and strategy that meets your real objectives. We must keep pushing for those conversations and keep showing the strategic value of what we do. Never start with the tactics, and always start with what you're trying to achieve and what the strategy is to get there.

Tabita Andersson: I couldn't agree more! Finally, if there's one thing you could be remembered for in your role, what would that legacy be?

Amy Lawson: I'm the first Chief Corporate Affairs Officer to sit on the leadership team at Sage. I'm proud that I made the case, and that the work of my team has made the case. I've been here nine years, so I'm personally very proud of that because I think the role will remain here at Sage long after I go, and I think the company will be all the stronger for having Communications and Corporate Affairs at the top table.

As a business, the biggest difference we can make is helping the company be successful. For us, that means creating an environment for small businesses to thrive, which is what our external campaigning is about. If I could pull that off, it would make a real, meaningful difference!

CHAPTER 14

David Burnand

Chief Marketing and Communications Officer Staffbase

David Burnand is the **Chief Marketing and Communications Officer** for **Staffbase**, a global leader in employee communication platforms. Staffbase is the fastest-growing employee communications cloud, equipping many of the world's leading companies with solutions to inspire every employee with motivating communication. With 2,000 customers, Staffbase helps organisations such as Adidas, Aldi, Coca-Cola, DHL, Samsung, Toyota Finance Australia, and Volvo to inspire their people to achieve great things together. Staffbase connects companies with their employees through a branded employee app, intranet, email, and Microsoft 365 integrations, all of which can be managed through a single platform. Staffbase is headquartered in Chemnitz, Germany.

For more information about Staffbase, visit staffbase.com.

David's LinkedIn profile: www.linkedin.com/in/davidburnand/

Tabita Andersson: Would you mind starting by giving us an overview of Staffbase and how you, as the Chief Communications and Marketing Officer, work within your organisation?

Chapter 14 | David Burnand

David Burnand: Staffbase is a SaaS (software as a service) company. We have just over 800 employees, spread primarily across Europe, North America, and Asia-Pacific-Japan. Our headquarters are in Chemnitz, a town in East Germany, which is closer to Prague than Berlin! As our Founders are based in Germany, we have a big presence there, alongside offices in New York, Minnesota, Canada, Australia, and London, and we recently opened an office in Japan.

Staffbase provides software for internal communications, which includes an employee intranet app. We started out as the original branded employee app after our founders saw a gap in the market for companies that didn't have an effective way of communicating with their high volume of frontline workers, so they came up with the idea of a branded app. For example, one of our largest app deployments in the world is for logistics company DHL. Their employees download the app from one of the app stores, and the company can then use the app to communicate directly with them. DHL has 600,000 employees, so it's a very large deployment. Because we originate in Germany, we work with most of the large German brands; in addition, we work with customers such as Intel, Audi, BMW, Adidas, and Sephora. It's a broad spread!

We were the first software business that originated in the former East Germany, outside of Berlin, to be valued at a billion dollars. It's been an amazing story over the last ten years. We keep going from strength to strength as we expand across North America, the UK, Australia, and Japan.

Tabita Andersson: Can you please expand on your role as Chief Communications Officer within a global company and describe the structure of your team?

David Burnand: I might be a bit different from some classic Chief Communications Officers in that my remit spans both communications and marketing, so we have everything, including internal and external communications, in one team together with marketing. My team consists of multiple global functions, including central marketing, product marketing, communications and PR, marketing operations, web, and brand. We also have regional teams that focus on local activities spread out across our markets.

Tabita Andersson: Are there benefits to having all these functions in one place, and do you see any synergies from better integrating activities?

David Burnand: I do, and it was a strategic change. Previously, internal communications were sitting in the HR function, and we made the decision to move it into the overall communications team because we believe in the idea of telling one cohesive narrative externally that is reflected by our employees. Our employees are our best ambassadors, and bringing the teams together helps create clear synergy between internal and external communications. It's important that our employees understand our brand, vision, and mission, as well as how things fit together within our strategy.

Another benefit of having an integrated team is that, from a business strategy point of view, one of our most important priorities is to build our brand and reputation in North America. PR is one of our most important channels to achieve that, so from that perspective, it makes sense to have our PR activities fully integrated with our marketing plans.

From my perspective, I have seen silos building up in other companies when people don't work together across the functions, which can make it difficult to ensure you're joined up around your brand externally in the various markets we cover. That's why we're structured this way.

Tabita Andersson: Thank you for explaining. It also depends on the type and size of an organisation and the goals of the different functions.

You mentioned that building an internal employee brand is core to what we do in internal communications. Do you also think internal communications can have a positive impact on an organisation's culture?

David Burnand: Yes, I do. I also say that based on what we see happening with our customers. From a Staffbase point of view, it certainly has an impact on our culture. It also has an impact on business performance. Quite frankly, the teams that don't buy into your mission and vision and understand the why of what you're trying to achieve as a company are far less likely to deliver the things you need them to deliver. We see the same with our customers, and I believe this is both the biggest opportunity and the biggest weakness in communications right now. Personally, I've always maintained a clear link between marketing and communications all the way through my career, even when I worked for Siemens. When we launched campaigns, products, and mergers, I used to sit opposite the communications leader at the time, and we were completely joined at the hip. He ran all the core communications functions, and I ran all the central marketing functions, so it didn't matter what we were doing; we would work together every single day.

Another big opportunity for communications is in technology. Marketing has moved on massively in the last 15 years, driven entirely by technology, and there's a huge opportunity for communications to do the same. To me, it falls into two categories. The first one is the connection with business strategy, which still isn't there for a lot of communicators. I see a lot of communicators still being catchers. They take whatever is thrown at them by the leadership in the same way that marcomms people used to do back in the day. They make the best of it, build the message, and use the most effective channels to get the message out to the market. It used to be the same in marketing. We'd take the product or whatever the business told us, and we'd try to project the best possible message. We tried to polish whatever message we were given instead of truly shaping the message. This is often why product marketing would sit separately from the rest of the marketing team. There is a huge opportunity for communicators to get more deeply connected to the businesses within which they operate. A part of that is down to a lack of confidence but a part of it is also down to an inability to articulate value so why would I as a senior leader take you into the inner circle and ask you to shape things if I believe that your value is just in distributing what I say because you've never shown me anything else. There's an imperative for communicators to prove their value.

One reason it's not happening in the same way it does in marketing, where we are able to tie our contribution down to the individual dollar, is our inability to use advanced technologies to articulate value. Software is not just about being the channel. For example, if you implement a new intranet these days, it enables you to run multichannel campaigns internally and measure the impact of those in the same way you would as a marketer.

What do I mean by impact? What I don't mean is open rates and likes because those are vanity metrics that we still overly rotate toward. What I mean is measuring sentiment shifts within an organisation, measuring the likelihood that employees are changing their behavior. We do that through things like micro pulses, data, and analytics. Within our own software, we have an analytics package that enables communicators to measure and then articulate messages to their businesses. As an example, we needed a group of employees to go through a re-skilling program, so we designed it as a multichannel campaign. At the start of the campaign, only 20% of them understood why they had to complete the re-skilling program, and only 10% of them were likely to invest their time to do it. At the end of the program, 60% understood why they needed to do it, and 45% said that they had committed time to completing it. That's powerful, and that's exactly where we want to be as communicators, being part of shaping how things are executed, rather than just catching decisions at the end and being told to send out emails and messages. This is a huge opportunity for communicators.

Tabita Andersson: I agree. The CCO's role is to help shift the perception of communications as a function from being a service delivery centre to a trusted advisor. Part of the role is about the message and making sure it's landing well, shifting behaviors and sentiment in the direction that the organisation needs. Part of the role is also about being a valued advisor at the executive level. Would you agree with that, and if so, how do you think we can improve?

David Burnand: Yes, I agree, but a part of it is generational. I also believe CCOs need to become much more deeply ingrained and build a better understanding of the practical uses of technology, which I still think is a gap. I notice this within conversations that are happening within the industry, where we talk about how technology is going to change everything—artificial intelligence is already changing everything—but if you ask people about it, they say that's an interesting opinion but what does it mean to me and how do I practically implement it within my business? The reality is that most people are not able to articulate the next step and the how, because, beyond using the basics, like dabbling with Chat GPT or Gemini, most people are just not deeply ingrained enough in technology. I know that's easier to say if you're the CCO of a software company where we think deeply about software every single day, but I think there's a real imperative for CCOs to move in that direction because ultimately, if you don't understand how it can help, how can you improve how you run analytics, how you measure your tactics and how you build the confidence to articulate the impact, then you will always be clinging to the most basic data and you will gravitate toward the vanity metrics which, let's be honest, most of the C-suite don't care about.

Tabita Andersson: That is true, but part of the reason we're not doing it is that it's perceived as difficult. How do you think we can improve? How can we get better at this as a profession, going forward?

David Burnand: It starts with taking the time to cut through fear and talk deeply with your organisation across functions. It can be a functional challenge, so it's about going out and educating yourself, spending time getting accustomed to it, and being aware of all the different opportunities that are now available to communicators within the world of technology. Go meet vendors, sit down with them, and see how solutions are used, even if you don't end up doing anything with those vendors. That's a practical way of closing the gap that I believe would make a massive difference. Otherwise, it will never happen because you're always talking about it at a very high level, not from a position of knowledge.

Tabita Andersson: Sometimes it's about trying things out and sharing best practices. For AI, for example, it's been interesting to hear about what CCOs and their teams are doing, which varies greatly between teams and organisations, and I believe there's an opportunity as a profession to come together and talk about the ten best ways of incorporating AI into our work to make us more efficient or effective. Sharing those best practices and knowledge is important to help the profession move forward.

David Burnand: I agree and would add that making space within organisations for more experimentation is key. A lot of companies talk a good game, but the reality is, ultimately, how much time did you put into trialing something new? How much space did you create for your team to go out and experiment? The majority aren't doing this right, or they're doing it at a very generic level. What I hear from communicators is that generic platforms can be a source of frustration because they are useful to a degree when it comes to completing some tasks, but it's also so easy to lose differentiation, brand sentiment, and all those soft things we add when we do something.

There's a far greater opportunity in the experimentation around impact and in how we can better measure our work. One aspect of that is to remove the fear. We have customers who use AI in incredible ways to experiment and help shift their entire business models. A high level of experimentation is deeply ingrained in those businesses.

I talk to some communicators who are, quite frankly, scared stiff of AI. They see it as a threat, something that's going to take away their jobs. They will literally say that to me. For CCOs, our role is to say AI will not take away your job; your inability to use AI to create outputs more quickly, to automate low-value tasks, and to gain deeper insights, will be the thing that takes away your job. Take the time to get to know these new areas because they are changing so quickly. If we don't move with it, the tide will wash us away. If we move with it, then it can add a huge amount of value to what we do.

Tabita Andersson: Do we need a bit more stick than carrot here to encourage our teams? Getting everyone on the team to get involved, to go and trial and test things, can be hard. When it comes down to it, quite often, only a small percentage of colleagues will go and do it. Most people say they want but don't have time, or use some other excuse. How do we encourage the broader population of communicators to go do?

David Burnand: I wouldn't define it as a stick because ultimately, you can't force humans to change their behavior. You just can't. Recently, I read Mel Robbins' book *Let Them*, and that's a perfect explanation as to why you can't force people to change their behaviors. It doesn't mean that you're powerless. What we can do is encourage people to think about doing things differently. For example, you could have an AI spotlight in your team meetings where you ask a different person each week to bring an example of how they're using AI in their role, what's good about it, what's bad about it, and what they're learning. Make it a positive thing, so to a degree you're enforcing, but you're doing it in a positive way, so other people within the team can learn.

Tabita Andersson: That's a great idea. Let's pivot to talking about your career path. You mentioned your time at Siemens, for example. How did you get into communications, and what has your career path been like?

David Burnand: I majored in marketing at university, and I had a passion for how companies communicated and projected their image to the outside world. I've always loved brands. Going back, as long as I can remember, I've always been fascinated more by how a company builds its brands than what they actually do, as in the mechanics of a company. Pretty early on at Siemens, my focus was on marketing. I started out in a services team in a training centre but moved quickly into marketing and software. I spent some time in sales, and in services, but for me the most interesting thing was always how we communicated what we do to customers and the outside world so gradually, over time, I made the move into the global marketing function and from there, it was my first time getting heavily involved in communications. Siemens was undergoing multiple transformations during the time I was there, including divesting the business I was in, which was a communications business. We moved it into what ultimately became a joint venture. We weren't sure at the start whether it was going to be a sale or a flotation, and this was the time when I was working formally with the communications leader directly on everything relating to the M&A, and ultimately on the foundation of a direct venture. When he left, I took over the communications function because we were going through multiple phases of restructuring the business, and internal and external communications were key to those restructures.

The scenario planning for the outcomes of those changing business processes was as much about communications as they were about marketing, so that's how I started thinking about the two functions working well together, and from there, I went back to doing primarily marketing.

In 2015, I joined Adobe and moved into software. My current role is my fourth software gig, and I've been involved with both marketing and communications all through that time, although this is the first time I've had global responsibility for communications at the same level as marketing.

Tabita Andersson: What advice would you give to someone more junior who wants to build a career in communications?

David Burnand: Be close to your market. The best communications people are the same as the best marketing people. Great marketers are deeply ingrained in the business; they're able to deliver great campaigns, but they also are involved in what the product looks like and how it fits in the marketplace. It's the same with great communicators. Communications people who want to be truly effective understand the business in which they operate. They understand the market and the nuances of their company, how all pieces fit together, and in that way, they can make better decisions and create better communications strategies.

My advice would be to first understand your business and then educate yourself about AI and analytics from the perspective of having an impact. Think about what you're going to do and how that will be impactful. The impact is not just running an event, launching a program, or sending an email; it's driving behavioral changes. When you run a PR program, it will boost awareness, and you need to understand which pipeline you want to contribute to and be as specific as possible about what you want to achieve.

Don't be afraid to ask questions. Communications people sometimes shy away from asking questions because we don't want to look silly, and our natural inclination as a comms person is to defend our reputation. You also think about your own reputation, right, and you don't want to be exposed so oftentimes, we don't ask the questions and then realize that you could have produced something much better if you'd had a deeper understanding of the business or the intent of the program that you needed to communicate. Be curious and don't be afraid to ask loads of questions! Go and find out about your business. Oftentimes, communication support is asked for in the bad times, or in a crisis, and you can be a lot more impactful if you have the trust of your organisation and if you've spent time with the business through the good times.

Tabita Andersson: You mentioned we get called on in a crisis, and crisis communications is a big part of what we do. Do you think this is getting more complicated as the world is changing, or are we getting better at it?

David Burnand: I don't know if we're getting better at it, but it's becoming more complex. It used to be the case that there were things you could prepare for in terms of crisis communications, and certain things were stable. You typically knew that the political environment would be stable, at least if you're in a Western country, and you'd typically know that the economy would go in cycles whereas now we live in a more dynamic and turbulent world so the general sentiment has a much more direct impact on your business and oftentimes, it's unpredictable so it's impossible to prepare for all scenarios, which is a big challenge. As a result, I think communicators have to be more agile than ever before.

Tabita Andersson: I agree. As a communicator in a global company, I'm sure you've also experienced the more global nature of the crisis we face today, with teams having to balance work between cultures, countries, and time zones.

David Burnand: Very much so. The other aspect is interconnectedness. We all feel like we're stakeholders in other places, not just our own place. These days, and especially in companies that are socially aware, there's oftentimes a feeling of ownership and participation in many countries, not just in the country you reside in, or the country from which you're from. That is a big change. Navigating this and deciding where an organisation needs to message something to meet their employees in that market but also meet the expectations of employees in other markets who may have strong, even opposing opinions, is a complexity we didn't have a few decades ago.

Tabita Andersson: I agree. As communications professionals, we can play a valuable role in helping an organisation make sense of what's happening and figure out what would make a difference to the people on the ground.

David Burnand: Something else I would add is that communications teams can't do that on their own anymore because if you look at the net volume of everything that must be done, it's too big. The other aspect that plays into this is that, in many cases, trust has been heavily shaken between companies and their employees. If you look at the *Edelman Trust Barometer*, a few years ago, we were in a situation where individuals trusted their companies more than they would trust the media or politicians. However, if you look at the data this year, it has declined. People now tend to trust their direct manager or immediate leader more.

As a comms team, this means you now have two choices: you can either choose to continue in the old way and keep sending messages out directly, top down from the CEO, with the corporate message. Or you can spend time and energy, using technology, to ensure that managers take over and own a large chunk of that communication. Of course, there are still going to be times when you need a top-down message, but there are also times now here you can act much more as a coach to the organisation and I believe the motion toward more individual communication will become powerful, and driven not only by the scarcity of resources within comms team but more importantly, by recognition that it's more impactful.

Tabita Andersson: Moving to a slightly different topic. What advice would you give to a CEO on how to best work with their CCO and communications team?

David Burnand: Take the time to explain your thinking if you want to be impactful. The elephant in the room for a lot of organisations is that they will spend no end of money and time developing a strategy, and then they spend a pittance on communicating that strategy. You will never win the hearts and minds of your people unless they understand the why. Your communications team can help you do that. If you don't believe that's the case, then get a better communications team. That's your answer. If you don't trust that leader, get a comms leader who will spend the time to get to know you and your business because if you don't, you're missing a trick because you will spend a lot of money on the big consultancies or with your leadership team to develop your strategies but you will never change things within your organisation, or as quickly or effectively as you could if you engage with your CCO and comms team.

CHAPTER 15

Dan Charlton

Chief Communications Officer Sussex Partnership NHS Foundation Trust

Dan Charlton is the **Chief Communications Officer** for the **Sussex Partnership NHS Foundation Trust,** which provides mental health, learning disability, and neurodevelopmental services to people living in the southeast of England. The Trust provides care in a range of locations, including people's own homes, specialist clinics, hospitals, low and medium secure units, and GP surgeries. The Trust employs almost 6,000 members of staff and is a member of the University Hospital Association and the Sussex Health and Care integrated system.

For more information about the Trust, visit sussexpartnership.nhs.uk.

Dan's LinkedIn profile: linkedin.com/in/dan-charlton-b8535ba/

Tabita Andersson: What is your role as Chief Communications Officer for the Sussex Partnership NHS Foundation Trust?

Dan Charlton: The organisation I work for is an NHS (National Health Service) provider offering mental health and learning disability services in Sussex, UK. My role is board-level, and I have responsibility for communications, complaints, information governance, patient experience, and the management of the CEO's and Board Chair's offices.

© Tabita Andersson 2025
T. Andersson, *Chief Communications Officers at Work*,
https://doi.org/10.1007/979-8-8688-1856-1_15

Tabita Andersson: That's a much broader role than perhaps a typical CCO role in a commercial organisation. You mention complaints, which is a different area than many other communicators would be responsible for. Would you mind explaining that function in more detail?

Dan Charlton: Yes, if I zone in on complaints, it's an area that is very well suited to the communications skillset. I'm the executive lead for complaints, and I have a fantastic team that manages the complaints process. We're in the process of an improvement journey where we are looking at the timeliness of our complaint responses, tone of voice, and clarity of content. All complaint responses come to me for final sign off, and I'm particularly looking at tone of voice and clarity of content. As someone who's not a clinician, I'll sometimes ask if we're using language that a complainant would understand or if we're relying too heavily on technical language or jargon, which is all too often the case in the NHS.

In terms of my broader, eclectic range of responsibilities, our chief executive officer says to all of us on the executive team, "you're a member of the executive team first, a portfolio holder second." We're a unitary board, so I'm expected to have as much interest, involvement, and understanding of finance, clinical issues, and strategy as my fellow board members.

Tabita Andersson: That's an interesting point and something that comes up regularly in conversations with CCOs. It's also something that could be quite disconcerting if you're a new CCO who hasn't worked at that level before. What advice would you give to new CCOs in that situation?

Dan Charlton: The bottom line is curiosity. Being curious and wanting to be involved in all aspects of the organisation's business, which, as communications professionals, we are anyway, because we must have an understanding of strategy, finances, and operations. Whether that's in response to a media inquiry, a public affairs briefing, or an internal communications activity that we're planning, it's not a million miles away from what we do day in and day out as communications professionals, but the most important thing for me is curiosity. As a member of a unitary board, it's my responsibility to pay as much attention to an area of the organisation's business that's not in my remit as I do to the areas of the organisation's business that are within my executive portfolio of responsibilities.

Tabita Andersson: How can we build that commercial awareness or business acumen as communicators? Should we focus on it during our early career years, or does it come naturally over the years as we progress?

Dan Charlton: That's an interesting question. I look at this through the lens of the professionalization of communications because all too often, we can still be seen as a profession that's primarily interested in cosmetic PR, media relations, and reputation management, pumping out press releases that say the world's all fine and everything we're doing is wonderful. It's that conventional, simplistic and out-of-date view of "spin doctors" whose main job is to put a positive gloss on everything.

In terms of your question about what that means for the development of communications professionals, I have another role as Deputy Director of the Centre for Health Communications Research, which is aligned with Buckinghamshire University. Just last week, we launched our new postgraduate program for NHS communications and engagement professions, which is about doing exactly that. It's about giving communications professionals a qualification, but it's also looking broadly at the nature of the role from an academic and practitioner perspective. It's incumbent on all of us as communications professionals, whatever level of seniority we occupy, to be constantly developing and learning, looking at our own skillset and where we need to develop.

Tabita Andersson: You mention that communications is a strategic function, what do you mean by that?

Dan Charlton: For me, it's about not seeing the function as one that is about cultivating relationships. When we're at our best, we're a profession that can help create an environment where people feel empowered, encouraged, and enabled to contribute to the work of the organisation through effective two-way internal communications and engagement. As professionals, we can help embed standards about the provision of clear information, whether that's to patients, carers, or families in our case, or whether that's clear information to staff or other external stakeholders. We're a profession that's essentially about helping build strong relationships with our workforce, with our partners, with the people who use our services, and we can also help be ethical advisors and advocates about how an organisation responds when something goes wrong, not just looking at it through a reputation management lens but through a public confidence lens. When something has gone wrong, how do we give the public confidence that we understand what's happened, that we're interested in identifying the underlying root causes, and that we're committed to mitigating the risk of something similar happening again in the future? As an organisation in the NHS, we need to learn from experience and, most importantly, act on what we've learned. That's what continuous quality improvement is all about.

Tabita Andersson: Do you think being a trusted advisor for reputational challenges, or when things go wrong, is something we do more now than in the past? For example, organisations are now much more inclined to comment on things that happen in the world. This is something that we didn't really do ten years ago. How can we, as communications professionals, help an organisation navigate these scenarios?

Dan Charlton: That is certainly my experience in this organisation, and it's helped by the fact that I have a CEO and a board who understand and value the role of communications as a strategic function. I think the old-fashioned perceptions of communications and public relations still exist.

Ironically, as a profession, we still have a bit of an image problem. One of the ways we can respond is to professionalize communications. That means demonstrating that there's an evidence base and a theoretical grounding to the work we do as individuals by being continuously involved in our own development. I have a personal passion for communications professionals being more involved in the academic space, which is one of the reasons I'm doing a PhD. You don't see many of us as professionals actively involved in that area. It's absolutely a space where we should be operating. We should be leading the evaluation of the work we do. We should be leading the work to inform the academic debate about what the gold standard in communications and engagement looks like, both in a public and private sector context.

Tabita Andersson: Why do you think that is the case?

Dan Charlton: It could be seen as remote from the work we do day in and day out as practitioners, and it's one of the things we're trying to address through the Centre for Health Communications Research program by getting people interested in academic research and discussion. Certainly, there are some research papers that I've looked at that I think what on earth has this got to do with anything in the real world, but equally, I've read research papers that absolutely speak to my job as a practitioner, to my responsibilities as a board member and my role as a strategist. I genuinely think we have a huge amount to learn from the academic discourse about communications and engagement. We also have a huge amount to offer, but that isn't always particularly recognised or valued. And, if we're not careful, that can feed into those perceptions that communications isn't really a serious profession, that anyone can do it and that it's somehow less weighty than a "proper" profession like HR or finance.

Tabita Andersson: You're right, and it's not something we encounter often. If you work in the academic world, you may be more involved and have easy access to research, but if not, it could be difficult to know where to go and where to get started, even if you want to.

Dan Charlton: That's exactly it. Interestingly, the postgraduate course I'm now involved in, I completed about seven or eight years ago. At that point, I had not done any academic work since way back when I was at a polytechnic college, so you're right, it's difficult to know where to start if you want to embark on that academic journey, especially, when as practitioners we're not sat around twiddling our thumbs every day! We have very demanding jobs with an action list of the 50 things that need to be done today and the other 50 things that need your attention this week. So, I can completely understand that practitioners might think they don't have time to think about scholarly discourses and rarefied issues around theory. I just happen to believe that it's relevant to what we do, and it's invaluable for us as practitioners in terms of what I describe as the professionalization of communications. If we're able to talk with clarity and confidence at the board table about what the latest academic research is saying, that can be one way for the profession to gain greater credibility.

Tabita Andersson: That's true, and that's another way we can prove the value and benefits of what we do. Often, we talk about the data and metrics to prove value in the numerical sense, but sometimes you need other proof points. What we could do is bring in the academic research as part of that validation and measurements of how what we do adds value. It's a smart way of looking at it, and it brings a new angle. Is this something you already do in your role, marrying data and metrics with research to evaluate the effectiveness of your work?

Dan Charlton: Yes, I do, and I'm sure some of my executive colleagues would say I bore them senseless about my PhD and the value of academic research! Over the last year, we've been doing work as an organisation on our five-year strategy. We've co-produced the strategy with staff, patients, carers, families, and partner organisations. I've brought what I've been learning from the latest academic research to the way we've planned and undertaken that work. I will often refer to academic research when we have discussions about strategy or about communications and engagement. I try not to go on too much about it, but it's another string to our bow that we can bring to the board table as communications practitioners.

Tabita Andersson: We've discussed how to work best with your executive peers and leadership team. What advice would you give to a CEO about how to work best with their CCOs?

Dan Charlton: That's a good question. If I talk from my own experience, I'm fortunate to have a board that values and understands the role of communications as a strategic function. In fact, we won an award for it as a board at the national NHS Communicate Awards last year! We won the NHS board's commitment to communications, so that's a good starting point. My CEO will constantly encourage me to be part of the discussion around issues that are outside of my portfolio of responsibilities. As I mentioned earlier, she will do the same with all the executive team because we're executive directors first, portfolio holders second.

I would also add that as a CEO, to get the most out of your CCO, lean into their expertise and have challenging conversations as an executive team and as a board. Traditionally, communications and PR people were the ones who were brought in at the end of a process to assess when something had gone wrong, or when there was a media inquiry or a problem that needed fixing.

That's part of the role and responsibilities and that's fine, but our expertise can be maximized if we sit right at the heart of those strategic discussions from day one, right from the outset, so that we're bringing our knowledge, experience, and expertise to the discussions that are at the heart of what the organisation is planning to do.

Tabita Andersson: Let's pivot to talk about your background and career path. I'd also like to dig into your PhD. How did you start in communications, and how did you get to the role you have today?

Dan Charlton: I trained to be a journalist, which was my career ambition. I always loved writing and the power of a good story, and I wanted to work for a local newspaper, so I went to the Polytechnic of Central London, which at the time was one of the very few places where you could study media as an undergraduate. As I graduated, one of the old regional NHS health authorities approached the course tutors to say they were looking to hire someone as a public relations or press officer, and did they have any graduates in mind? I put my name down and got the job, so that started me off on a completely different career trajectory!

The skillset I developed through my journalism training was very well suited to the role. I loved a good story, I had technical writing skills, and could write a press release. That job got me started on a communications pathway, and I've been working for the NHS pretty much ever since in various communications roles, and for most of that time in mental health services.

Tabita Andersson: What then led you to the CCO role, and what advice would you give to younger communicators who want to build a similar career?

Dan Charlton: My first most senior role came up because we were in the middle of an NHS merger. I was working at the time in what became the South London and Maudsley NHS Trust, which is one of the big mental health trust providers. At quite a young age, I was very fortunate to be appointed to the role of Head of Communications, and I worked there for a long period of about 15 years before moving to a different NHS provider organisation in a more senior role, initially as Director of Communications, and then Chief Communications Officer.

My advice to younger practitioners would be to stay curious and stay interested in your own development. Keep pushing yourself because whatever role you're in, whatever profession you're operating within, we have an understandable human tendency to stay where we're comfortable. There isn't a week that goes by when I don't feel distinctly uncomfortable at least once, but that's a good place to be because it challenges you. It enables you to draw on your experience and expertise, and it really pushes you. As communications and engagement professionals, I believe there's a risk, especially when you get to my seasoned stage in your career, to think that you know how to do things.

That isn't the case. There's no right or wrong way to do communications and engagement. I'm frequently learning new things and being challenged, whether that's from a member of my fantastic comms team or from a fellow executive director. To my mind, that's the most important thing to pay attention to. Your own development, your own willingness to learn, your own willingness and interest in being challenged.

Tabita Andersson: I often say that we work in the grey. Some of the other functions within an organisation work in black and white because there are rules and regulations that dictate if you do A, you get B, and so on. However, we live in a world where quite often you could go either way, and both would be okay, but they could turn out differently, so it's much more about being open and able to work within that type of environment.

Dan Charlton: Exactly, and not everyone can do that. It can be quite difficult. When I think about my current role, taking on responsibilities for other areas that are outside of my natural skillset and comfort zone has felt challenging, and it is challenging, but that's one of the many things that keep the job interesting.

Tabita Andersson: You mentioned your team. What's the size of your team?

Dan Charlton: In terms of my full portfolio responsibilities, I have just under 50 staff in the Directorate. Across the communications function, that's a team of eight, which includes creative graphic design, media relations, public affairs, internal communications, and behavior change.

Tabita Andersson: What skills and attributes do you look for when you're looking for new people for your team? What makes for great communications professionals?

Dan Charlton: The technical skills, at a basic level, particularly writing skills, the ability to digest complex information and translate it for different audiences, and an interest and understanding of digital media.

More broadly, to me, it comes down to energy, enthusiasm, and willingness to learn. Those are more indefinable attributes that make for a gold-standard communications professional. When I then meet with my communications team, it doesn't matter how difficult and pressurizing things are, I see a team where there's energy, commitment, and willingness to help each other out. With the right attitude, we have a team that has a desire to find a solution to problems and, most importantly of all, there's a desire to think about how we can be innovative and do things differently and better, which brings us back to the point about being interested in constantly learning and developing.

Tabita Andersson: We've mentioned your PhD a couple of times. Let's dive into the details. How did you end up doing a PhD, and what is the subject?

Dan Charlton: I did a postgraduate qualification a few years ago, and I hadn't done any work in academia since way back at the Polytechnic college, which was a long time ago, and I really enjoyed it. I found it challenging, and it stimulated me. It made me stop and think about the job and the profession, and it made me concentrate on one thing at a time, whether that was the next assignment or the next lecture. One of the things about our jobs that I find personally enjoyable is that we, at any one time, are balancing 20–30 different things, and you're constantly going from one thing to another. You can go from strategy to media handling in the blink of an eye, and that is one of the things that is so exciting about the role. When I got back into academia, I enjoyed stopping and thinking about one thing at a time, so I got the bug and went straight to doing an MSc. I then thought it would be interesting to do a PhD.

I was a bit hesitant about it, wondering whether it was the right time. Work and life are always busy, but I concluded that there's never a right time to do something like this, so I took the plunge!

Tabita Andersson: Tell us about the PhD, the subject and topic you are researching, and the goal.

Dan Charlton: I'm looking at organisational change leadership, staff engagement and communications in the NHS. I've done that by interviewing 20 CEOs within the NHS. Part of the reason I'm doing this is that I found organisational change very interesting to study during my MSc, and there was very little out there about it from the perspective of CEOs and barely anything at all from CEOs in an NHS context. That strikes me as a gap in research knowledge, because of the pivotal role CEOs play in organisational change.

As a result of the interviews and research, I have developed a conceptual framework called grounded optimism. This is about having a hopeful, realistic, and plausible vision for change that's rooted in recognition and acknowledgement of the real challenges that come with change, and that's informed by authentic engagement with staff and an understanding of the emotional impact that change can have on people. This conceptual framework is designed to respond to the problem of excess leadership positivity, where you get a disconnect between leaders and the workforce because the vision for change that leaders are promoting feels overly optimistic, unrealistic, and out of step with the difficult reality that staff experience day in and day out. My contention is that when you get that disconnect, it's one of the reasons that organisational change efforts fail. If you look at the academic literature on organisational change, only 5% of that research includes emotions, or has emotions as a keyword attached to it, so there's still a view that organisational change is seen as a technical, rational process that involves following a prescribed series of steps. My contention is that it's all about people, and the emotions they bring with them as people. That's especially true in a context like the NHS where our business is all about people. NHS staff are dealing with incredibly difficult and complex pressures every single day. You have to be attuned to the sheer amount of change that NHS staff are managing all the time. You need to be mindful of the emotional impact of change, and you have to be sensitive to that impact. As a leader, you need to be interested in exploring it with staff rather than pretending it's not there.

Tabita Andersson: Even in the commercial world, when we go through big changes, which are almost part of the normal now, I've witnessed the excessive positivity that you talk about, which can create dissonance with what's happening on the floor.

Communications can play a great role in facilitating organisational change and creating the right environment, but I've seen scenarios where communications is used as a sticky plaster, which can be seen as the easy way rather than thinking strategically about the various aspects of the change. It can be so much easier to send out five emails and then consider things done rather than doing the hard work of thinking through all aspects and challenges.

Dan Charlton: It's fascinating, and as this is live research, I've been able to feed that straight into our organisational discussions about our own strategy development and where we are as an organisation in terms of the changes, we're looking to make to meet the needs of the local communities we serve. I find the literature interesting about the risks of excess positivity. There's one paper by a researcher who talks about Prozac leadership, which is the idea that leaders are going around pretending everything is wonderful, and the future is full of excitement without any problems, which is completely unrealistic! But that approach exists and can literally place patient lives at risk when it's coupled with systemic quality problems that go unrecognised. We had an example of this at Mid-Staffordshire NHS Trust, which was brought out by an independent inquiry and subsequent academic research into what happened. One study identified the problem at Mid Staffs as a "narrative of silence" taking hold, where people felt unable to voice any concerns that threatened the organisational image. When you have a leadership team that's disproportionately focused on reputation in an unhealthy way, you can end up creating an environment where staff don't feel able to speak up about concerns, where they don't feel able to highlight problems, and challenge thinking. This is where I think the role of communications and engagement professionals comes in. We can help create that environment that promotes two-way engagement, debate, and disagreement. Disagreement is important and healthy in organisations to scrutinize future plans, gain perspectives from across the workforce, and ensure that it's taken on board when planning, rather than the vision for the future being designed in a dark boardroom somewhere by a bunch of leaders and then being imposed on the workforce.

Tabita Andersson: What are some of the tactics that we're missing in communications to help with organisational change? What can we do better?

Dan Charlton: There can be a tendency within organisations and within the profession to focus on a compelling vision for the future and broadcast it to people. The change orthodoxy suggests that you absolutely must have a clear, compelling, incredible vision, and we need to communicate it, which I don't dispute for a moment. But there is a risk for all organisations, private and public sectors, and for all communications professionals, that you focus too much on communicating the uplifting vision for the future, and you pay less attention to crafting a clear, credible message that acknowledges the difficult challenges. If you do both, you get to a place of grounded optimism, where you hold hope for the future and what we can achieve together within the organisation, but it's grounded by the acknowledgement that it's tough, and that staff are dealing with pressurized situations, and being bombarded with information from multiple sources every single day. If you can acknowledge the reality and hold the hope, you stand a better chance of bringing the workforce with you on a vision for the future and, most importantly of all, enacting that vision so that strategy is translated into practice to deliver the intended change. It's all about talking to people. We know from research that leaders are nearly ten times as likely to be criticized by staff for under-communicating than over-communicating

Tabita Andersson: I like the phrase grounded optimism. It explains the approach very clearly. If you recognise that, as a communicator, you're sitting in the toxic or excessive positivity camp right now, what can you do to get your leadership along and become more grounded?

Dan Charlton: That will come in part from constant, authentic engagement with staff. Leaders must be out there and be present in the organisation to listen to staff. And listen to staff in a way that makes them feel heard. As a leader, you are in a powerful position, and if you can demonstrate that you are interested in listening to other perspectives, despite your ability to ignore those perspectives, that can be a positive, powerful force for change. Where staff feel able to speak up and raise concerns, where staff feel empowered and enabled to be innovative, there is a demonstrable impact on both staff experience and patient outcomes. It's not something to do to keep everybody happy; it's fundamental to the business we're in, which is improving outcomes for patients.

As a communications professional, I keep coming back to the point we discussed earlier about drawing on academic literature to demonstrate the value and evidence for effective staff engagement. This is not a way of persuading people to do something different, but an opportunity to listen and have your own ideas challenged. Having different perspectives brought to you as a leader is important to shaping your thinking. When I was looking at this in my PhD research, you can see that those NHS organisations that have a higher score for engagement in the annual NHS staff survey tend to have better ratings on quality of care.

Tabita Andersson: There's the other side of the coin as well, the negative side, where you could end up fearmongering, or where it's grounded and authentic but super negative, which is almost as bad. This is sometimes where we as communicators need to sit in the middle of the spectrum.

Dan Charlton: That's absolutely it. Balance is, in essence, what we need to achieve. We talk a lot about resistance to change in academic literature, but my view is that it's easy to label people as resisters. It's easy and convenient because you can put them in a box and think that they need to be managed. I believe we need to reframe the context. Reframe the notion of resistance to change, and rather than seeing people who resist as oppositional, irrational, or difficult; there's an opportunity to see those as people who may have genuine and valid concerns. They simply have a different perspective to bring to the table, especially when it comes to organisational change. If you can bring those perspectives to the table and show, as a leader, that you are interested in hearing them, you may then be able to get to a point where you can say that you've heard the perspective but you're going to proceed with plan A anyway. That's perfectly legitimate. If you demonstrate that you're willing to hear other perspectives, that can help you create a positive organisational culture where people feel interested in the work of the organisation, feel able to contribute to the work of the organisation, and feel they have a voice in shaping how it goes about its work.

Tabita Andersson: I was just going to mention culture because that's one of the organisational aspects that we can contribute to as communications professionals. Would you agree with that?

Dan Charlton: Completely! I'm a big fan of the culture eats strategy for breakfast quote, and I think we have a big role to play here as communications and engagement professionals. However, far too often, culture is, or can be seen, as fluffy stuff. It's a nice thing to do. It's not as important as managing finances or operational performance. My contention is that it's more important than either of those because if you get the culture right, you deliver the financial and operational performance. If you get the culture right, you create an environment where people will raise concerns and speak about problems. You also have a workforce that feels valued, energized, and enabled to be innovative because, in the very best organisations, private or public sector, innovation comes from within teams. It doesn't come from the boardroom. It comes from the people who are closest to the problem, or who have the ideas and expertise in their teams. As communications professionals, we can play a role in shaping culture. It's very tempting organisationally to think that culture means having a nice set of values and putting them on a poster, on screensavers, or in social media posts. Job done. But the real work in embedding values is to live them in your organisational conversations and behaviors, every single day. And calling it out when people behave in a way that's not aligned with your values.

It's about ensuring that the values and behaviors are modeled by leaders. It's about ensuring that those values and behaviors are real and relevant to the job or work that staff are doing across the organisation. You don't do that just by producing a pretty poster and sticking it on the wall. You embed values by a constant, continuous process of engagement, discussion, and disagreement, using multiple channels to share information, while at the same time being transparent, grounded, and optimistic in your approach.

Tabita Andersson: To achieve that, we must be collaborators because we need to work with the rest of the organisation. It's not something we can do on our own. We need to partner with our HR colleagues and finance and IT colleagues because culture is everyone's job at the end of the day.

Dan Charlton: That's it in a nutshell! It's all about collaboration. If I think about the NHS and public sector environment, when we're operating in a resource-constrained environment with complex, sustained levels of needs within the communities we serve, within non-clinical corporate services, it's now more incumbent on us than ever to maximize our resources and work in partnership across functions. We need to avoid working in organisational or professional silos because it's only by collaborating and working together that we can maximize our energy, expertise, and effectiveness. That's also more fun and rewarding!

CHAPTER

16

Joanne Trout
Chief Communications Officer Omnicom Group

Joanne Trout is the **Chief Communications Officer** for **Omnicom** (NYSE: OMC), a leading provider of data-inspired, creative marketing and sales solutions. Omnicom's iconic agency brands are home to the industry's most innovative communications specialists who are focused on driving intelligent business outcomes for their clients. The company offers a wide range of services in advertising, strategic media planning and buying, precision marketing, retail and digital commerce, branding, experiential, public relations, healthcare marketing, and other specialty marketing services to over 5,000 clients in more than 70 countries.

For more information about Omnicom, visit omnicomgroup.com.

Joanne's LinkedIn profile: linkedin.com/in/joanne-trout-65b5aa1/

Tabita Andersson: What does a typical day look like for you as Chief Communications Officer for a global house of iconic agency brands?

Joanne Trout: No two days are alike! Right now, we're making a huge acquisition that we believe will change the advertising and marketing landscape as it reduces the number of big players from four to three. This means we're working on a major communications plan, which is internally focused as we haven't closed the deal yet. We have a workstream focused on employee and client communications to help bring everyone along until the acquisition closes. This planning takes up a lot of my time.

© Tabita Andersson 2025
T. Andersson, *Chief Communications Officers at Work*,
https://doi.org/10.1007/979-8-8688-1856-1_16

We no longer have a 1–3 year communications plan because I don't believe it works today. Ten years ago, we would have had a comms plan with all projects planned out in advance. Today, we have mini plans for major initiatives so we can work at pace and pivot, if necessary. One of these initiatives is focused on our Generative AI platform, Omni AI. We're working on the messaging and internal rollout plan first, then on the client messaging, and then for the rest of our external audiences.

The other part of my daily work is reactive media relations. This could be absolutely anything, but it currently includes working on communications regarding current issues, such as the ongoing tariff changes. For us, this means we need to monitor the news and examine how changes affect our industry.

The last part of my daily role is the big events. The major annual industry event for us is Cannes Lions, where all advertising and marketing agencies and competitors meet. We will have a big presence there at the end of June, so a lot of planning is being done to make it successful.

Tabita Andersson: What functions do your remit span, and what is the overall structure?

Joanne Trout: It's an interesting CCO role because even though we're a Fortune 200 company, our roots were as a holding company. When I started here 12 years ago, we were just the back office for our 1,500 agencies around the globe. At the time, we hadn't decided if Omnicom was a masterbrand or if we were a house of brands, so there was no big push to build a reputation for what Omnicom stands for or create brand messaging for all our different stakeholders. We were purely here to support our companies—our agencies—and we never really did any internal communications until COVID. We didn't even have a distribution list for our 75,000 employees! If you worked for one of our agencies, such as Fleishman, Ketchum, Porter Novelli, or BBDO, your CEO would communicate with you as an employee of that agency. You'd never hear from Omnicom, and some employees probably didn't even know that they worked for Omnicom. That changed during the pandemic because suddenly, everyone wanted to hear from the parent company, what was going on, what we were doing in terms of working from home, and they wanted to hear from the CEO. As a result, we started to engage with everyone regularly.

The communications function here has evolved in the last decade, but we're still lean because I use our PR agencies as my arms and legs. Even though I look after external communications, which is what I was brought on to do initially, it's expanded to be maybe 30% external and 30% internal communications, and then there's executive communications working with my CEO, there's our digital channels, including our website and social media, and I also manage CSR (corporate social responsibility). Overall, I have a very small team; it's a handful of people, but we can lean on our agencies to help with resources when needed, which is very helpful.

Tabita Andersson: That's quite unusual, doing PR for PR agencies. On the one hand, it's helpful because you can draw on the experiences of many, but on the other hand, it must be tricky because they're also scrutinizing you more!

Joanne Trout: It is, and sometimes we can be our own worst enemy. For example, about a year ago, we started to define our brand, and with the current acquisition, we're going to have to do this again. This means looking at our vision, mission, values, and what we stand for. We had a small task force, but everyone was a critic; all our marketing and branding agencies had a point of view. We wanted to come up with a halo that our agencies and networks could ladder into, and we wanted everyone's buy-in, but we didn't land on a position, and now with the latest acquisition, it will need to change, so we'll need to go through the process again.

To your point, this can be very challenging because everyone in our industry knows what we're doing. When I worked at MasterCard, the product people didn't know what the finance people were doing, and the finance people didn't understand what the communications people were doing, so they didn't get involved. That's very different from here, where everyone is in the same industry and has a very strong viewpoint.

That can also be a strength, so if I need anything for our website, I can go to our digital agencies, but it's more difficult to define the overall framework.

Tabita Andersson: In that situation, with so many opinions, how do you build a reputation as the Omnicom brand, so it's not just about your agencies and their brands?

Joanne Trout: It's not without challenges. Today, we are a brand because our clients dictated it. They now come to us and ask for holding company solutions. They want the best branding agency, the best PR agency, the best digital agency, and they want everyone to work together. Our clients have definitely influenced our brand evolution because they are now coming to Omnicom, rather than just one of our agencies, so we've had to respond and come up with a business development point of view. We've had to consider what we stand for, how we're different, and what we will communicate to our clients. I work very closely with the business development part of Omnicom, and those requests from our clients led the way in defining who we are and how we work with our agencies. Many of our agencies have their own positioning, one is a disruption company, and one of the others has just changed its positioning to Think Big. But they still see the benefit of coming together on larger pitches and being part of the Omnicom family. So even if we haven't landed on a final sentence that describes what we stand for, or our vision, mission, values, there's more openness and receptiveness to looking at us like an operating company. They see the benefits of a strong Omnicom narrative.

Tabita Andersson: You mentioned working with your CEO. How can a Chief Communications Officer work best with their CEOs?

Chapter 16 | Joanne Trout

Joanne Trout: I'm fortunate that our CEO has been at Omnicom for over 25 years, which is a long tenure for a Fortune 200 company, where the average tenure is less than a decade, and we don't have a lot of layers. We're a small, lean team working closely with our CEO.

At one of my previous companies, there were so many layers you had to go through to get things done. There was executive management, there was a product organisation, there was communications, and we reported into marketing. Hence, we had to get marketing on board before we could do anything, which meant there were all these steps before we could even get to talk to our CEO. Here at Omnicom, we're a small C-suite, and I just go straight to our CEO and walk him through our plans. We don't have a lot of management layers, so it's a very streamlined process, which I like because I'm not really into processes and politics. I just like to get things done!

I think it's easier here because we've evolved from a holding company to more of an operating company that still hasn't implemented big management structures. I speak to my CEO daily. Sometimes, it's about a press inquiry, and other times, it's about plans and actions. That doesn't necessarily happen in other large companies.

Tabita Andersson: What are the organisation's benefits of the CCO having such a close connection with the CEO and a seat at the top table?

Joanne Trout: It means we can make decisions quickly. In our industry, things move at such a fast pace. We no longer have weeks to respond to something, like we used to. Now, we must consider how we respond to the latest press inquiry or critical issues. In the past, we'd had time to go back and forth to create a reactive press statement and go through various layers for approvals, but now, we sometimes must respond in minutes. From a reputation management point of view, it's great for the organisation that we have close access to our CEO and executives.

Tabita Andersson: Do you think having that close access to the CEO and the C-suite also helps prove the value of communications because everyone can see it up close and firsthand?

Joanne Trout: Yes. It's evolved a lot since I joined Omnicom. I've built trust with my CEO over the years, so the planning is much more seamless and easier for everybody. This also stretches across my team, my agencies, and my networks.

Even though I have a very small team at the headquarters, I have communications people in our subsidiaries who look to us to help with messaging around major industry topics like Generative AI, M&A, reputational issues, etc. They will look at us for guidance on messaging so they can cascade those messages down to their organisations. It's great to have that connectivity and quick decision-making we need today.

Tabita Andersson: What are some other ways we can show value as a function and a role?

Joanne Trout: Our CEO is a finance and businessperson first, so we must tie value to business results. Before I joined, he'd experienced what a negative story in a major business publication can have on a company's reputation and, ultimately, shareholder value. As a result, he has a firsthand experience of the value of a good reputation. On the flip side, you need to show how your actions are connected to growing the business.

For example, when you've done something great and clients have seen it and commented on it, that's when there's a clear connection with the communications function.

You need to connect the function to the results. Every company is different and has different metrics; it could be business development, for example, getting more clients to come in through the door, or it could be products, for example, increasing sales of certain products. Communication departments sometimes lose connection with how their objectives and strategies contribute to the company's growth.

Another aspect of value we never get credit for is keeping things out of the news. Damage to a company's reputation can lead to a company's stock price crashing, just because of one bad article in the Wall Street Journal. Helping to eliminate those negative stories and keeping us out of the limelight is very valuable.

Tabita Andersson: That's an interesting point. Another CCO said that the best crisis communications is when no one knows there's been a crisis. That is the best thing we can do: take care of it so no one knows what could have happened.

Joanne Trout: Yes, and it's important because that's hard to demonstrate to your leadership. We're seeing some of that now with today's divisive political environment. We try to remain neutral both internally and externally on any given issue of the day, so we don't appear to be taking sides, and it doesn't lead to negative press coverage. Reputation management and keeping a company out of the news is just as important as taking a leadership position publicly.

Tabita Andersson: I agree, and sometimes that can be tricky, especially when you're in a global company and must think across countries or regions and balance your messaging. Is that something you've experienced?

Joanne Trout: Yes, and it is tricky. About 50% of our business is US-based, and we're headquartered in the United States, but the UK is our second biggest market. Because we don't have a large team with people all over the world, I have agency people in the regions who can be my ears to the ground. It's important to have them tell us what's happening in London or Australia so we can balance the messaging correctly.

The global nature of what we do became clear with COVID. It was when I developed closer connections with the communications people in our agencies. We had bi-weekly communications meetings with everyone because we needed updates on what was happening in different parts of the world to provide the messaging needed. I still hold these meetings, they are now quarterly, and the extended team has become my eyes and ears around the globe. It's an informal network that has connected us much better, and it means that if a story breaks in China and it'll make its way to the United States quickly, we can get in front of it.

Tabita Andersson: What are some things that CCOs didn't do well in the past, and what should we do better going forward? How can we improve as a profession and function?

Joanne Trout: First, have a seat at the table and make sure your value is established. Second, like anything else, you need to continually build on that value, whether rolling out a new employee engagement plan or whatever it might be to support the business. Third, you must have metrics that your CEO and CFO can understand. If you base your metrics on likes, impressions, or share of voice, many C-suite execs around the table don't necessarily understand what that means. Those were metrics we'd often used in communications, but they just don't resonate with the current CFO or CEO. On the other hand, if you have metrics showing the value of reputation and what that means to the business outcomes, it will help.

My advice would be to find what might work for your organisation to prove the value and understand it from a business point of view. If you're in a publicly listed company, CEOs care about their stock price, shareholders, and clients. So, look at your organisation's stakeholders and what metrics will resonate with the C-suite. Most of them wear financial hats, so as a profession, we need to do better with our measurement frameworks.

Tabita Andersson: We've already made great strides in improving our metrics. Ten or 15 years ago, measuring communications was very basic. It involved looking at the share of voice or even advertising value equivalent, so we've improved a lot and now have a wider range of data points available. However, we can still improve how we gain insights from the data points and how we use that insight to prove the value of what we do.

Joanne Trout: I agree; we've come a long way. When I started in communications, we didn't have metrics, the role of Chief Communications Officer didn't exist, and there was no connectivity between the communications disciplines.

Early in my career, I worked at Sony, and we had a small internal comms team that was disconnected from the external comms team. The internal team would be off doing their own things, and in external comms, we worked on press releases, media relations, product launches, etc. We had a huge external comms team but only a small internal comms team. Over the years, the disciplines have become connected, and internal comms have grown in importance. That's good because our employees are active on social media and the company's biggest advocates.

Here at Omnicom, we're trying to get everyone excited about the pending acquisition of IPG, and we want them to talk about how excited they are because that's more valuable than getting an article placed somewhere. As the world of social media has evolved, everything is connected, which means we also hold more power in communications than in the past. Understanding that value and then communicating the value to the rest of the organisation will help the profession. We've certainly come a long way and need to keep improving.

Tabita Andersson: You mentioned internal communications, which can sometimes be perceived as the communications world's poor cousin. Did COVID bring internal communications to the forefront and help more leaders see the benefits? Is the value of internal communications now on par with external communications?

Joanne Trout: Yes, and perhaps even more so. When I worked at MasterCard, I saw a huge shift in building out that team. It's important for CEOs to have internal engagement, and many CEOs are measured on that, too. It's expensive for a company when people are leaving all the time; no one wants a high turnover, so it's become important to keep people engaged, keep your employee engagement scores high, and communicate more often than you do externally.

For example, during COVID, we would send a note from the CEO to all employees on a weekly basis, and they all appreciated receiving it. They got to know him, what he stood for, and where he was taking the company. At the end of the day, we're a people business, and clients hire us because of our people, so engagement is important, and internal communications has come a long way. As a discipline, employee communications has proved its relevance and importance.

Tabita Andersson: Culture is more frequently mentioned as an aspect of building a great brand and a great company. Can we, as communicators, contribute to building a company culture?

Joanne Trout: Yes, because if you are in communications, you are creating and bringing to life a company's vision, mission, values, which are integral to the culture. Today, when you look at some of the chaotic parts of the world, knowing where you work and what you stand for is important, especially for the younger generations. The average employee is 28 years old at Omnicom, so you must understand that demographic. At that age, most people want to work for a company that knows what it stands for and has values that resonate with them. We've seen it happen in our agencies. For example, one of them is known for being a disruptive company, and they have built a culture of going against the status quo, which is articulated as being pirates. It's more fun to be a pirate than a captain! They have a very creative way of explaining what they stand for, and it's important because they are our creative marketing agency that goes against the grain, so they need to attract a specific type of employee who fits into that environment, into that culture.

I agree with Peter Drucker that "culture eats strategy for breakfast any day of the week," and internal communications is important for keeping the culture alive and well.

Tabita Andersson: What trends do you see on the horizon for communications? We've mentioned artificial intelligence (AI), which is probably the biggest trend, but is there anything else you see that will impact our profession?

Joanne Trout: I agree that AI will change how we work, and I probably see that more because I'm on the front lines of advertising, marketing, and communications.

Another trend I see, which is more visible as I work in a holding company, is that clients come directly to us asking for a holding company solution. They want the best PR people, the best branding, and the best advertising. I liken this to how social media was introduced, and in communications, we'd say that's earned media, so we own this, and the marketing department would say no, it's paid media, so we need to own those channels. The trend is that we now must work better together.

I teach for the Newhouse School at Syracuse University, a communications school. Although my classes are PR and Advertising majors, students need to understand all marketing disciplines, whether branding, media, digital, or experiential, to work effectively with these teams.

Often, when we put a holding company solution together for new business pitches, there's still a lot of jockeying regarding roles and responsibilities. In contrast, I believe everybody needs to play nicely in the sandbox and understand the value that each one of these disciplines brings to the table, because it's changing. Disciplines are merging into one; you can no longer say this is earned, this is paid, or this is owned. It all should connect. The media world is fragmented, and as that continues, it's important we understand how to partner and know each other's swim lanes. Working more closely with the various marketing disciplines is a trend.

Tabita Andersson: Let's move to the other big trend, AI. How has AI impacted your team and your role at Omnicom?

Joanne Trout: It's still in the early days. We have a platform that we experiment with. From a communications perspective, we're playing with using it for writing and researching. It's not going to replace people, but it might change jobs, and it might change our job descriptions. If everybody has the same tools, all the writing will look the same, but what will make it different is your take on it, your creativity, your angle, and your special sauce, which will make it better than everybody else's. Everyone will use the same prompts, meaning you will see similar press releases and earnings releases. AI will help us spend more time on strategy and improving plans vs. spending hours on research.

At the moment, it looks like the early 2000s, when the craze of digital started. People were worried that it would replace our jobs, which didn't happen; it just changed our job descriptions. It's a phenomenal shift, and I tell my students that they should be well-versed, go play with the tools, and understand the different large language models. It's the same thing as 15 years ago, when we relied on the 20-year-olds to understand social media and help us figure it out.

Tabita Andersson: There's also a good opportunity to come together and share best practices because it's easy to think about the simpler tasks we can automate, such as helping with writing, doing research, or coming up with creative ideas. However, there are other areas that we could look at as a profession.

Joanne Trout: It would be helpful to share best practices and different use cases. For example, someone recently told one of our PR agencies how they're using Generative AI to do more research on reporters. They can find out much faster what they work on, what hobbies they have, and what topics interest them, so they can craft better pitches. There are a lot of opportunities for using AI, so coming together and sharing best practices would be helpful.

Tabita Andersson: Let's pivot and talk about your background and career path. How did you get into communications?

Joanne Trout: I always tell my students it wasn't a straight ladder; it was more like a meandering, curvy path! I started on the account side of advertising, and I didn't enjoy it. I like to write, and I like the creativity of doing a lot of different things, so I pivoted from advertising to public relations.

I started on the agency side, in a mom-and-pop agency. It was a small agency, but I got to work with clients such as Sony, Prince tennis rackets, and underwear brands. I often tell my students to start in a small agency where you can get a wider view and do many different things, from media pitching to writing and strategy. From there, I was regarded as a consumer electronics expert; I went to work for the agency that did communications for Sharp and Pioneer.

After that, I was hired on the client-side at Sony, where I stayed for a while, working on many cool product launches. This was in the 1990s, and Sony was launching Discman, Trinitron TVs, etc. I had a great boss, and we worked together for 15 years, and I owe a lot to her mentorship. I had four different jobs with her over a long period of time, and she was very supportive as I was growing my family at the same time, so I could balance work with caring for my children. That was a big deal back in the 1990s and 2000s. In fact, when I worked for Sony, a Japanese company, I was one of the first to do a job share where I worked three days a week and someone else worked two days a week to cover the role. At the time, this was unheard of in a Japanese company, and it was all due to my very supportive boss. Later, when my children were older, I returned to full-time work with Waggener Edstrom and their biggest client, MasterCard. They were conveniently based about ten minutes from my house, and many of my career moves have been so that I could have a good work-life balance, which is important. At the end of the day, you're not going to say you wish you'd worked more!

MasterCard then hired me, and I worked for them as they pivoted from being a payments company, grounded in financial services, to becoming a technology company. I worked on emerging payments at the time, so it was still consumer technology, but I also gained experience working in a large global corporate communications function. After a decade with MasterCard, I started looking for another challenge, and the Omnicom role came up. It was like MasterCard in that they were also looking to transform their reputation to be more digital and tech-focused. This was when we had many digital agencies starting up, so our competitors were buying a lot of new agencies to transform their businesses from the "Mad Men" era of advertising to becoming digital, future-forward businesses.

When I first joined Omnicom, it was just me in communications. We then started the journey toward becoming an operating company, and I hired a few people for the team. I've been here for 13 years, working with the same CEO, which is great. There's a lot of staff turnover naturally at the agency level, but people have been here a long time at the holding company level, which shows it's a well-run company that cares about its people.

Tabita Andersson: What advice would you give yourself if you could return to your early career?

Joanne Trout: To not stress so much! I've been lucky that I've been able to develop skills, and the jobs kind of came along the way, but there's also a lot of hard work, and you need to keep in touch with people to create those opportunities. I've spent too much time stressing that I'm not doing well, or that I should get out of communications and try to get a job elsewhere, so my advice would be to believe more in myself and believe it will all work out in the end.

To me, it's about the people, not the money. Money isn't going to make you happy. I've had bad bosses, and I probably could have handled the situations better, but it made me realize the importance of being with people I respect, who will look out for me, who are good people, and that's very important.

Tabita Andersson: What advice would you give to the young students you speak to when they ask about building a career in communications?

Joanne Trout: I never started out wanting to be a Chief Communications Officer; it wasn't even a role when I started in the late 1980s. It's good to have an intention and a goal about where you think you want to be, but my advice is to keep your aperture wide open. It's so competitive now. I was a psychology major and minored in Asian studies. Now, so many colleges offer majors in PR or advertising, they have amazing internships, and it's still very competitive for them to get a job, so I tell them to keep their aperture open. Even if you take a job you don't like, and I've had plenty of those, where you know it's not a fit in week one, and you start thinking about how to pivot, and that's okay. You will learn something from it, so take the good, leave the bad, and it will help you navigate your way.

Today's younger generation sometimes tends to be laser-focused and wants to do, for example, fashion or work for a specific company. I tell them to keep their options open because you don't know where something will take them. I didn't know I'd like consumer technology until I started working in that industry. It's important to keep an open mind and take the opportunities that come up; you never know where it will lead!

Tabita Andersson: That's great advice. Also, as communications professionals, we must build business acumen and commercial awareness, which can be difficult if you've been stuck in one PR role for a long time. You need to widen out if you want to continue to grow. It's not always just about growing upwards, but sideways, too.

Joanne Trout: Yes. I teach a course called Integrated Agency Live. I've seen the same issue across several universities where they teach PR and advertising separately, so I came up with this course where every week we take the students to a different Omnicom agency where they get a deep dive into what the different agencies do, across PR, digital, advertising, etc., and we talk about all the different roles, from strategy to creative, or account management. The point is to help them understand all the different disciplines and functions. Many students will then tell me that they've changed their interest from PR to advertising, or something else they like better. The benefit of doing this is that in real working life, we must have both PR and advertising working together., Many of today's US universities don't offer courses that span different marketing disciplines, so I believe academia needs to figure out how to integrate their public relations and advertising schools to better reflect the real business world.

Tabita Andersson: In summary, what do you like so much about communications?

Joanne Trout: It's such an exciting discipline. I've been doing communications for 35+ years, and I keep learning. Every day, I learn something new.

Also, it's such an exciting time to work in communications. The role is no longer the poor stepchild to advertising. It has taken a prominent seat with the C-suite, and COVID certainly influenced that development. Communication departments became so important to any business when the world shut down. Working more connected and hand in hand across all marketing disciplines is exciting and a huge opportunity!

CHAPTER

17

Craig Spence
Chief Brand and Communications Officer
International Paralympic Committee

Craig Spence is the **Chief Brand and Communications Officer** for the **International Paralympic Committee (IPC)**, the global governing body of the Paralympic Movement, based in Bonn, Germany. Founded on September 22, 1989, as a non-profit organisation, the IPC aims to be athlete-centreed and membership-focused in all endeavors. Working with 200+ member organisations, the IPC oversees the delivery of the Paralympic Games and uses Para sport as a vehicle to advance the lives of the world's 1.3 billion persons with disabilities.

For more information about IPC, visit paralympic.org.

Craig's LinkedIn profile: linkedin.com/in/craigwilliamspence/

Tabita Andersson: Can you tell us about the organisation you work for and your role as Chief Brand and Communications Officer?

Craig Spence: The International Paralympic Committee is the global governing body of the Paralympic movement, and my job is the most awe-inspiring job anyone could ever wish to do! We oversee the delivery of the Paralympic Games, which is the world's third biggest sports event right now. We're here to serve and advance our member organisations so that our athletes can achieve excellence around the world. It's such an amazing job because, through sport, we are changing the world for 1.3 billion people with disabilities. Many people want to work in sports, but to also work in a sporting organisation with a strong purpose is tremendously rewarding.

I'm the Chief Brand and Communications Officer, and I oversee a team of around 20 individuals who look after all communications. We work with organizing committees to oversee the delivery of all communications around each edition of the Paralympic Games. We create a ton of digital content for our various channels, and we look after the Paralympic brand. This includes how it's used, not just by us internally at the IPC but also throughout our 208 member organisations, commercial partners, and broadcasters. It's a very diverse role, and when I joined about 15 years ago, we were a team of two, so it's been rapidly evolving.

Tabita Andersson: What functions and disciplines does your team of 20 now cover?

Craig Spence: The function is split into three areas. First, we have the communications team that primarily looks after media inquiries and proactive media outreach in terms of engaging with traditional media and telling people about the work of the IPC. The workload varies a lot. At the moment, we receive limited media inquiries: on average, five a week; and when we get closer to the Games, we can receive up to 250 inquiries per day. We step up and bring in temporary staff to help with the event.

The second and biggest team is content. This team is responsible for creating digital content for our multiple different social media channels. We have a video production team, an editorial team, and a CRM team. We do a lot of direct, one-to-one communication through our CRM database of about one million people.

Lastly, we have a brand team that manages the brand as well as the in-house design studio.

Tabita Andersson: You mentioned the brand, which is very well-known in some parts of the world, such as here in the UK. How do you work to help protect your brand?

Craig Spence: We serve 208 member organisations at the IPC. Each one is allowed to use our brand, so you need the strictest guidelines possible, but also allow flexibility for those organisations to use the brand. We manage those guidelines and help the member organisations use the brand.

We also work with some of the biggest companies in the world, who are our marketing partners. We want them to use our brand as much as possible because they have huge audiences that can amplify what we do and reach far more people quicker than we can. We work with them on how they can utilize our brand in their campaigns and tell our story.

In addition, we work with our media rights holders on how to use our brand. For example, for the Paris 2024 Paralympic Games, we had 225 different media rights holders, which included traditional broadcasters such as Channel Four in the UK, NBC in the United States, and NHK in Japan.

Lastly, we work with the various organizing committees that organize the Paralympic Games on how to use our brand, which is used within the Paralympic Games symbol and the look and feel of the Games. We work ten years in advance on organizing the Games, so we're already working on the Salt Lake City-Utah 2034 Paralympic Winter Games.

We did a brand identity update in the build-up to the Paris Games which caused a whole lot of issues because it then needed changing in so many places. Even if we're just doing a small tweak here and there, or changing the colors slightly or the shape, it causes a lot of challenges. We must appreciate that when we update our identity, it's not an overnight delivery. It can take five to six years to complete the rollout. It's like the airline rebrands, when you can still see the old brand on the airplanes for years later, because it's so expensive and difficult to rebrand everything at once. It's the same for us, managing a rebrand is not something we can do overnight, it's like an oil tanker that takes a while to turn around.

A good example is our 183 national Paralympic committees, each with its own emblem, including the Paralympic symbol. Some of these committees are run by volunteers, so when we tell everyone that we've updated the Paralympic symbol and we ask them to update their content, they will come back and tell us they have no resources to do it. Sometimes we then need to do it for them, or for the larger committees who may already have produced their uniforms for the next Games, for example, we may need to be flexible with our deadlines. We must always appreciate that we can't change everything overnight.

Tabita Andersson: That's a complex scenario to work through to protect and manage your brand. How about building the reputation of your brand? What approach are you taking to do that successfully when you're already relatively well-known?

Craig Spence: Well, I'm flattered that you say we're well-known because in certain countries we are well-known, especially where we've had the Paralympic Games, but in other countries there's a limited brand awareness and understanding of what we do. For example, Great Britain had the Games in London in 2012, and therefore everyone knows the Paralympic Games, but if you go to the United States, where we are going to be for the 2028 Games in Los Angeles, we don't have such a great profile. They tend to ask if we're part of the Special Olympics, which has a higher awareness, so there's a bit of brand confusion in the US market. We need to treat each market differently, and that's difficult when it comes to implementing global communications with a team of just 20 people. We can't create bespoke plans for 183 member countries, so we focus our attention on certain territories by educating people in those countries about what our brand stands for and how we transform the world through sports. Often, people don't want to hear from a global governing body; we're often regarded as stuffy and corporate. People engage much better with athletes than spokespeople of organisations or corporate governing bodies, so we utilize our athletes to be advocates for our brand and to engage people in what we do. There are no greater advocates than the athletes who are role models and change makers for the future. That means it's important our athletes understand the brand and what we want to achieve in our efforts.

Many people believe we're just a sports organisation, which is great because ten years ago, we weren't considered a sports organisation. We were considered a disability organisation, with the essence of sport. Now, we want to be known as a sports organisation that transforms the world through what we do, and that's the evolution of our brand as we mature as an organisation. The IPC is still a young organisation. We were founded in 1989, and we're still evolving. We've gone from being a startup to a more mature organisation, but we're still in our infancy. For us, it's about ensuring we have great Paralympic Games, but also ensuring we can serve our members successfully. Now that the Games are much more well-known, we can focus on the impact we have around the world and how the Games and our development programs advance disability rights. Through our work, we change attitudes toward disability, and we empower persons with disabilities to live active lives through sport, so informing people that this is what our brand stands for is the most important activity for us right now.

Tabita Andersson: What role does communications play in helping you tell that story?

Craig Spence: It's an integral role. For example, I've just done a lecture to 16 master's students studying journalism from a local news channel here in Bonn, Germany. They all knew that we organized the Paralympic Games, but none of them knew the impact we have on changing the world through changing legislation and creating legacies. Communications is front and centre of everything we do in this organisation. That's also why I love the job so much and have stayed here a long time!

Before I joined the IPC, I worked in Rugby League in the UK, where you end up doing the same activities every year because of the seasons. Here at the Games, we work on things in four-year cycles, so by the time we get to the next Games, communications have evolved so much, and we need to keep up, which is very cool!

To arrange the type of Games we want to achieve, we need to sell up to 3 million tickets, and we want people around the world to watch. Communications is at the front and centre of achieving those goals. We also want people to not only watch the Games but also understand the impact that the Games have on changing attitudes and driving disability inclusion. We're front and centre on that, so it's great that communications is at the heart of everything the IPC does.

Tabita Andersson: Where in the structure do you sit as the CCO? Do you have a CEO and classic C-suite structure, and how do you interact with each other?

Craig Spence: We have a six-person strong C-suite and a very flat structure, which I love. The CEO wanted a flat structure where we could all contribute to the business decisions that need to be made. We meet twice a week to discuss everything that's going on in the organisation. My job isn't just communications for the organisation; it's the welfare of the organisation and ensuring we're building a great place to work and do business with. It's a dynamic, diverse group. Our Chief Executive Officer is a two-time Paralympian, so a person with a disability, and we have a 50/50 gender split, which was the goal for our CEO when he took over. Across the IPC, we have 135 staff from 48 different nations, so we deal with a multicultural team. The CEO reports to our governing board, which is elected every four years. The board is led by our President, who, luckily for me, is a former journalist who understands communications!

Under our governance structure, you can serve a maximum of 12 years in a position, so you can only do three terms, which ensures some continuity. Our current President is sitting his second term, and we have some board members who have reached their limit, so they will be termed out this September when we have elections. That will bring a few new faces, and it's always good to refresh the group as we go forward.

Tabita Andersson: What value do you think a CCO brings to the conversation at the top table?

Craig Spence: Communications is the eyes and ears of an organisation. We typically know more in our team about what's going on in the organisation than in any one department. That's what we bring to the top table. We can see what's going on outside in the world, the latest trends, and the latest events, and we can flag what an organisation needs to be careful of. At the same time, we're very good at working across functions and seeing how we can bring things together and tell stories or identify where we may need to protect our brand if issues are happening.

Communications people are naturally creative, and if you're creative, you're usually a problem solver, which helps us face issues as an organisation. I always thought I was creative and innovative, and then I joined the IPC. I now work with people with disabilities, who are the best problem solvers on earth! 18% of our workforce has a disability, and they have been solving problems since birth if they were born with a disability, because there are barriers to everything that we want to achieve in life. They just work around those barriers, and we learn so much about problem-solving from working with people with disabilities. That's been such an unexpected benefit I've gained from working here.

Tabita Andersson: I can imagine! What are some of the ways you measure the effectiveness of what you do for brand and communications?

Craig Spence: This is one of the evolutions I've seen when it comes to communications. When I started working here, it was all about securing column inches and TV coverage. Now, the easiest way to measure is by using traditional digital figures. What's the engagement? What's the reach? What's the viewership? Securing coverage for Paralympic sports, 365 days a year, every year, is very difficult for an event that happens only once every four years, but we still want to keep the audience engaged throughout. We measure what's working, or not, monthly and primarily focus on digital numbers. We don't have the budget for the traditional media clipping agencies because doing clippings for 200+ countries regularly would take up our entire communications budget! The IPC is a small organisation with around 25 million in revenue per year, so we must spend our money wisely.

Our finance team does something we call data-to-insight, which is to ensure that each department delivers to their objectives and that we get the best value for our budget. That's how we assess our functions. I will always want to do more things in communications, but I need to evaluate whether the same budget would, for example, introduce 10,000 more in Africa to Para sport for the first time. Those are the budget discussions we have on a regular basis.

One challenge we face is getting people to understand our metrics. For example, last year, around the Paris Games, we had 1.6 billion video views across our digital channels. We were supremely proud of that number, and our CEO challenged me, rightly so, and said: Is that good? To what end is that number good? What did that number achieve?

As a result, with our plans going forward, we're now not just measuring the viewing figures but working out, with our digital channels, how we can capture whether watching a video changed their attitude toward disability, or did it challenge the stigma that's attached to disability. We don't have the budget to commission an agency to help, so we're working with the digital channels to see how we can integrate surveys into our existing content delivery. Thankfully, the digital channels themselves want to work with us due to our viewing numbers and events, so we can go a bit deeper on metrics. I'm a keen believer in having KPIs for the team so we have a clear direction for what we want to achieve during the year and how we can use our activities to change the world.

Tabita Andersson: How do you think we can improve the way we use data better in the future? We have done enormously well, as you stated, in terms of the evolution of the type of data we now receive, but we seem to lack expertise in turning data into insights. What are your thoughts?

Craig Spence: One thing we can do better is to streamline the data we collect. When I first joined the IPC, we were paying research agencies that would come to us with 150-page reports, which were amazing. We would sit through the presentations and comment on how great the data points were, and you'd then never look at the report again, apart from two pages with the key data points. It's important when you get the facts that you also have the resources needed to act on the findings. There's nothing worse than receiving tons of data and coming up with loads of ideas about what you could do, and then you look at the resources that are available to you, and they don't match! As a non-profit organisation, we need to use our budget wisely, and it's important for us to focus on the data sets that will help set us up for success in the future or change our strategic direction. We can't collect data just for its own sake.

Tabita Andersson: Even in commercial organisations, we still have limited budgets, and we must make sure that what we do is targeted at supporting our business objectives. That also means understanding what the business needs, and there is a need for the CCO and the communications team to have a good commercial understanding of the organisation they work for. Would you agree with that?

Craig Spence: Yes, we must be able to understand what we're trying to achieve as an organisation. We're constantly communicating our vision, mission, and strategic plan to our colleagues. One of the things we've had to focus on during the last five years, as we're a small organisation, is not to say yes to every single opportunity that comes along. When you're in a startup mode, it's so easy to do that, and when you review what you've done at the end of the year, 30% of what you delivered had nothing to do with the strategy that the board of your membership asked for. So, for the last five years, we've started to say no to some projects and made sure that we focus on the core projects that deliver on the strategic plan. That has been difficult to do with the team, because everyone who joins this organisation goes above and beyond the call of duty because of what we do. People here quite happily work long hours doing everything they possibly can to ensure that we deliver the most successful Paralympic Games. They believe in our vision to change the world through sports but sometimes, we have to say no, we must deliver on the strategic plan first, and we also have to look after everyone as people. We have a duty of care to ensure, under German law, that everyone works a 40-hour week. It means focusing on what's strategically important to the organisation, which has been a challenge, especially for people like me who have been here a long time and who were used to saying yes to everything!

Tabita Andersson: That's a slightly different challenge than most commercial organisations, where it might be easier to ask the team to focus on strategic objectives.

Let's pivot to talking about your background; you mentioned working for the Rugby League. How did you get to your current role as CCO for the IPC?

Craig Spence: I started by doing a three-year public relations degree at the University of Central Lancashire in Preston, the UK. Originally, I wanted to be a journalist. Someone I knew, a family friend, was a journalist, and they told me not to do journalism because it's a dying industry. Getting into communications is probably the best piece of advice I've ever received!

After the degree, I worked in a PR Agency for nine months, and then went in-house to Yorkshire Water, promoting tap water and sewage, which on paper sounds quite boring, but it was the most fun job in the world. Creativity is one of my strong points, and when you promote tap water and sewage, you need lots of it! We had a lot of fun, for example, launching diet tap water on April Fool's Day on GMTV. The serious message behind the joke was that water is the most cost-effective health drink you can get. You don't need zero-calorie drinks!

After Yorkshire Water, I went to another PR agency and worked predominantly on consumer accounts. During my early years, I wanted to work both in agencies and in-house to see which one I liked best. At the agency, I worked on B2C accounts, such as banks, energy companies, and sports sponsorships like the Ashes for the England Cricket Team.

As a former rugby player, when the job as communications manager for the Rugby Football League came up, I jumped on it. I stayed there for two and a half years, and I didn't particularly enjoy it. It surprised me, but it's like the saying that you should never meet your heroes! One of the sponsors of the sport told me there's an opportunity at the IPC, and I'd never even heard of them. At that time, I'd realized that I wanted to work in-house, so I joined the IPC in 2010. The opportunity to work on the London 2012 Paralympic Games was amazing, and I fell in love with everything we do here, so 15 years later, I'm still here as passionate as I was on day one.

Tabita Andersson: What an amazing career path! What advice would you give to younger communications professionals in the early stages of their careers?

Craig Spence: It's a question I get asked a lot! During my first year at University, I was always looking at every job description that was advertised, and they all said you needed two years of work experience. As I wanted to go straight from university to a job, I had to work out how to gain two years of experience when I was not working. That's why I ended up volunteering and working for various organisations during all my holidays. I did some work for a local PR agency, I volunteered for charities, and I even did a weekly newsletter for the local pub where I worked evenings. By the time I graduated, I'd gained 18 months of good work experience, and I was able to say that I'd done as much as I could while studying for my degree. My first piece of advice is to get as much work experience as you can while you're studying. It gives you a step up, because when you graduate, there will be about 2,000 other people like you looking for work.

My second piece of advice is that you may have an aspiration of where you eventually want to end up, but you may not get there straight away. I always wanted to work in sports, and I knew it would be difficult and challenging to get there. It took me about ten years to get into sports PR, so my advice is not to try and achieve your objectives in year one after graduation.

Also, be prepared that you might have a change of career path along the way. If you'd asked me when I graduated if I'd ever end up working abroad in Germany, I'd say not! It's the best career move I've ever made because it's not only giving me an opportunity to work for such a great organisation as the IPC, but when you work with people from 48 different nationalities every single day, you learn so much about the world. As a result, my advice is to be open to new ideas and new horizons. Be willing to learn and adapt. I'm a completely different person today than I was 15 years ago when I started here, in terms of cultural sensitivity.

Tabita Andersson: What are some of the great attributes someone needs to have as a successful communications leader? What attributes do you look for when you look for new people to join your team?

Craig Spence: First, excellent communication skills. It might sound stupid saying that, but surprisingly, you come across people who work in communications who are not very good at explaining things. Clear and concise communication is the number one skill.

I'm always looking for people who are better than me. Leaders shouldn't be afraid to appoint people who are more talented than they are. Our Head of Content, for example, knows 100 million times more than I do about social media and how it works. I don't need to know that level of detail, but I can shape him and direct him in the right direction. I look for people who are good in their fields and who know more than I do. When I look for leaders, I look for people who have a clear sense of direction on what they want to achieve and who can make people buy into it.

I like people who are different. Here at IPC, it's all about diversity. Previously, I would have appointed people who were like me, and after joining the IPC, I've learned that diversity and difference are a massive strength, and employing people with different backgrounds and different experiences brings so much more to your team. When I joined the IPC, I was suddenly working with people from Africa or South America, and they were bringing totally different viewpoints to what we were wanting to do. I quickly realized how much you can learn from each other. I've always tried to embrace the difference, and I ask my team to do the same. We have 20 people on the team and 17 different nationalities. It brings so much value to the team.

In addition, I like people who have fun and who have a sense of humor!

Tabita Andersson: I agree. We spend so much time together working, so it's important to be able to have a laugh!

Is there something in your background that's not communications-related that you think helped in your career?

Craig Spence: Team sports. I played rugby league from the age of five to 19, to a very high level. From 11 years onwards, I was captain of my team, my region, and so on. When I look back now, and when I recruit people, I can always tell those who have been in a team sport because they are disciplined and embrace teamwork. My team tells me they like my leadership style, which is a result of being the captain of a rugby team and learning how to motivate a team. My rugby team wasn't particularly good—we lost more than we won—and you learn more from defeat than you do from winning, but I always had to keep the team fully motivated going into the next game. Here at the IPC, I'm leading a team of 20 people who are all living away from home, sometimes struggling with their mental health because they're homesick, and I have to motivate them to keep going. Growing up playing team sports has helped me massively in terms of my day-to-day work of building teams, harnessing the energy, and getting the best out of people.

Tabita Andersson: How do you think communications as a function has changed in the last few years?

Craig Spence: When I first joined the IPC, we were all about securing column inches and gaining broadcast coverage in traditional news channels, and now, very few people read newspapers; it's all about digital content. As a result, we now go directly from our office to the end user on social media, or via the CRM system, telling wider audiences about our news without a third party having to interpret it, or reduce its size. With the Paralympic Games, it's always difficult to secure coverage, especially outside of the Games, because the sports media around the world is so dominated by football. It's hard to convince a sports editor that they should be doing Paralympic Games coverage on a regular basis. It's like women's sport and how hard they have had to push to become visible. Being able to embrace digital media to help push our news has been integral to our growth, and it's one of the biggest changes I've seen.

In the last 12 months, AI has started to sprout, and it will change everything in the years to come. Right now, with AI, you're either jumping in or you're sitting on the sidelines waiting and seeing how it goes. We're sitting on the sidelines and watching, but it is something we will jump into eventually and embrace because it will make our lives a lot easier. The challenge right now is that you have to train the tools, and the Paralympic content isn't there yet to train the tools accurately. As an example, ahead of the Paris Games, we had various companies approaching us, telling us they had AI tools that could help us clip video content easily, and they were already working with other sports organisations. When the Games then came around, they realized that they couldn't do it because they had to train the tool, and the tool didn't have a clue about the Paralympic-specific sports terms. It helped us understand that if we're going to jump into AI, we also need to train the tools so they're familiar with what we want them to do.

Tabita Andersson: What are some of the other ways that you think AI will shape the communications profession in the future?

Craig Spence: It can help streamline content around the world, writing content, and planning for us, but that's still depending on the right training. We often test the tools to see how they're progressing. The other week, I asked AI to write a biography for me as I was speaking at a conference and needed a short synopsis. To my surprise, I died in a car crash in 2016! AI is not foolproof yet, and in parallel, there's not a lot of content available from the Paralympics, so it's not ready for us to use to write stories, but in terms of project management and planning, it's there. For example, it's very good at helping metatag athletes.

After the Paris 2024 Paralympic Games, we had 1,400 hours' worth of video content from 22 sports that went into our digital archive. Everything in the digital archive is meta-tagged, so if you type in the name of an athlete, you can pull up a library of that athlete in action at the Games. We work with a third party for that tagging, and the platform is then used by our broadcasters, marketing partners, and members who use our archive footage in coverage. This is where AI is helping us right now. Previously, we were tagging the clips manually, but for the last three years, it's been done by AI.

During the Games, we live stream everything across our website, and we clip every single race so it can be viewed on video on demand. Up to now, a person used to sit and do those clips manually. In the future, we will be able to bring in AI to do the clips and upload instantly, which will be much more efficient.

Tabita Andersson: That's a great use case! We can do a lot to share best practices and examples of how to use AI for communications.

On a different topic, when you think back over the years, what are some of the mistakes we've made as a profession, and some of the things we've not done so well?

Craig Spence: Something that frustrated me in my early career was the arrogance that communications should be at the top table just because it's communications. We must earn our stripes and move up the career ladder accordingly. You're not going to get up the ladder because you've been somewhere for two years, and I think it's the same with communications. It needed to prove its worth to organisations and prove why it should be at the top table. We've improved. Fifteen years ago, all the textbooks talked about why communications needs to be at the top table, without demonstrating the results or the evidence of how organisations can flourish when communications sits at the top table. Everyone wants to be there, so prove your worth!

Tabita Andersson: Do you think it's easier to prove your worth today because we have fake news, and there's so much distrust around us, so we need communications more than in the past?

Craig Spence: No, because fake news works both ways. When I look at some of the fake news that people are preaching today, it's clearly not coming from a communications professional. The leaders are saying things anyway because some people will believe and vote for them, so the fake news has almost come about because the communications people have not been listened to.

One thing I love about working here is that I'm involved in decision-making. There are organisations where the communications person might have a seat at the top table, but they're not involved in the decision-making; they're only involved in the communications of a decision. Ever since I joined the IPC, we've made big decisions, such as suspending Russia for doping or the invasion of Ukraine, and communications has been involved in those discussions to help discuss the consequences and move forward. I've previously been approached by organisations that have asked me to come and work for them. My first question is, what type of communications person am I going to be for you? Am I involved in decision-making, or am I communicating decisions? If they say the latter, we're done with the conversation. Some people are really surprised about that, but it's important to me that communications people are integral to decision-making. Often, I see communications as a game of chess, where you must think two to three moves in advance about how something could play out, not just tomorrow but over the next six to several weeks or months. The decision you make on day one could influence where you are in six months. You need to look several moves ahead.

Tabita Andersson: How can we, as communications professionals, improve? How do you think we can shift from being a service delivery to being part of the decision-making process?

Craig Spence: Take the chance to prove your work and speak up. Don't sit on your hands; otherwise, you're always going to be the service delivery person. Every time I'm involved in the decision-making, it doesn't mean my suggestion always wins, but I'll give my view, and then I'm at peace that at least my view has been heard. Even if you sit in a service delivery role, you can still go to your bosses and say you disagree with an approach and give your legitimate reasons. They might ignore you but if things go pear shaped your boss will certainly consider you for advice about the next decision because you've forecasted what might have happened. This is where you can earn your stripes and prove your worth. You don't prove your worth by knocking on the door and saying I should be here because I'm communications. You prove your worth by giving a rational explanation of why certain approaches may work or not.

Tabita Andersson: Maybe that's one of the hidden skills that CCOs and senior communications leaders need to have. The ability and bravery to go against popular opinions and say something different in a conversation?

Craig Spence: Sometimes it's easy for me to say that, but it differs between organisations and what culture you have. We have a fantastic culture here at the IPC, where in our C-suite, we're all empowered to speak up and share our views, even on the governing board. I have worked in organisations where the CEO's view was rigid, and no one felt empowered to give a view, but you were the first to hear if things went wrong, and you hadn't warned about something. This is where the culture of an organisation is important, and as a communicator, you should be able to try and influence that culture, but it can be very difficult when the person or people at the top want the culture to be their way, or no way.

Tabita Andersson: You mentioned culture. What are some of the ways that communications can influence and contribute to building a good culture?

Craig Spence: Culture is about two-way communication, transparency, listening to people, harnessing energy, and appreciating different cultures. With 47 different nationalities working in the same organisation in Germany, which has a very specific culture, we try to bring it all together through listening, embracing views, and shaping policies and decisions. Communications can be at the heart because we're the eyes and ears of the organisation, both internally and externally.

Tabita Andersson: Finally, what does a communicator need to thrive in an organisation?

Craig Spence: Trust is important. I work best when I'm given a clear brief and clear direction on where to go and then empowered and trusted to go away and do it. That works for me, and it works for my team. People work in communications here because I trust them. Otherwise, they wouldn't be part of the team, because there are thousands of people who want to work here. Many leaders don't fully trust or empower their teams; they want things done in their specific way.

I often use a Satnav analogy. I need you to go from A to B, but you need to find the best route and that might be completely different to the one I would suggest but ultimately, if we've travelled from A to B, we've not gone over budget and we've achieved the objective, then that's great! It's important that people are given the ability to thrive and find their own way sometimes, because you learn more from mistakes. You don't want people to make mistakes all the time, but mistakes are not offenses; they are learning opportunities, and I'm a firm believer in throwing someone into the deep end and seeing if they sink or swim. Most of them happily swim to the surface and go on to even greater things. There's no finer privilege as a leader than seeing one of your team thrive in your organisation and then move elsewhere to go on. That's where we as communications leaders need to get to.

One of the best pieces of advice I've ever received was from one of my bosses at Yorkshire Water. I'd been there a few years, and I'd won every single award I could. I was a press officer, I'd won the award for Young Communicator of the Year, I'd been recognised for many projects, and I loved working for the organisation, but I wanted to be a manager, so I asked my boss. They said no, we have a structure here, and until someone leaves, you can't be a manager. I decided to apply for a sewage tank driver position at Yorkshire Water, so HR came to me and asked what I was doing. I said I've done a degree, I've won many awards for you, but sewage tankers earn twice as much as I do, so I want to be a sewage tank driver! My boss then took me to the side and told me I wouldn't progress at Yorkshire Water because people in managerial positions often had been there years and were unlikely to leave. So, his advice was to go get employment elsewhere, and you will absolutely thrive. He told me to be prepared to move around a bit to help climb the career ladder, because you could be waiting 30 years if you stay here to move up a position, due to the nature of the business. Within six months, I was gone, and it was the best advice I've ever received. I've passed on that advice to many of my team here who have been outstanding in their roles, but there are no further opportunities, due to the structure, to move them up, and I've told them to go. That tends to surprise them. I love nothing more than looking at some of my former colleagues who are in high positions now. They always say they remember the conversation where I told them to leave, and it surprised them, but it was the best advice I'd given them. It's funny how the same advice has been passed from another communications leader to me, and now he's helping others as well!

CHAPTER

18

Lucy Henry

Chief Communications Officer Avanti Communications

Lucy Henry is the **Chief Communications Officer** for **Avanti Communications**, a global satellite technology company. Founded in 2002, with a mission to help the world become better connected, Avanti leverages satellite technology to create custom solutions that protect communities and unlock opportunities for individuals, communities, businesses, and governments all over the world.

For more information about Avanti, visit avanti.space.

Lucy's LinkedIn profile: `linkedin.com/in/lucy-henry100/`

Tabita Andersson: How would you explain your role to someone who doesn't know what Communications entails?

Lucy Henry: In its simplest form, it's about making sure that when anybody interacts with your brand, the experience makes a good impression and lands a message with you, be that through a social post, reading about you in an interview or magazine, or meeting an employee at an event. The aim of communications is to ensure that everyone is aligned about the company and its products, giving a good impression of who the company is, what they stand for, and, most importantly, being clear about what the company is selling.

© Tabita Andersson 2025
T. Andersson, *Chief Communications Officers at Work*,
https://doi.org/10.1007/979-8-8688-1856-1_18

Chapter 18 | Lucy Henry

The brand experience sits with communications. This is a company's language, engagement tactics, culture and feel. We are always challenged in our role because you can't necessarily measure a brand's feel and experience, but it stands for so much, which I think most people would understand when it's done well.

Tabita Andersson: How do you interact with other functions within your organisation? What you just described isn't necessarily within the communications function's control.

Lucy Henry: It's the age-old conundrum about where communications reports into and where it sits within an organisation. Communications needs to work with everybody. We're in a unique position where our stakeholders are not just one group of people. We have external and internal stakeholders—our audience is everyone. In contrast, if you look at the other areas of the company, invariably, they tend to be focused on one or two stakeholder groups, like employees or customers. This means that our internal relationships with every head of department and function are paramount to our success. We need to understand what they want and need, and vice versa. Additionally, the relationship with our CEO is incredibly valuable.

I'm fortunate to sit in an organisation with a CEO who believes in communications because he understands its power when executed well. He's a great orator, and he brings me to the table from the beginning when something happens. Communications is not a second or third thought, which changes everything for us. When you're involved from the start in shaping a decision, you can work on strategy from day one rather than hear about something the day before it happens. This is fundamental. You need to work with everybody in the organisation, but your relationship with your CEO and senior decision-makers impacts your daily job.

For me, and this might be unique and debated, I sit in the people function because so much of what I do is internal employee engagement. I cover both internal and external communications, so being able to work hand in hand with our Chief People Officer has been a blessing. I've learnt a huge amount working for her in the People function.

Tabita Andersson: You mentioned the importance of the relationship with the CEO. What advice would you give to CEOs on how they can better work with their Chief Communications Officer?

Lucy Henry: Please bring communications to the table at the same time as you bring finance, legal, and marketing. The boundaries between communications and marketing can sometimes be blurred. Still, you can't do one without the other, and the messaging needs to be agreed upon in communications before we take it externally. Understanding the value of communications in the chain is important. Having an open dialogue with your

C-suite is key because what you think we should do and what I think we should do could be different, but the outcome will be brilliant if you can discuss it at conception.

This is where communications can be at its strongest. Having an open dialogue is so important. Also, being flexible on both sides is paramount and rare, especially if you want to effect change. We can't stand still in our world, so CEOs and CCOs need to be comfortable flexing and changing, considering things you might not have considered 12 months or five years ago. We must move on, and it's our job to deliver the vision.

Tabita Andersson: You mentioned earlier that you sit in the people organisation but are still responsible for external communications and work closely with the CEO and C-suite. How do you balance your stakeholders because priorities can be equally high on both sides?

Lucy Henry: I dial up or down depending on what's happening, and I've built trusted relationships with all stakeholders. My entire background is in media and brand. I've worked for Discovery, UKTV, in television production and Conde Nast, to name a few, and that's one reason I was brought to Avanti. They wanted someone to come in and do things differently. I'm fortunate that I'm trusted as an expert in my field and what I do, so I balance that with the priorities of our different stakeholders. They are comfortable with risk and with us having a personality, which I embrace. We can go out externally and talk about our opinions, and that's led me to a great place because we have something different to say compared with other people and the balance of what that is, and how it resonates with all stakeholders, sits with me.

Tabita Andersson: Having an opinion on something is often called "thought leadership" in the industry. What does thought leadership mean to you?

Lucy Henry: I benefited from having completely fresh eyes when I joined the satellite industry. I hadn't worked in technology or the satellite sector before, so I quickly noticed the untapped opportunity to mine our technology teams for thought leadership ideas. We also had a brand-new CEO and a new leadership team. We have world-class people with fascinating insights into the satellite world, which is now exploding, and people are open and interested in hearing their thoughts.

Second, we were operating in a new era of space. The rate of change has never been so massive. With Elon Musk and Jeff Bezos entering the industry, satellite communications has gained heightened media interest. If you're experiencing disruption in your industry, there's a huge opportunity to speak about it.

Thought leadership is opinion-based. You don't want to read something reiterating someone else's words. You must have a company point of view. It gives you a license to question whether you agree with something, discuss whether we want to say something publicly, or think there's another angle to the same topic. The satellite industry is zeitgeist in mainstream media, and it allowed us to start responding to a conversation. Avanti employs people with deep knowledge who have built and launched satellites for 20–30+ years, so bringing this knowledge to the table felt natural.

Thirdly, we have a big footprint across Africa. No one has been on the ground in these countries, reaching these ultra-rural areas and connecting schools, villages, and hospitals in the same way we have. We are very passionate about this work and can easily talk about it because we are doing it, as opposed to many others who are just talking about it theoretically.

When you do something you care about and have an interesting point of view, thought leadership becomes easier, and you have a great opportunity to tell your company's story.

Tabita Andersson: What are some outcomes you have seen from that approach?

Lucy Henry: When I joined, we had a new executive team that primarily came from the telecoms and technology industry, not necessarily the satellite field, so we had to establish them as leaders, building their profiles step by step within the satellite industry by leaning on their areas of expertise. It was a real challenge because our company wasn't widely known—we went from pitching and perhaps landing one in ten media opportunities to getting picked up regularly, and now we are proactively offered opportunities.

It was a relatively linear process. We went from starting to build our brand and the reputation of the people running the organisation to establishing them as interesting, reliable, and specialist experts. Now, when you pick up the phone and chat to someone and mention that you're from Avanti, they respond, "Okay, we know you," which makes our sales teams' jobs much easier. For example, Virgin Atlantic had its first-ever horizontal launch out of Newquay, where our largest technology hub is located. Media came to us for our opinion on how it went, as we have become a trusted specialist in our area.

Tabita Andersson: You mentioned your team's broad reach across various functions. What are those functions, and what does your structure look like?

Lucy Henry: When I started at Avanti, it was as Head of Internal Communications, and that remit then grew. I now oversee public relations, social media and brand, including design, and we cover events internally and externally. We're not a large organisation, so we're a lean team, but what we cover is broad.

Tabita Andersson: What are some benefits you see from having all communications functions under one umbrella, working together as one team rather than siloed?

Lucy Henry: The benefits are endless. If you're coming up with ideas as a collective group, and everyone is adding value from the start, what you create feels much more rounded than something that the PR or marketing teams have created independently. If you have a creative idea together, and then collaborate on your vision, output, target audience, and what you feel it should look like when finished, the outcome will be much stronger.

If you have all these experts in their fields, why wouldn't you lean on all of them for their ideas? What you do should be cohesive, but there's a reason we all have different specialisms, so when we put them together, it works brilliantly! We're not dealing with hundreds of people in each function; it's a small group, so we're known to be very agile and quick with what we do, which works well. You can't be as agile if you're all set apart, working independently and only coming together once a week to discuss your work.

Tabita Andersson: In terms of measurements, we mentioned the emotional side of a brand is hard to measure, but what do you do to measure the rational side of what we do?

Lucy Henry: It's a good question because it's fascinating how our world has changed from measuring AVE (advertising value equivalent) and number of likes to the broad way you can measure now. This is also a challenge because, yes, you can measure the number of articles you get, and that's great, but that's just one tiny slice of the pie. Who was talking about it? How many places was it shared? What platforms did it appear on? How was it perceived?

Having an internal measurement tool is also incredibly important. After COVID hit, the archaic once-a-year survey doesn't cut it anymore. I pitched to our executive team to bring a platform to conduct weekly pulse surveys. It's five questions once a week and takes less than a minute to complete. We then have ten metrics against which I measure the responses, such as happiness, reward, recognition, and their relationships with peers and managers. We can then plot that against feedback and watch how our employees feel week-by-week. That changed everything because our rewards package completely changed based on those metrics. How we recognise people changed, giving us tangible results to go away and highlight when we didn't get something right. Those conversations are far easier when we have the data to back up the findings rather than a feeling.

Tabita Andersson: What can we do better in the next few years? How can we keep improving? We have evolved so much over the last 20 years. Where do you see us going in the next five years?

Lucy Henry: The next five years will radically change our profession. We're only at the beginning of an explosive technology journey. Technical literacy is hugely important, but we also operate in a more decentralized organisation than we used to be. That allows us to measure what we do differently, but it also poses a real challenge because when you're not face-to-face with people, the role of communications needs to change. You can't feel or engage with someone on Zoom in the same way as you can in an office.

I can't tell you the answers, but I'm a technology adopter. I fully embrace AI, which is difficult because of its challenges for our profession and the value we add. We live in a moment where creative industries, not just communications, are being wildly impacted by AI. I hope AI will become commonplace in the next five years, but not replace people. It's easy to spot when someone has written something on AI, but that will get increasingly harder, and the technology becomes smarter—I'm fascinated by what will happen in the next few years.

Tabita Andersson: Everyone is on the journey with AI. Right now, that seems to be a different type of journey. Some teams are already heavy users with great examples; others are standing back, watching and waiting for improvements. Yet others would love to do something but are unsure what that looks like. There's a real opportunity here to share best practices.

Because of its position in an organisation and often with a small team, the CCO role can be lonely and isolated, and it's important to keep learning.

Lucy Henry: Absolutely. I'm an avid reader and sponge for information about what's happening. Still, I don't have a peer equivalent to throw ideas around with, so I always take the opportunity to speak to other like-minded professionals about what they're doing because we're in such a fascinating period.

Tabita Andersson: How do you think we can continue to elevate the role? We have done well over the last ten years, but what can we do to continue that journey?

Lucy Henry: The irony of making our companies and teams look good is that we're always last in promoting our function! Typically, we are behind the camera, the interviewer, because our job is to make other people look great, and our brand looks great. In its most basic form, we need to use our skill set to elevate what we do, clearly articulate what we do, and find the right way to share the measurement of our success.

We have elevated our role, but we also need to be the person who can have sparring dialogues, offering different points of view and perceptions. We're in a fascinating global period, where it's easy to stick with what you know and surround yourself with news, information, and opinions that match yours. Our job is to look at them and bring them all to the table. For example, we've never lived through a period where we've had so many generations in an organisation. How do you talk to those in their 60s, who are experienced in a traditional office, as opposed to those who are digital first and have never worked in an office? How do you align communications to cover those differences? This is something I spend a lot of time thinking and talking about.

Tabita Andersson: Many communications professionals talk a lot about our multigenerational challenges, but what are we doing? What have you seen in terms of actions? What are organisations doing to help?

Lucy Henry: My first job was with Tiger Aspect, an amazing production company, and I had this incredibly vivacious boss who took me to all his meetings. I didn't say a word, but he took me to a wide variety of meetings where I had no place to be, but I sat there and soaked up everything. I have a lot to thank him for because I learned by osmosis. I learned how to have a conversation with someone very senior, and I learned how to manage stakeholders because I started my working life in television, where everyone has incredible personalities, and you're dealing with talent, agents, and production companies, so you learn how to talk to people properly. EQ is incredibly important in business, but it's often underutilized or missing for those who have entered a remote workforce.

Our job in communications is to try to get our entire organisation on the same page, and that can be challenging when everyone wants to work differently.

Tabita Andersson: Exactly. For example, some companies recruiting graduates during lockdown and then asking them to return to the office a few days a week caused some initial challenges because they had not worked in an office before and had to learn how to structure their days. They didn't know how to manage their time or plan the commute when they were used to taking calls at any time.

Lucy Henry: That's such a good example. We appreciate the hybrid working so much because we've done the five days throughout our careers. It built up an important level of grit and resilience. If you're not in an office, you miss everything that happens outside of meetings. There is value in having social conversations about what's happening in our lives; it helps us understand personalities and circumstances, and build relationships, which is crucial for us in communications.

Tabita Andersson: Especially from an internal communications and culture perspective. You can pick up on nuances, which is hard in a virtual setting.

Lucy Henry: Exactly, and I'm fascinated to see what the future holds because that's unknown. Also, the skill set that's coming with the generation is digital-first and digital natives. We're working in an amazing period.

Tabita Andersson: To build on that, the even younger generation will now grow to be AI-first, which will be a complete game changer.

Lucy Henry: Yes, I'm currently raising young children, which I must continually balance. They can just pick up a mobile phone and use it without explanation—it's second nature to them. I want them to learn how to write with a pen and paper, and it's important to me that they can apply critical thinking and analysis to a problem. You can understand their response is to question why, when there are tools that will do it for them!

That's also why I'm a technology adopter. It's important to embrace what's coming because it's not going anywhere, and the speed of change is so rapid that you have to get on board or else you get left behind.

Tabita Andersson: Let's pivot and talk about your background. You've mentioned your background in the media a few times, and everyone seems to have had their journey into communications. How did you get into communications?

Lucy Henry: I studied English literature and drama. It had always been my intention to be an actress. I never wanted to do anything else, and I had two wonderful and sensible parents with two sensible jobs who told me I had to get a degree. Thank you to them! I knew that I wanted to do a degree and a job where I could mix people, entertainment, and writing.

When I first moved to London, my first role was with Tiger Aspect Productions, which was an incredible company to work for. The company produced big prime-time programs for the BBC, Sky, and ITV. I moved to London on a short-term contract and signed a one-year lease for a flat, thinking this was it! It was a fantastic time.

During my first interview with the person who later became my boss at Tiger Aspect, he told me to never change my accent. He's from Scotland, and I'm from Yorkshire, so his advice stuck with me. In essence, he instilled in me that you are good as you are. It's such an important lesson, and it's carried me through a lot.

Tiger Aspect helped me cut my teeth in PR in its most basic form. I learnt how to write. I also learned to deal with talent and production companies, selling and pitching stories.

After that, I was allured by the bright lights of Conde Nast, which didn't suit me at all, so I quickly went back to television, working for UKTV as a publicist. They own a suite of channels, including Dave, Really and Watch, and I was assigned my own campaigns, so I was running my own television launches, which was fantastic and a really vibrant industry to work in.

I then had the opportunity to move to New York, which changed everything for me, as I had the chance to work in television in NYC. The change was staggering; the working culture and hierarchy were completely different, but I'm thankful for my time there because I've never worked so hard. I had a global job as the international publicity manager and worked for Scripps Networks, now owned by Discovery. We were launching channels worldwide. This is when my stakeholder engagement skills were honed because I was working at a level multiple steps away from the senior team. I had to learn to deal with senior leaders in a large organisation within a structured hierarchy. It was my first exposure to such an environment because when you work in television in the UK, or a small production agency, the leadership is more accessible.

When I moved back to the US, Avanti Communications approached me. At the time, I was questioned why they wanted to hire someone with no experience in the satellite industry. I knew nothing about satellites, and that's exactly what they wanted. They were looking for somebody who understood brand, the power of communications, and how to sell a story. They were in the early stages of a turnaround and wanted to radically change the personality and brand of the company. That's how I got the job, and my role has grown since I've been there. I'm a grafter and work hard, but I'm fortunate to work with a leadership team that believes in communications.

My career has been quite linear in terms of communications but varied hugely sector-wise. I'd always be open to returning to media or trying something entirely different because, in our world, our skillset is very transferable.

Tabita Andersson: I agree. It seems that the tools and skill set of the profession are the same regardless of what industry we're in or whether we work in a business-to-business or a business-to-consumer organisation. If you've done a communications role in one industry, gaining new industry knowledge is much easier than building a communications-specific skillset.

Lucy Henry: Yes, and I'm a walking example because I knew nothing about satellites and was open about it during the hiring process. My manager was all for that. She wanted someone looking at things differently who could help build a brand and company culture. It worked well, and I wish people were more open to that idea because I think you come in with a different point of view, which can be very beneficial.

Tabita Andersson: What advice would you give younger communications professionals just starting their careers?

Lucy Henry: I cannot undersell the importance of being around people, leaders, and mentors in person because what you will learn by proximity is unquantifiable. It will change who you are.

My number one piece of advice in terms of tactics is to ask questions. Asking questions of the people around you is important because people love to share what they do. People are open and empathetic to those climbing the career ladder and willing to share their knowledge, which is an untapped source of advice. Learning online or taking qualifications is great, but what you will learn from real, in-person interaction is important, specifically in communications.

Also, in a world where you can be filmed at any moment, you could be photographed at any moment, or recorded, making sure you take care of your brand and understand the speed at which something can grow in the world we live in, is quite often presumed but not said out loud enough. A brand is exposed in many ways now, and you can't undervalue how quickly something you say can become public.

Tabita Andersson: That's an interesting point. How do you protect your brand and reputation today when anything can pop up on any channel?

Lucy Henry: There are two things here: your personal brand and your company brand. For the company brand, when anybody is going to do an interview or speak to anyone externally, we prepare properly and talk about what we want to discuss ahead of time. Anything that will be said externally on social media, for example, goes through a two-stage approval process; nothing goes online without us reviewing it.

The people who talk most about your company are your employees and ex-employees, so giving people a good journey and experience with you is hugely important because they advocate for your company. They can post their thoughts online at any time. It's the classic question we all receive after we have used a service: Would you recommend this company, and is it a good place to work for? When I joined Avanti, one of my big goals was for us to become a "best place to work" in the UK. We had a journey, but we were awarded it in 2024. Our results were so high that we went from a "great place to work" to "best place to work." You only win these awards if your employees are happy.

Tabita Andersson: As a CCO in the technology industry, do you think there are fewer CCOs overall who work in your industry?

Lucy Henry: It's an interesting observation. I've seen more mixed roles with communications and marketing in the same remit. When I joined Avanti, the role didn't exist here. It was something that has grown over time. If you look at many technology startups, the role will have similar trajectories because you won't hire a CCO in the early days. You need to grow the company, and there will come a point when you need to hire someone to look after the company's reputation. Or you go through a transformation, or a crisis, and you suddenly realize the value of communications. It could be that the rate of startups in the technology sector is so fast-paced, and not all of them make it through the early growth years, so that throws the balance out.

Tabita Andersson: I wonder if there's a tipping point, perhaps when a company reaches a certain number of employees or revenue or starts to cater to certain sectors, that could impact the need for the role.

Lucy Henry: Without a doubt. Unfortunately, you're not often an early hire, but a company will get to a point where they need somebody dedicated to communications and get it right, because you're growing so quickly. People are suddenly interested in what we're doing. So, when the need becomes apparent, there will be a moment in time, be it revenue, volume, or a big customer win.

CHAPTER

19

Paul Barrett

Chief Communications Officer Davie Group

Paul Barrett is the **Chief Communications Officer** for **Davie Group**, a privately held international shipbuilder with operations in Canada, Finland, and soon the United States. Davie Shipbuilding has been based in Québec, Canada since 1825, is a world-class designer and builder of highly specialized ships—particularly icebreakers for government and commercial customers. Davie became a partner in the Government of Canada's National Shipbuilding Strategy in 2023. This historic agreement is for the design and construction of the world's biggest order of large and technologically advanced ice-going ships. The initial $8.5 billion work package includes seven heavy icebreakers and two large hybrid-powered ferries. Also in 2023, Davie acquired Finland's Helsinki Shipyard, the world leader in icebreaker design and construction. In 2025, work will begin on the Polar Max icebreaker for Canada. Uniquely, this ship will be built between Davie's facilities in Helsinki and Quebec. When delivered in 2030, Polar Max will be the most advanced, powerful and capable icebreaker ever delivered to a Western government.

For more information about Davie, visit davie.ca.

Paul's LinkedIn profile: linkedin.com/in/pmabarrett/

Tabita Andersson: I was reading The Wall Street Journal this morning and saw a great mention of Davie in a story about the ship-building industry. What's the background to that mention?

Paul Barrett: That is the first meaningful mention we've ever had in the Wall Street Journal as a company. It shows that we're coming of age because the journalist wanted to bring our interesting backstory to their readers' attention. Right now, we have an empty shipyard because we're only starting to build in a couple of months, and the reporter came and took pictures of our dry dock, which is a very impressive 300-meter-long empty rock bath! That said, the story is about how the world is about to flick a switch in our industry. As a Western company, we're about to start building the types of ships Russia and increasingly China have built for decades, which is positive for global commerce and the specialized shipbuilding industry we operate in.

We're pleased with the mention and the fact that more people are interested in icebreakers and what we're doing, which is fantastic validation. A mention like this will help us build reputational equity and do business.

Tabita Andersson: You mentioned building reputation, how do you go about doing so in your industry, which is quite specialized?

Paul Barrett: It's not easy, and that's not just because we're in a niche industry; it's because we're in a tricky position. For example, our Canadian company was 200 years old this year, and we've only owned it for about 12 years. The business has undergone several boom-and-bust periods, where it almost faced bankruptcy and flatlined for several years. The perception was that the company was dead, had fired many people, and was struggling, leading to it being reputationally challenged.

You build a reputation through the organisation's actions, and then the communications and engagement you do that support those actions. Yes, we could do a stunt, which we have done occasionally when we needed immediate media traction to support a short-term goal. Still, when you make a promise to the market, and we're not a listed company, we have more latitude in what we say; however, if that's not backed up by us delivering on that promise, then you've got a big problem.

We bought the company 12 years ago, when it was essentially bankrupt. We then started on a journey to build trust with our stakeholders by saying, "Look, you give us any work and we will deliver on that, in a cost-effective way and on time. We will employ people while doing so, ultimately, we will be your best ally. You will love us because we're going to deliver the assets you need, and we can also help you develop your public and political reputation." The way to do that is through our actions, and it's also about building trust.

The pillars of trust, stakeholder management, communications, and marketing are the glue that helps you move from a license to operate to a license to innovate and grow the business.

I've seen trust deficits in other companies that I've worked for over the years. For example, in a pharma company with great insights to suggest that they have a transformative drug coming to the market, that type of data can fuel a spike in share price because everyone gets excited. At the same time, to be successful, you also have to properly educate patients, doctors, and investors. You don't want a situation where the data converts immediately into big sales opportunities as soon as the drug is ready, but you haven't prepared the market. That's when you get a trust deficit, which can take a long time to rebuild.

Something else that's incredibly important for a company's reputation is to ensure you're not a pushover. Some people will say that the customer is always right, except when the customer isn't right and doing something that will hurt the customer, us, or the public. We've always tried to be intelligent in explaining the risks and rewards.

There's a good example of this in our current scenario. We're about to start building a huge ship, the Polar Max icebreaker, for the Government of Canada between our facility in Finland and our yard in Canada. For such a complex project, it normally takes a very long time to work with the governmental procurement system because the government controls the entire process. After all, it's taxpayers' money, but naturally, the government has far less expertise in how to build ships than we do. This means that typically the government is involved in every single step and has an opinion on what to change or what costs to control, without always fully understanding the long-term consequences of completing the project on time and budget. It could be easy for the shipbuilder with a "cost-plus" government contract to say, "That's great because you're paying us for pretty much everything we do on the project, regardless of when it's delivered." However, the Polar Max is a desperately needed ship, and we need to stand firm and let the customer know that a normal procurement process will turn into many years of delay and rising costs in the long run. While you think you're saving money, you're wasting money and won't have the ship for many years. That's very difficult to say to a group of people who may have been working for decades in a system that's been around for a very long time. Perhaps the system is no longer working, but we have a solution for you. We will build the ship on commercial fixed price, fixed schedule terms. We are a disruptor that delivers on its promises. As experts on shipbuilding, we go to the government with the list of things they need to build the ship they want, the plan for how we will deliver it, and a clear timeline. If we do it the other way around, they won't get their ship for another ten years! It's about building trust while being disruptive. This doesn't always make us popular with customers and competitors.

This means communications and engagement become an incredibly strategic driver of the business. As a result, our CEO and owner, James Davies, often does stakeholder engagement work for over 50% of his time. Communicating our story and messages to various stakeholders, building trust, and showing that we're a company that can deliver where others can't means we're differentiating ourselves. In that sense, communications as a function is front and centre of the business rather than a peripheral support function. If, for example, James goes to the White House, I go to the White House. We develop the narrative and our content together. The key is that communications is in the room so we can help build reputation, relationships, and trust.

In any senior role, you must be a business leader, not just a functional expert or functional leader. I've seen so many times when communications hasn't been allowed in the room because they're seen as "just the comms person." To help with that perception I will often predicate what I say, "Look, I'm not an engineer, and I'm not in finance but I understand the dynamics of our business and I believe we need to think about this." Often, I get to comment on the reputational container that wraps itself around everything we do. Everything we see, say, and produce has a reputational component, which can be both hard and soft dollar value. When you're a CCO, you need to be the person in the room who can talk with authority about the business and communications.

Tabita Andersson: How can we build business acumen as communications professionals? It could be easy if you've been in many traditional PR or communications roles and have become excellent at the trade, but being a business leader is a different role when you get to the CCO level. How can you make that jump or journey?

Paul Barrett: First, you must let go of your functional excellence or competence, because it's a given. When you get to a senior position, you're expected to be good at the fundamentals, so it's about the value and how you become organisationally savvy. That's important and related to stakeholder management. It's something I've done extremely badly at different times but also extremely well at other times, so it's a skill we need to develop.

Secondly, it's about being relentlessly curious about things. For example, many people get an MBA, which is fundamentally good, but just having an MBA doesn't mean you know everything! It can be worthless unless you can immediately show that the MBA will help you make that jump and be a business leader like the other business leaders around the table. I'm sure it's an amazing experience, but unless you can show how it's changed you into something more than a communications person, that you're that person who's like the other leaders, then we have a problem.

If you look at my background, I have worked in multiple industries, as a consultant and an in-house communicator, and I've jumped from logistics and shipping to life sciences and then back to shipbuilding. Some people tell me that it's schizophrenic, but the reality is that you can do it because you have fundamental competence. Many of your skills are transferable if you've worked as a corporate communicator. What matters is that you fundamentally understand the business you're in. To build that knowledge, you need to speak to people. You need to have mentors and a network within the organisation.

When I joined Davie, the first thing I did was write about their strategic journey. I interviewed about 40 people within the organisation to get to know them and get their perspective on the part of the business they run. Writing it all down then helped me understand the business myself. This is how we work as communicators! It was a 32-page document, which I received some good feedback on. Still, more importantly, it helped me fast-track my understanding of the business, and I had an output that helped me get buy-in from internal and external stakeholders for what I wanted to achieve. Not everyone needs to go and write an annual review document, but everyone should get to know and understand the business. Another tip is to team up with someone who knows the business in detail, knows the good and bad about the organisation, and is the most experienced person.

Something important for a CCO is to be confident even if you're not certain about something. Don't say many irrelevant things, but contribute, especially in the early meetings, even if it's seemingly a stupid question. I do this all the time. Asking what might sound like a daft question will result in the expert in the room giving a download in simple language, and that's a good exercise for everyone around the table.

It's about being relentlessly curious and trying to find a way to fast-track your understanding of the industry and organisation. For me, doing a piece of writing was a good thing. I imagine many people would now just go straight to ChatGPT to do something similar. I would use generative AI for research, but find it counterproductive to my creativity and understanding. I advise putting ChatGPT to one side and doing it yourself!

Tabita Andersson: You've been in the communications profession your whole career. What changes have you seen in the last few years?

Paul Barrett: The only constant is change. Parts of our function have been commoditized, and in terms of its status in general, it's lost some of its luster. We live in a world of narratives and storytelling, which is awesome for the profession, but at the same time, everybody believes they're a great communicator—until they're not! We have such an overload of information all around us, so how can we as communicators ensure that we're not the breaks, or the barriers, to great communication.

In the past, we worked as gatekeepers. We advised leaders and colleagues that they couldn't say anything unless they came through the communications person. Now, that's impossible, so we need to consider how we can advise people on how to communicate in the best way possible and how that will impact both themselves and the organisation. We can no longer tell people what to say; we must advise everyone how to position the organisation. In that sense, the role has somewhat been commoditized, which worries me.

On the other hand, the corporate affairs function has grown. While straight communications is in some ways in jeopardy when you look at companies that don't have a CCO or similar role, there's no path to the executive team or board. Sometimes, you see the role reporting to HR or other functions. Still, we have a real chance of knowing if a company wants a proper corporate affairs function. You will be ingrained in the company's license to operate. If an organisation needs to deal with stakeholders such as governments, you might go into the room and lead those conversations on behalf of the company. If you're operating across these broader issues, government relations, public affairs, and investor relations, it becomes easier to show value.

I recently spoke to someone earlier in their career who sees the writing on the wall in the sense of what's going on in their organisation, and they asked me, "What's the next step?" For me, the next step is how you move into a place where you're the person leading conversations for the organisation. You're a company representative, not just a media spokesperson, someone in the room talking with authority to a wide range of people. This comes back to my point about being an expert in what we do. Being a business leader means understanding the business and the broader dynamics, and then going out to speak about it.

Tabita Andersson: To continue that thought, how do you prove value as a CCO in the organisation?

Paul Barrett: I'm ultimately remunerated for the success of the business. I've recently been part of securing a new business contract, and I hope to secure a few more as we move forward. My contribution to that is how I'm rewarded, and my contribution involves being the person who's helping to get us into various places where we need to be to deliver our message. I'm in the room alongside engineering, finance, legal, etc., when we talk to a customer about a contract because I've seen the contract, I've helped produce the content that's included and at times, I'll be the person who will be called up to give an overview of how we've engaged with stakeholders. My role is often to tell the story of why they should buy from us because we've helped create a positive opinion climate about our organisation.

Another way of cutting through is to be data-driven. The Wall Street Journal article we mentioned is a great example. It's a conventional way to show value because we can point to the audience.

I keep what I call a magic circle of media. Whichever market we work in, the magic circle is quality over quantity. It's identifying who the elite media are for an organisation and its stakeholders. Then, we will look at the demographic data to understand who reads that media outlet and how information is disseminated. For example, we know that everyone in the White House reads The Wall Street Journal, so it's hugely important to us to be positioned as central to Finland's story of building icebreakers.

I always try to be genuinely embedded in the commercial side of the business. Later today, for example, we have business development meetings; a big part of that is who we're talking to in different government bodies, so I work closely with our business development folks.

The old school ways of measuring value, such as the comparative value of media to advertising, have less relevance. For me, it's more about what meetings we have locked and how important they are. Mostly, I work directly with our CEO and senior leadership, so when I go to him and say, "I've got 20 meetings set up over the next three days," he will ask, "How many of those are truly relevant to what we're trying to do?" Sometimes you must be brave and say we've only got three meetings, but that's with the president, the prime minister, and the mayor. Then the CEO can work on something more important to the future of our business.

Tabita Andersson: You've mentioned how closely you work with your CEO. What is your advice to a CEO about best practices for working with their CCO?

Paul Barrett: Get to know them much more! It depends on what sort of person you are, but you need to understand what makes the person tick at quite an intimate level. Take time to build a good relationship, not just during the job interview, and understand that somebody can give you sage advice, beyond writing a speech or producing a 50-page strategy document.

I've spent so much time in my career building slide decks to run up and down the hierarchy of leaders to get an audience with the CEO. When I finally got there, I was immediately asked what I would do to create value for the organisation, rather than walking through my 30 slides! I advise the CEO to ensure the CCO keeps things as simple as possible and holds ambiguity. Tell me what I need to do to act in the way that's in the best interest of what we want to achieve. Be solution-oriented. I don't want you to come with a load of problems. We will be working very closely, and we need to trust each other, so you need to know what makes me tick. Here's that key theme of trust again! Don't come to me with a ton of details. I have the details ready if I need them, but overlay with something easy, simple, straightforward, and tied to the strategic imperatives of the business. It can't be an offshoot; if it is, it won't fly.

Tabita Andersson: You've mentioned previous roles a couple of times. Let's go back to the beginning of your career. How did you end up in communications, and what's been your career path to your current role?

Paul Barrett: I was the first person in my family to be educated beyond high school, so I come from a supportive blue-collar background. I was always extremely sporty and reasonably academic until the age of 14, when I became academically challenged! At the time, I was destined to go and work in a trade or a shop, which I started doing. I played semi-professional football and left school at 16 with poor exam results, except for English Language and Literature, which I was always good at.

For about a year and a half, I worked on a building site and played football before realizing I wasn't cut out for that life. I had an epiphany that I needed to do something different, bigger. I told Mum and Dad that I had to feed the fire that was burning inside me. They were fantastically supportive and told me to do whatever I wanted, but they didn't know how to make it happen for me.

Because the only thing I was very good at was English Language, I enrolled to do my A-levels again, which I did at my local sixth form college. After that, I got an internship at the local newspaper, and after eight weeks there, I loved it. I covered everything, including the local duck race, and they gave me stuff to write that appeared in the newspaper, which appealed to my skills and my ego as I could see my name in print!

After redoing my A-levels, I applied to various universities and ended up at the Polytechnic of Central London journalism school. At the time, it was located right next door to the BBC and Channel Four, and Fleet Street, where the major newspapers were situated, was only down the road. I had to take a test, writing headlines and stories under time pressure, and I was accepted. That's when my journey started, and I enjoyed it. I essentially learned traditional print journalism and a bit of broadcasting.

I then landed an internship with the BBC World Service by simply applying. At the time, they were churning out loads of budding journalists, but they asked me to come in and do shifts for them, working in radio, at a couple of magazines, and in the BBC bookshop. It meant that in the second year of my studies, I worked at the BBC World Service, which I continued after finishing my degree. Working at the BBC as my first job was fantastic, and I feel very lucky to have had such a great start.

I left the BBC after a few years, not because it wasn't a wonderful place to be, but because the pay was very poor back then, and I needed to figure out how to stay in London. I went to a publishing house called eMAP, where I worked on an austere and not remotely cool publication called the Local Government Chronicle. Interestingly, it was a proving ground for many journalists who went on to do other things in much bigger, better places. I worked there for a while, first as a chief sub-editor, then as a reporter and journalist. I left them because I was offered another job in a different industry: shipping and logistics. I was part of launching the first-ever online news service for that industry, called the Liner Shipping Network. It was super interesting, but it ended up a bit of a disaster because it was still dial-up Internet! We would present it to customers offline, and it looked amazing with flashing dials, stories, and content. However, the reality was that it would sometimes take me several hours to upload one picture for a story, and users would be upset because what finally appeared online wasn't great. From there, I went to Lloyd's List, a shipping newspaper and had the opportunity to move to Hong Kong and be their local correspondent, and that's when I moved into communications.

While I loved journalism, I didn't feel like I had a journalist's soul. In my sense, being a journalist means being perfectly balanced with a chip on each shoulder! I generally have a sunnier disposition, which is more suited to the communications profession. I left Lloyd's List and started my own communications and writing shop. I worked for various clients, sometimes in the shipping industry and sometimes outside, while still doing some work for the South China Morning Post.

Those experiences led me to decide that I wanted to start working in corporate communications, so I went and spoke to all the big consultancies and PR agencies. None of them were hiring then, so I continued working for myself until a job came up in Singapore with their national shipping line and logistics company, Neptune Orient Lines. This was my first real step into communications, and I started to build experience in internal communications and corporate affairs above and beyond public relations. It whetted my appetite for the job, so I then ended up going into a public affairs consultancy, working across a range of different clients, including some in the shipping industry, but also some in technology, before going back to the Neptune Orient Lines to lead on external communications and some government work.

When the global financial crisis hit in 2008–2009, our industry was a bellwether for the global economy. If you're not transporting goods, that's bad for business, so I felt like I became a merchant of doom because I was communicating about restructuring, laying off tons of people, and mothballing ships. As a result, I went to look for a new challenge.

That new challenge was with agri-science leader Syngenta running corporate affairs for Southeast Asia. Within 18 months, they asked me to go to the global headquarters in Basel, Switzerland and interview for the group head of media relations, a job I landed. I was moving up the organisation, getting a different perspective and enjoying myself because the industry was fascinating and very "issues-rich."

After five years with Syngenta, I was headhunted to join Novartis as their group head of external communications, a key stepping stone to a CCO role. It was a much more challenging role than I could ever have imagined. I took over a team that was not in good shape because they hadn't had a leader for a while, so they were just doing their own things. I turned the team around, and we did some interesting stuff together. For example, I led communications for several mergers and acquisitions worth more than $100 billion in value, stock market listings, and divestments.

The last thing I did for Novartis was to run communications for the spin-off of the Alcon eye care business unit. It looked likely that I would join Alcon in Geneva. That didn't work out, so I had time on my hands, wondering what to do next. I interviewed for various jobs that ultimately weren't filling me with passion, and I spoke to my very old friend, who said, "Why don't you come and visit us in Canada. We're on a massive growth trajectory, and we need a CCO who will be the custodian of our reputation and relationships and who can build our capability." That's what I've been doing here during the last five years.

In summary, I had no idea what my career would be other than that I've always been curious and driven.

I've also always been a staunch defender of communications, what we do, and the importance of a good reputation. It's so important to an organisation, and it gets run down and underestimated all the time. It has been my crusade and mission to move from being asked to "just tart up a presentation," which, when you open it, is full of gibberish, or super arcane and long, to being strategic about what we want to accomplish.

Tabita Andersson: Another classic question that irks me and I've often faced is, "Can you just send this email out to the whole company tomorrow?" without context or time to ask strategic questions.

Paul Barrett: You're right! It's that situation where we need to know everything to do our jobs properly, including what the person who wrote the original email thinks. It still happens to me today, at my level! People often think that the communications person is, by definition, a blabbermouth who's just going to go and talk to people about the company's secrets. I'm not saying people mean it, but if you're working in the engineering or science space, your credentials have been established over decades.

Tabita Andersson: In summary, is there anything else around the role of the CCO that you feel is important to mention?

Paul Barrett: Being relentlessly curious is incredibly important regarding what you do and how you carry yourself if you want to be or act like a CCO. When you're meeting with the executive team, make sure you contribute. It might just be feeding in tidbits of information to start with.

One of the tactical things I did when I joined Davie was to send out a weekly update to the most important people in the organisation to ensure they knew what was going on.

Ensure you stay in clear line of sight, have everybody's trust, and are indispensable. Also, defend the function with your life! Defending the discipline is important because if you capitulate, you could go from having a big budget to a small one. Use all means possible to show the value of what we do.

CHAPTER 20

Katherine Neebe

Chief Communications Officer Duke Energy

Katherine Neebe is the **Chief Communications Officer** for **Duke Energy** (NYSE: DUK), a Fortune 150 company headquartered in Charlotte, N.C., and one of America's largest energy holding companies. The company's electric utilities serve 8.6 million customers in North Carolina, South Carolina, Florida, Indiana, Ohio, and Kentucky, and collectively own 55,100 megawatts of energy capacity. Its natural gas utilities serve 1.7 million customers in North Carolina, South Carolina, Tennessee, Ohio, and Kentucky.

For more information about Duke, visit duke-energy.com.

Katherine's LinkedIn profile: linkedin.com/in/kneebe

Tabita Andersson: You've had an unusual path to being the Chief Communications Officer (CCO) at Duke Energy. What is your background and career path to date?

Katherine Neebe: My core background is in sustainability and stakeholder engagement. I spent about seven years with the World Wildlife Fund (WWF), managing one of the world's largest corporate-non-governmental organisation (NGO) partnerships with the Coca-Cola Company, focusing on water, agriculture, and climate. I then moved to Walmart, where my career evolved to include stakeholder engagement, strategic sustainability initiatives, C-suite support on sustainability, international policy and other thorny, complex business challenges. I joined Duke Energy almost five years ago as Chief Sustainability Officer, with an expanded portfolio to include public affairs, the Duke Energy Foundation, and federal policy. I stepped into the Chief Communications Officer role in February 2025.

Tabita Andersson: Congratulations on the relatively new appointment! Being new to the role, what do you find most exciting about the function?

Katherine Neebe: What I love about the corporate communications function, particularly at Duke Energy, is that we have an obligation to serve our customers and communities, and we also provide an essential service—energy—which is critical to economic mobility and development. You can't do anything in the modern economy without power. Our fundamental value or purpose is one of service and enablement.

Beyond that, it's an incredibly exciting time to be in the energy sector. New technologies emerge as we power rapid growth across our service territory, stemming from AI, onshoring, and economic development. Now, I get to tell that story, which stretches me personally into issues beyond those traditionally addressed in sustainability and philanthropy. It also requires me to grow as a leader to learn the strategies and tactics of communications.

Tabita Andersson: Does having a public affairs and sustainability background help you in your communications role?

Katherine Neebe: To some degree. As I stepped into this role, it felt incredibly familiar to what I was doing before. In both my previous role and this one, it's important to understand the relevant external environment and social trends that help a company navigate. It's about how the company positions itself on those issues and tells its story while thinking through the most effective strategies and tools you would use to engage the audience.

I'll also add that public affairs was folded into the corporate communications function at Duke Energy a little over a year ago. So, I helped build and launch the team and was lucky enough to have it returned to me.

Tabita Andersson: What lessons did you learn from your previous roles that communicators can learn from?

Katherine Neebe: At this moment in time, no matter where you sit in a company, what's important is authenticity, credibility, and trust. Figuring out how you do that in a way relevant to your brand and that meets the needs of your stakeholders, customers, policymakers, suppliers, and others is vital to getting it right. Plenty of communications professionals do that very well, and there are others for whom this is a new muscle they need to build.

Tabita Andersson: How do you build a successful reputation for a brand in a heavily regulated sector such as energy?

Katherine Neebe: At its most basic, utilities implement their company strategy as well as public policy—largely federal and state-led energy policy, but with strong ties to environmental and economic growth policies. We implement what our policymakers believe is important, and our regulators provide oversight. With any policy, we need to navigate stakeholders with different views about how best to approach these topics. Beyond those issues, stakeholders might prioritize reliability, affordability or clean energy outcomes differently. Hence, the opportunity for utilities companies is to be the honest broker that sits between policymakers, customers, companies, and NGOs to explain an incredibly complex system in an accessible way so that everyone has a seat at the table and can determine the future path forward.

Tabita Andersson: That involves working with many stakeholders with various priorities. How do you balance that?

Katherine Neebe: This is another area familiar to me from the sustainability world. One cool thing about a utility company like ours is that there's something for everyone to like about our sector, regardless of where you sit.

At the top, we're a very large energy provider. We provide essential services, helping power important economic development across our service territory, from AI and data centres to manufacturing, industry, and other growth drivers. We have some real proof points we can point to with respect to jobs, economic vitality, and GDP (gross domestic product).

In addition, our service model requires that we serve all customers in our territory. As a vertically integrated utility, we manage generation, transmission, and distribution. In other words, because we have to serve everyone and we have insight into how the entire system needs to function, we can plan in a way that enables us to optimize for reliability and affordability. We're essentially democratizing access to energy, which is not the same service model across the United States and is a nice access point for our customers.

As we continue to modernize our energy infrastructure, we'll also continue to see climate benefits. One of my key proof points is that the US utility sector has already reduced actual emissions by 40% relative to 2005.

Plenty of people would argue that the pace of our transformation is too fast. How it happens is complex, involving physics, ideology, and costs. We need to balance all those factors.

For me, the opportunity is to find common ground with a variety of stakeholders and figure out how to optimize our business and messaging around these interests. We, as a function, need to balance clearly articulating who we are and what challenges we face.

One tactical way we do that is through integrated resource plans and stakeholder engagement, which is part and parcel of that. These are filed in the jurisdictions where we operate and identify our planning and recommendations for the next ten or 15 years of operating our system. We then invite stakeholders to provide us with their perspective.

Tabita Andersson: You mentioned earlier that one of the key aspects of the CCO role and function is building trust, and what you just mentioned sounds like a really good way to build trust in your brand. What are some other ways you build trust with your specific stakeholders?

Katherine Neebe: First, trust fundamentally starts with transparency, and it's very hard to establish trust if you're not transparent. It helps that we have integrated resource plans, but we also have our annual impact report, climate report, and climate resilience plans. We're very forward-leaning in the amount of information we disclose as a utility company, both in what we're mandated to disclose and in our voluntary disclosures. It's an area of real pride for Duke Energy over the last decade, since well before I joined the company. Being incredibly transparent is important.

Second, we need to identify where interests start to collide and compete, so we're clear about what we need to solve as a company and then make it clear to our stakeholders where their input would be addressed and where the tensions and trade-offs exist.

Third, being real, using real language, being accessible, and not being afraid to go into a room and address the hard stuff, rather than avoiding a topic, matters. In corporate America, there's often a reluctance to talk to people who disagree. At Duke Energy and some other organisations I've worked for, we have prioritized sitting down in a room with people who will disagree with us. That's where the magic is unlocked.

Tabita Andersson: Is this a trend in communications? For a decade or two, PR and communications professionals tended to be positive and always said glowing things. Are more organisations moving toward a more open, authentic, and transparent communication tone?

Katherine Neebe: I don't know if it's a trend so much as something essential to communicating in today's world. People today often get information from their neighbors or friends rather than directly from traditional media, and often more informally or casually. The more leaders and communicators can identify how information flows and then show up in those spaces in a way that humanizes the company, the more effective we'll be.

Tabita Andersson: What other trends in the communications function do you see that will propel us forward?

Katherine Neebe: The way people consume information is evolving rapidly. They're not just going to their friends and neighbors, but social media, podcasts, and short-form videos are such powerful tools. These are not necessarily revolutionary; it's more of a natural evolution of how people consume content.

In addition, people's attention spans are getting shorter, and the timeline to respond and be heard is tighter. The opportunity for a communications professional is to figure out how to tell a story in a 15-second soundbite rather than a 150-page report, whether that's a video or a tweet, and to get it out there quickly.

With that said, there's an inherent tension we need to balance. Transparency and trust go hand in hand. On the one hand, there's a need to publish and disclose fulsome information. On the other hand, you need to figure out how to match that with the soundbite approach. Hence, the information is digestible and targeted to the audience segment, be it the customer, investor, or employee.

Tabita Andersson: How about artificial intelligence? How has AI impacted your role so far, and will we be able to use technology to our advantage to improve our function in the future?

Katherine Neebe: AI will play a huge role in transforming corporate communications. I'm excited about the potential to eliminate some of the drudgery of our jobs and move us toward a more strategic place where we have more capacity to add the intelligence of the human brain to our work.

For example, I often struggle with the first draft of a document or a statement. If I can get AI to help me overcome that initial hurdle, which can be a time sink, I can get to a place where I can improve it and make it stronger much more quickly. I also think about how much time a communications professional can spend analyzing data, such as employee comments on a survey. Now we can leverage AI to analyze in minutes, so that we can spend the time instead to develop and implement the strategic communications plan.

Every technological advancement, however, has its pros and cons. As communications professionals, we must consider leveraging these advancements' strengths to enhance and improve our jobs. At the same time, we need to be mindful of some of the pitfalls companies may face when using AI. That will be important.

Uniquely for the energy sector, AI is driving a lot of demand. We have shifted as a company from being a utility you don't often think about to being front and centre in the news. People want to understand how our company and sector are meeting the explosive energy demands to serve AI and data centres, as well as all other economic developments. AI, for us, is not just going to help internally in communications; it's also transforming our company.

Tabita Andersson: How can you make the best of that as an opportunity for communications to prove its value?

Katherine Neebe: You use the word value, which is interesting because, in the United States, energy has been reliable and affordable for decades, and it's been a hugely important component of society. However, when people walk into a room and switch on a light or charge a device, they don't think twice about all the magic behind making that simple thing happen. Unlike other sectors, we do not provide a product people can hold in their hands. We need to think through how we articulate that value when we're not always top of mind for people. Even now, when we appear in the media more often, we need to translate those headlines into the value customers receive from us.

Tabita Andersson: What are some of the tactics you would use to do that?

Katherine Neebe: We typically use research, polling, and focus groups to understand how we resonate today with our residential consumers. We also sit down with our larger industrial customers to understand what energy mix they need and how they think about their company's growth. This means we need a lot of stakeholder engagement. We can then refine all these insights and evolve our work based on what we see from data, such as net promoter score (NPS) or media quality scores (MQS).

Tabita Andersson: You touched on NPS scores. How about measuring what we do in communications? How do you measure what you do at Duke Energy, and how do you think we can improve going forward?

Katherine Neebe: Measurement is so important to me, and it's another area where I've brought some perspective from my previous roles.

I consider measurements in three categories: input, output, and impact. I would argue that in the communications function, like so many others, it is easiest to measure input, that is, how many press releases did we issue in one year? In terms of output, we'd look at how many times that press release was picked up, whether it was covered in the news, and how many impressions it generated. Then, to measure impact, we examine whether that coverage fundamentally changed hearts and minds about an issue or cause related to the corporate brand. However, my holy grail is to find measurements that indicate whether we fundamentally changed a behavior if that's what we were trying to achieve. And did they change behavior in the right or wrong way?

Measurement takes a lot of professional courage because there can be fear around doing something wrong or making a mistake. In my experience, many professionals don't want to know if their projects failed or had the wrong results. They're wary of measuring in the first place. Creating space for people to look at the data, however you measure it, to understand what's working and what's not. Not to name and shame but to learn and understand what to do more or less of, and to test new opportunities. This is where social media and other methods, like communications audits, can be helpful, as you can check and adjust more frequently and in a less costly way.

Tabita Andersson: I agree. We want to see the real impact and whether there was a behavior change. That can often be quite difficult because people aren't always rational. We don't always make decisions based on what we read from the communications department!

Katherine Neebe: Oh yes, and I have a great example from my previous roles: people will fill out surveys all day long saying they are willing to pay more for something with certain environmental or social attributes, but when they get to the store, they pick the brand they know at the price they can afford!

Tabita Andersson: Let's talk about the structure of your team. How is your communications team structured, and what functions sit underneath you?

Katherine Neebe: We have an internal/external communications function focused on C-suite support, our senior management committee, social media, and business areas like human resources and legal.

A second area is jurisdictional public affairs and communications. As a utility, we're part of the fabric of our local communities, where we operate with frontline workers, so we must be engaged with the state-level policies driving our move forward. A big focus for this team is the stakeholder engagement and communications needed at the state level.

A third area is focused on business operations and crisis communications. This team focuses on how we operate our systems, communicate with our customers, and respond to storms or other crises.

Finally, we have a brand and creative function, including an in-house creative agency leading advertising and promotional design.

Tabita Andersson: As you own internal communications, do you believe it can contribute to organisational culture?

Katherine Neebe: We have a new CEO, Harry Sideris, who has just stepped in, and he has been pushing us to think through what we refer to as a circle of success, where an engaged employee leads to a satisfied customer, which leads to a connected stakeholder, which leads to invested shareholders. Having an employee who understands our strategy, where we're going, and their role in advancing the business is fundamental to our success. When I think about internal communications, particularly when our industry and company are in a growth phase with a lot pulling at us, we must be able to provide employees not just with what they need to know, such as HR deadlines. We also need to paint a picture for them about where we're going as a company and how their role aligns with helping drive company success.

Tabita Andersson: You mentioned you've got a new CEO. What advice would you give to a CEO about how to work most effectively with a communications function and the CCO role?

Katherine Neebe: I will go back to transparency and honesty. I need a CEO to tell me what they want from corporate communications. I need them to be honest with me about where they believe the company is going, its strengths and opportunities, and where they see themselves in the discussion. Do they want a big public persona? Or do they want a more behind-the-scenes role?

As a corporate communications professional, it's my responsibility to understand where and how the CEO wants to be positioned, where they want to take the company, and to be a strong thought partner. I need to sit down and provide a perspective from my seat on where I see the opportunities, too.

Tabita Andersson: What is the role of the CCO as part of the executive leadership team? Where can it provide the most value?

Katherine Neebe: Corporate communications is one of a company's or enterprise's most fundamental, external-facing arms. Many people within a company are engaged with various audiences, but corporate communications touches almost all of them, almost all the time. As a result, we have the best sense for where our stakeholder groups are at a given moment, what they care about and what they're asking us to do. Our role is to be a voice for those communities in the boardroom, to bring their perspective forward.

We also must be able to challenge our business partners in how they think about the business today and how they can think about it tomorrow. By the nature of our role, we see around corners in a way that many other functions, just by nature of their work, don't. That enables us to share where our stakeholders are today and uncover the blind spots that various leaders may not see, so that a company can navigate successfully.

Finally, our role in a crisis is essential. For example, as a utility with operations in Florida and the Carolinas, we deal with severe weather and hurricanes. We need to help our customers prepare in advance and let them know what they can expect once the storm has passed. But it's more than storms, we are also continually advising our senior leaders about how we can successfully prepare for and, if needed, navigate other crises, and whether there's a need for speed for additional information or something else we can advocate for effectively.

Tabita Andersson: Would you mind elaborating on crisis communications? This is often when communications get brought in and where we can prove value. We can also greatly impact how an organisation navigates and works through that crisis. What's your experience?

Katherine Neebe: I've been fortunate that we've not yet had a major enterprise-wide crisis since I stepped into this role, but I've appreciated how prepared we are. I've already sat down in maybe a dozen meetings where someone has walked me through the playbook for various scenarios, and these playbooks are not sitting on a dusty shelf or in a drawer. Our playbooks are continually updated and refreshed, so we're prepared for whatever may come.

As we touched on governance, one of the measures we have in place is a Crisis Management Team that is stood up as soon as something significant happens. This team includes our senior management committee members (our CEO and his direct reports), plus me, so I'm automatically in the room when something happens.

Tabita Andersson: That is so beneficial because you can help immediately with a strategy rather than being brought in at the last minute, being asked to do something when you haven't got the full picture, making it difficult to put forward the best approach.

Katherine Neebe: You touch on something so important for corporate communications. I talk a lot about trust with our external stakeholders, but trust with our internal business partners is also essential. Being brought in early and often is important to the success of the communications function and the whole enterprise. We can help a company think through the early phases, provide feedback and an external lens and then evolve the strategy and tactics to respond in real time. And it doesn't have to be a crisis; we need to be brought in early in discussions about any issue. This is where we can add a lot of value and insight, as the business is trying to figure out what to do, if we're doing anything differently, or changing something.

Tabita Andersson: What are some of the other factors that contribute to success in these situations?

Katherine Neebe: Listening, not telling, is an important success factor. Operating from a place of no judgment is another. And then, having a plan.

If you're brought in early, you don't need to arrive automatically with a plan, but knowing where you're going once you've aligned on a direction and then executing against a plan is essential. It helps keep the work strategic and advances what we do, and it stays out of the tactics, which are important but only when they're part of a larger, strategic plan.

Tabita Andersson: It's so easy for everyone to see the tactics. They see the CEO's email go out or the press release being issued, but the strategic piece behind planning isn't necessarily as visible, which is a shame because it's so important.

Katherine Neebe: Yes, and that's a challenge for the communications function, which I've observed from my previous work. Everyone communicates all the time, so it's easy to think you're conversant in a professional function's tools, tactics, and strategies. For the corporate communicator, there's an opportunity to appreciate people's insight and perspective on how we need to do our jobs, but also make sure that we as professionals carve out the space for ourselves to execute because we have much more expertise to bring forward.

I'm not the only one who, in a previous role, has said, "Well, why don't we just do a tweet?" The team has always been so nice about saying, "That's a great idea. How about taking a step back and looking at what we want to achieve before we do that?"

Tabita Andersson: As communications professionals, we need to bring that solutions-focused attitude when we work with such a range of internal and external stakeholders, which brings me to my next question. What are some of the skills and attributes that are necessary for communicators to be successful today?

Katherine Neebe: A strong communicator needs to eliminate jargon and corporate language. They need to look at what's available to glean insight from research, or figure out if we need to go out and do work to gain better insight to inform our plans. They need to be students of the business. By that, I mean they need to have or build strong professional, business, financial, and social acumen. They need to understand how a business operates, makes money, executes its strategy and be conversant in the enterprise strengths, weaknesses, opportunities, and threats. They need to establish relationships with key internal partners and have a bank of friends and mentors to reach out to. Many of the issues we need to navigate are complex, so having perspectives inside and outside the company is critical.

Then, there's the basics. They need to be strong writers and speakers. They need to understand how to reduce a complex topic from a 45-second soundbite to a 10-second soundbite. They need to know when to challenge and when to execute. In today's polarized landscape, they should understand when to be nuanced about topics, to make sure it's landing appropriately and how it positions the company on the more controversial topics in a way that suits the company.

Tabita Andersson: Your last point might be tricky for someone who has recently moved into a CCO role and works at an executive level for the first time. What advice would you give to someone in that position?

Katherine Neebe: This is where I benefited from having the background I have because I was already working in a space where issues were intractable and where there were a lot of different opinions and biases. Many companies in that situation would ignore, refute, or not speak on issues, but I got very comfortable with people internally and externally having a different opinion from mine. It's natural for reasonable people to disagree. It can be uncomfortable for a company or a leader to navigate, but this only underscores how essential the corporate communications function is.

It's also incredibly important for a CCO to help right-size how big of a story an external controversy or campaign really is to leadership. Often, there is an opportunity to explain how big and wide a story is, what's breaking through the noise vs. what's staying in a bubble.

Tabita Andersson: What advice would you give to younger communications professionals who aspire to become CCOs?

Katherine Neebe: I mentioned it before, first become a keen student of business to understand how the organisation makes money, how it makes its products, and what its customers want and expect and so on. It's incredibly difficult to communicate if you don't understand the fundamentals.

Second, be comfortable with managing through ambiguity.

Third, bring solutions. It doesn't have to be the right solution, but be the problem solver, not the problem maker.

Finally, people younger than me in their careers communicate very differently. They use an entirely different language from what I'm using and are on different channels. For example, I've learned that my emojis are no longer the cool ones to use. This is an opportunity for the younger professional where they can add real value. And I think it's important to gain that confidence earlier in your career to give you insights and a window into a world that more seasoned professionals don't even know exists. Bringing those ideas forward will help advise the company or non-profit about how they can think about the development of the overall function over time.

Tabita Andersson: You touch on the difference between generations in terms of how we communicate and consume content, which is very different. I hear many communicators talk about the issues, but they do not necessarily do much. Is this a challenge you're facing too, or are you already ahead of the crowd here?

Katherine Neebe: A bit of both, if that's a fair answer! The way people communicate and consume information and their tools constantly evolve, so I don't believe anyone can be ahead of it. You're just trying to keep pace and understand what's relevant so you can choose the strategies, tools, and tactics you want to leverage. At the same time, we've done a lot of work as a company and in our communications function to improve. It's exciting to see how we're researching all these new ways of communicating; they're not even new anymore!

For example, we had hurricanes Helene and Milton in 2024, which was an unprecedented and incredibly tough hurricane season. We put our communications team out in the field, wearing hard hats and protective gear alongside our lineworkers, and did live videos as we were rebuilding and restoring power. They were telling the story visually in fast sound bites, not only talking about the important work we were doing to restore the power system in the wake of a devastating hurricane, but also telling the story with a visual behind it, which was so powerful. By leveraging short-form video and social media, we moved quickly and humanized the company, highlighting our frontline heroes. Then, we leveraged all the different channels to ensure we were reaching our customers where they were getting information, so they could appreciate the work underway to respond in the wake of the storm. We received a lot of kudos for that approach.

Tabita Andersson: That must also have been powerful internally, showing employees across the organisation what was happening on the front lines.

Katherine Neebe: It did so much to shine a light on heroic work, and there's so much pride in this company when we're responding to our communities. Seeing it, talking about it, and amplifying it inspired employees during a long stretch of hard work.

Tabita Andersson: What do you think the future of communications will look like, and how will it differ from today?

Katherine Neebe: I wish I were a futurist who could tell you exactly how it will look in ten or 20 years! I know it will look different! Part of that is because the energy sector is transforming rapidly, and our company is keeping pace with immense change. Hence, communications has to partner with the business and evolve alongside it. As the company moves forward, we're moving from being a utility company quietly providing power behind the scenes to an important and exciting part of the next chapter of energy modernization. As a result, we as communicators must evolve as the industry and the company evolve.

Tabita Andersson: What would you like to be remembered for as your legacy at Duke Energy?

Katherine Neebe: A culture of transformation. Here at Duke Energy, we provide reliable, resilient, affordable energy to power the economy of today and tomorrow in a way that will decarbonize the energy system and grow the local economy through jobs, supply chain, and so on. This is a story of the transformation of a company, but it's also a story of the transformation of society in a positive way.

When I think about any team I've led at Duke Energy, ensuring that everyone understands and sees themselves in this story benefits not just for them and the company but it's also brilliant for our communities. I'd like to be remembered for being part of that story of transformation and helping everyone take pride and be engaged in what we're doing.

CHAPTER

21

Christian Stein
Chief Communications Officer Renault Group

Christian Stein is the **Chief Communications Officer** for **Renault Group**. Strengthened by its unique expertise in electrification, Renault Group comprises four complementary brands—Renault, Dacia, Alpine, and Mobilize—offering its customers sustainable and innovative mobility solutions. Established in over 130 countries, the Group sold 2.235 million vehicles in 2023. It employs more than 105,000 people who embody its purpose every day, so that mobility brings people closer.

For more information about Renault Group, visit renaultgroup.com.

Christian's LinkedIn profile: linkedin.com/in/christian-stein-b698344/

Tabita Andersson: As Renault Group's relatively new Chief Communications Officer (CCO), can you describe your journey to the role?

Christian Stein: This is my first CCO role in a publicly listed company, and I've held most jobs across sales, marketing, and communications in an automotive company.

The first part of my career was in the Peugeot sales and marketing team, working across different roles in different countries, including five years in retail. After that, I moved to a global role with SEAT (VW Group), where I first handled the global marketing role before moving to the global communications and public affairs job. When our CEO at the time left the company, I rapidly followed and landed as head of communications for the brands here at Renault. My next role was responsible for product and customer experience at Ampere, a subsidiary of Renault dedicated to EV cars. Finally, I was called on to take the global CCO job for the Renault Group in September 2024.

In my current role, I oversee all the internal and external communications activities of the group and its brands in France and across the globe.

Although I'm a French national, my experience is almost exclusively outside of France. Up to 2020, I spent many years in Belgium, Spain, and the UK, which gave me great international exposure. In the automotive industry, communications tends to be related to the country and origin of the company, so having global experience is unusual. The other aspect of my experience is the wide sales, marketing, and retail expertise I've built, which has been extremely useful as, ultimately, the customer pays our salary!

Tabita Andersson: What are the benefits of a dual sales/marketing and communications role? What advantages does that bring to the company?

Christian Stein: There are several advantages. First, when you work in sales and marketing, you are very close to the business on a day-to-day basis, so you get a great understanding of all activities that are taking place. The automotive sector is not the simplest, regardless of where you work, whether in engineering, manufacturing, procurement, or sales. It's more complex than many other sectors.

Even when a company in the automotive sector is not the biggest in the world, you still have to integrate the full value chain, and every part of that value chain is a world in itself. You always face engineering, manufacturing, procurement, and human resource aspects. Each company has blue- and white-collar workers worldwide, and there are different aspects within each country where it operates. Each activity in itself requires a specialist. When you work in communications, you're supposed to communicate about anything relevant and worthwhile that stems from the company. This means you can't be a specialist in everything, but you need to be extremely open and curious and understand your business well. Having a background in sales and marketing doesn't give you all the skills or all the knowledge you need, but at least it gives you a good understanding of what's happening in the field, what customers look like, and how the company is profitable.

Second, by nature, you need to work on long-term plans in marketing, but that's not always the case in communications. It can be much more reactive. When a crisis or news item appears, you need to be able to flex and react. However, that's just one part of the communications job. Simultaneously, you need to be able to set a strategy for the long term and adapt plans regularly.

Having a marketing background helps because you're good at defining a long-term strategy, and it gives you a good understanding of marketing. Marketing and communications go together in some companies, typically not retail-oriented and often in the business-to-business sector. In the automotive sector, we have strong advertising power and very specific press, so for me, it's better to split them out because owned, earned, and paid media are very different channels. We need to speak together, but have clear swim lanes. This is where it helps having a mixed background because you understand the goals for activities on both sides and how to adapt and align with each other.

Tabita Andersson: You mentioned that the automotive sector is very complex, so you also have to work with many stakeholders. How do you build a company's reputation in such a disparate environment?

Christian Stein: There are so many ways to build a reputation. The first thing is to measure it properly, so you know what to focus on. If you're a good communicator, you measure the impact of the articles we get, PR values, tone of voice, share of voice, and so on. Nevertheless, those metrics don't give you the coverage's impact on reputation. In some cases, you might have a nice article, but it does not impact reputation.

The reputation of the company goes beyond the brand image. In the automotive sector, the brand image is related to business activities and products. When you try to impact the company's reputation, you must move beyond speaking to only clients and speak to a wider range of stakeholders. For example, we have unions, investors, analysts, and students with whom we need to build trust, and impact is measured on many more topics than just the pure image of the product. It includes your executives' credentials, attractiveness as an employer, innovation skills, and so on. It's important to identify the most relevant stakeholders to your business.

Once you have clarity on your objectives, you need to define the strategy for reaching those objectives. That's a precise job because an automotive company has so many assets. We could easily have news to communicate every day, but that would be information overload, so we need to select the type of news and products that nurture and feed our strategy.

Then, it comes down to storytelling. Your story needs to be supported by facts because one of our main targets is the press, and reporters love facts and figures for their stories.

In summary, with today's wide variety of stakeholders, you need a clear storytelling approach with the right facts and figures and a 360-degree perspective.

Being nimble and capable of speaking to different target audiences is also important in this environment. Today, in the automotive industry, the classical target is the press, and we have two types of press to work with. On one side, it's the corporate economic press; on the other, it's the traditional product press. Beyond that, we now have influencers discussing the product, its green credentials, and technology. Some of these are as influential for us as journalists. This means we must include social networking and influencers in our strategy. LinkedIn, for example, is probably the best and preferred channel for us because many of the audiences and influencers we want to reach are present, and it still feels like a safe harbor because it's less political than some of the other social networks.

All in all, building a reputation is a puzzle with many pieces! We increasingly see the trend of personalization, which means companies talk directly to individuals rather than groups. We are lucky to have a very charismatic CEO keen to communicate. Still, we can't rely just on him, so we're also developing a network of expert spokespeople within the company, which we are using increasingly. We create individual communications plans for each of them, targeting engineering, manufacturing, and different brands to ensure we spread the message in line with our overall strategy.

Tabita Andersson: As we've seen with some high-profile examples, negative press or opinions can quickly impact a company's reputation. This is often where communications and CCOs can help guide their companies—would you agree?

Christian Stein: It's true that a reputation can be impacted very quickly and spread very widely via social media today. If we go back 25 years, you could handle situations properly via a few key printed publications. This is no longer true. Today, opinions can come from anywhere, and the smallest news one day can become the biggest news three days later. This is why we now have a well-organized monitoring system where we look for signals if something might be happening, and we can prepare for it should it blow up.

Communications professionals need to develop their skills in crisis monitoring and market watching. These are crucial in our jobs. Building a reputation takes time, but it can be smashed quickly.

Also, you need to keep pace and direction. If you have a long-term strategy and vision, you need to be capable of adapting to the crisis you might have at hand, and jump the hurdles you might encounter on the way, but you need to stick to your path and your direction.

Tabita Andersson: You mentioned handling a crisis is a good skill for a communications professional to develop. What are some of the other skills and attributes the younger generation of communications professionals needs to develop to thrive in their roles?

Christian Stein: First, handling crises, which require skills related to understanding data. You need to quickly understand what the social networks are telling you. This means understanding the words, of course, but also the behaviors of people and the benchmarks for where you currently stand and where you can move toward. This new skill has become more crucial in the last few years.

A more traditional skill is absorbing a lot of information and explaining it clearly to your target audiences. For example, a press officer needs to understand the company well enough to explain news and information clearly to the press.

In addition, we need communications professionals who can write stories that can be used in multiple formats and channels. Once you've set the overall strategy, you need to build many stories. Historically, we needed communicators who understood all the company assets and could deliver a clear message. Today, we've moved from messages to stories. We've also moved to different channels, which require different formats.

Recently, here at Renault, we entered a new world: documentaries. This is something we've never done before. Currently, Amazon worldwide is streaming a documentary of four episodes, each lasting 40 minutes. To do this, we had to let the cameras into our organisation to see what's happening. We captured some good news, some great moments, but also tough negotiations or simply sad moments, which tick so many boxes for us because they show the real story behind closed doors. In the automotive industry, this is a first. We've never seen a documentary like this, where many of our employees worldwide are interviewed. There were risks, of course, because we let the cameras in unfiltered, but after two years of shooting, the documentary is now out and I'm very proud of it.

We often talk about digital formats, but it's a false statement because everything now is digital. As communicators, we need to understand the differences between channels. Instagram doesn't do the same job as LinkedIn, for example. Those are the key new skills we need to have beyond crisis understanding and monitoring. We need storytellers and people capable of handling different channels and adapting the story to each channel. For example, video and image content is often stronger than words. You still need the words because the press needs to write their story, so you still need a strong press release that helps you keep the story consistent, and if you move too quickly toward the visual content, without aligning with the strategy and story, it's easy to make mistakes. It all must align. It pays off to take the time to develop everything carefully because when it's out, it's out, and you can't change anything. It takes a lot of effort to correct something once it's been published, so it's much better to take the time up front.

Tabita Andersson: That touches on the point of protecting a brand. How do you protect a strong, iconic brand like Renault in a world where stories can appear anytime, anywhere?

Christian Stein: I greatly advocate for this within our company. The key is getting the internal information as early as possible. Of course, you can't plan or forecast everything, but you can anticipate much more than you think if you go right back to the source of information.

One of our challenges is ensuring we're embedded in projects as soon as possible. Sometimes, the perception about communications is that we handle the press; therefore, there's a fear that if we tell communications about something, the press will know. This is an urban legend! If there's a leak, the communications person is the first to be in a very awkward and uncomfortable position, since they don't have an answer. The last people in the company who want to have a leak are the communicators! People might still think this is how things happen, so unfortunately, they may be tempted not to share information, making our jobs more difficult. I spend a lot of time explaining that the sooner we are part of a project, whether positive or a crisis, the better we can be prepared. I have to say we have made a lot of progress on that matter at Renault.

The best way to protect a company's reputation is to prepare and anticipate what might come. A lot of this work is completely invisible to the rest of the company and those outside, because a good crisis is the crisis that nobody saw. This happens a lot; they may not be big scandals, but small things that you want to be presented in a specific way or not covered at all. Our job is in anticipation and preparation. It's about identifying the right stakeholders inside the company, crafting the right story, and defining the right communication channels. That's classic crisis communications and management.

To best protect your company's reputation, you also need to be reactive because threats can come from everywhere, inside and outside an organisation, and at any time. The key is to have good news to communicate regularly and sometimes go beyond what you've planned. The more you show openness, the better your chances are for setting a positive tone for your story. It's not a mathematical equation, and if you have a problem, you have a problem, but the market is sometimes more forgiving when something happens if you've been open first.

When I arrived at Renault, one of the first things I advocated for was to open our doors to show how we work, where we work, and the projects we are working on. Sometimes you need to embargo news, but transparency and sharing as much as possible about strategy progressively creates a positive environment, and you will be rewarded for that openness. That's the way to build a great reputation. Press and influencers are keen to understand where you're coming from and where you're heading, and they will help you improve your reputation if you open the books.

Tabita Andersson: Your documentary is a great example of opening the books and letting media in. I once worked with a CEO known for physically removing the doors from his office to illustrate the openness with which they wanted to operate.

You mentioned earlier that being brought in early on a project is very important. Is this easier as a CCO because you're in the boardroom with the rest of the C-suite when decisions are discussed and agreed on?

Christian Stein: Communication is not just one way. I'm a strong advocate for being a strategic partner. On the one hand, there's the way communications can help build the story that everyone must tell, but on the other, there's also the communication strategy that needs to be nurtured by each stakeholder.

I've seen many communicators being service deliverers rather than strategic partners. Of course you need to be close to the CEO; however, you have to start from the company strategy, then build a communications strategy that's shared with your peers, demonstrating how you will communicate the key pillars of the strategy, and then how you're going to nurture all the different activities that are going on within the company. That way, you can successfully position communications on an eye-to-eye basis with your partners. After that, you need to help them.

For example, I have an executive communications business partner who helps all executives with their social media handles. We provide them with the right media and social media training, and we do so with the end goal and company strategy in mind.

Tabita Andersson: You've mentioned your CEO a couple of times and how important it is to work closely together. What advice would you give a CEO about best practices for working with their CCO?

Christian Stein: First, you need good chemistry. You don't need to be the best of friends, but you need some professional and personal chemistry because you spend a lot of time together, whether in interviews, event preparation, etc. You need to have a good understanding of each other.

Second, the role of the CCO is no longer just handling situations when something has gone wrong; there's also a positive, proactive side that amplifies what's being done in the company. This is especially true in the retail world, where you have a lot of impact on the final customer.

Third, you have the defense role, which is part of the CCO's job. Today, in a world where people trust less media or online information, they need to be able to find the facts. They need stories and transparency. In this environment, the role of communications will become more important. To achieve this positive role and contribute to building the company's reputation, you need to access information in the first place. That's why it's important to be a part of the C-suite.

At the same time, you need to gain the trust of your CEO so they are comfortable sharing information beyond the facts. To do that effectively, you need to show them that you understand their convictions and vision, which may not necessarily be finalized, but you need to understand where the CEO wants to head. I'm not saying you need to be aware of all the confidential projects—that's up to the discretion of the CEO—but you need to have trust, an open mind, and open books to make sure that communications isn't by mistake going in one direction when the company is going in the other direction. Transparency and trust between the CEO and CCO can become real assets to the company.

Tabita Andersson: How can we continue to elevate the CCO role and ensure that communications as a function is solidified at that level?

Christian Stein: This might not be the same for all sectors; however, first, it's a shared understanding that the role of communications is beyond the traditional activities of internal messages and press releases. It handles the company's storytelling and all the related channels. If I list all the touchpoints we have today, beyond the classic ones like having a salesperson in the dealership meeting a client, sending out a press release about a product launch, or being present at a conference, that list goes way beyond, and we could end up with 20-30-40 touch points that we must be aware of. You need to ensure that the story and messaging across all these touchpoints align with the company strategy and are consistent with what you want to say.

I'm working hard to elevate communications by being a hub of information inside and out. Because there are too many touchpoints, it's impossible to achieve 100% alignment to ensure message consistency, but you need to put everything in place and have a good view of what's happening.

Tabita Andersson: How has artificial intelligence (AI) impacted what you and your team are doing?

Christian Stein: It's a game of two halves! First, Renault is very advanced. Thanks to AI, we almost have a digital twin of the company. In our industry, machines are connected, which enables us to analyze activities and issues in real time. Sometimes AI is used, falsely in my opinion, to refer to big data. For example, machines can quickly analyze a vast amount of data and draw conclusions. AI makes the process faster and more intelligent, but it's not the same as big data.

Second, we have generative AI, which is capable of helping much further. For example, in design, you can help design a car or generate design ideas much faster.

We are currently exploring different ways of using AI in communications. An example could be when we launch a car. We will see coverage in the media worldwide. Having an AI tool to easily input all the articles and mentions would mean we could generate a summary of all the data in just a few minutes in an easy-to-understand format.

We are also looking at ways of using AI to become more efficient. We are heavy users of Microsoft PowerPoint, and AI might help us improve our use of the tool. We haven't started using AI to draft press releases or articles yet. We've tested it, but I'm not in a hurry because, in my opinion, machines will not replace talent. I want to regard AI as a help for the team, not a replacement. I'm prepared to optimize costs by having AI do jobs that can be cumbersome, for example, when creating a video or a series of social media posts. But there's still a lot we need to learn, and we have completely embraced the learning journey by standing up AI Captains within the team who train others to spread the skills.

Tabita Andersson: If you had a crystal ball and could see into the future, how would the communications function have changed in ten years?

Christian Stein: I don't know whether it will completely change. I've had a long enough career and heard many gurus tell me that we won't have any dealers in five years and will only sell cars online. This has been said every five years for the last 25 years, and we still have dealers that sell cars!

Whatever happens, human relationships will remain key to communications. The fact that we are already very much AI-oriented doesn't mean we don't speak to each other. Building a strategy, crafting the messaging, and handling a crisis remain based on people, relationships, and discussions. This will remain the case, and perhaps even be reinforced, in the future.

AI may remove many basic tasks, so we can focus on more interesting activities. This could mean that the communications of tomorrow is reinforced in terms of storytelling, channel management, reactivity, and people management, inside and out. As a result, the technology and training of AI might just increase the role of the human being. We need to know how to use technology so it can be effective, and we need to know how to differentiate. Technology is accessible to everybody. Humans are unique. Therefore, I believe tomorrow's communications department will rely even more on people and storytelling. With the multiplication of stakeholders, we need to be able to reach more people outside the company, so we still need people in the communications team.

I hope this is how it will be because that's one of the reasons I like the job. I prefer to manage people rather than machines! It's not easy every day, but as a leader, you can make a difference to people, and that's a pleasure.

Tabita Andersson: What would you advise an upcoming CCO who's new in the role?

Christian Stein: Your personal credibility is extremely important. It's so easy for employees to look at the CCO as sitting in an ivory tower, only spending time with the CEO on strategic topics, and not understanding the business, so building professional credibility is important. For example, even though I have a sales and marketing background, I'm very interested in understanding the technology and manufacturing sides of our business, so I can talk to my peers and advise them on how to look at different communications issues in their respective areas.

More than anything, communications is a people business. Be interested in people and help them grow. Don't be scared of the people who want to take your place because they are easier to manage; you always need to prepare for the next steps anyway.

Stay curious, which is hard because we're time-poor, but stay open to everything and understand what's happening in the world so you don't become outdated. Everything is moving quickly, so I like having young people around me to keep me on my toes!

CHAPTER

22

Kate Humphreys
Chief Communications Officer Banijay

Kate Humphreys is the **Chief Communications Officer** for **Banijay Entertainment and Banijay Live** (BNJ.AS). Launched in 2008, content powerhouse Banijay Entertainment, with Banijay Live, is home to over 130 production companies across 23 territories and has a catalogue of over 200,000 hours of content. The business represents some of the biggest global brands, including Survivor, Big Brother, Peaky Blinders, MasterChef, Black Mirror, Deal or No Deal, and Temptation Island. In 2024, the collective companies reached €3.3bn in revenues.

For more information about Banijay Entertainment and Banijay Live, visit Banijay.com.

Kate's LinkedIn profile: www.linkedin.com/in/kate-humphreys-884787a

Tabita Andersson: Although the Chief Communications Officer traditionally owns public relations for a company, sometimes we're not very good at doing public relations for our profession and role. How can we do this better, and what core value do we need to amplify?

Kate Humphreys: I've always sought to find businesses that believe in the value of communications from the outset. It's incredibly hard to permeate a business with communications and be successful without the buy-in and belief that communications is a vital pillar of the business. When you look at any corporate entity, there will always be a Chief Executive Officer, a Chief

Financial Officer, a Chief Human Resources Officer, a Chief Legal Officer, etc. Those are valuable roles an organisation can't be without, but communications often doesn't make it to the C-suite; it often stops at the director or head of level, depending on what type of business you're in. It's unusual to see the role being promoted into the C-suite, which gives you a sense of how undervalued it is as a function. I've been fortunate to work in businesses that believe in the value of communications, and even so, I've often had to come in and give leaders a sales pitch to start with.

A big part of the role is building trust with the leadership team you work with and the leaders for whom you're building a reputation, which they often value greatly. Building trust is one of our biggest tasks when you come into a new role, above all else. Yes, it's about how good you are with your network, how much you can push the company out there, and how ambitious you are about pushing the boundaries of what you can achieve. The biggest job is still building trust and relationships, becoming embedded with the board because that's where you're most often playing, depending on where in the business you sit.

In my role, I work with an executive team and senior executives worldwide. Yes, the first stepping stone is always the CEO, but then it's about building trust with everyone in the C-suite and the layer below, including any type of spokesperson within the business. This is often the biggest challenge for someone new to an organisation. It's about personality, but it's also about listening. Few people listen, which is the key.

I went through executive coaching last year, and it's one of the most invaluable tools any leader can use. Not only do you learn so much about yourself, but you also learn so much about the people you work with and how you can be better. Being the best you can be as a leader and a communicator is vital to building trust and positive PR for the role.

Sometimes people can have tunnel vision and a one-track relationship model, just homing in on certain topics or issues. It's easy to get into this model with C-suite leaders, especially CEOs who are often time-poor and whose door is not always as readily open. But you shouldn't overlook your relationship with various leaders and the information you can glean from them. I report to the Chief Strategy Officer, which is an interesting model because that person holds the keys to much information about the business. Leveraging your network internally ensures you get the information you need, which doesn't always have to be at the cost of the CEO's time, but rather in advance, so you're readily armed before you knock on their door.

Tabita Andersson: What is your advice to a CEO on best working with a CCO?

Kate Humphreys: Be transparent. We appreciate that a CEO needs to build trust before they can hit the ground running, so spend time building a two-way relationship. Spend time getting to know the person, be transparent and trusting. The only way it will work is if the CEO entrusts the CCO with the most confidential information, so they can be better prepared for what's coming down the track. It means you can be better prepared for any issue and be more entrepreneurial in how you do this job.

Often, people think they do "just communications." They write press releases, send them out, and make announcements. However, the communications strategy will be more effective if you can get under the company's bonnet, build a strategy, understand the finances, and get deep within the business. It means you can become a vital asset and an entrepreneur within your organisation.

After seven years here, I've got really strong relationships, I'm trusted with information, and I sit at a high table that I imagine some of my peers don't, depending on the CEO you're working with. The CEO has to be open to having you work as part of the central executive team.

Tabita Andersson: What advice would you give to the wider C-suite on how to best collaborate with the communications function?

Kate Humphreys: Everyone in an executive seat is a business partner to the communications function. Regular interaction and making an effort to spend time together is important. It's about information flow. The better the relationship, the better the information flow. You will get the information you need when you need it, and every project we work on together is much more effective because it becomes collaborative. It also typically means everyone listens better.

When I first started in communications, I worked in a multifunctional business-to-business agency, covering communications, marketing, and digital. I operated in a very traditional environment, writing press releases, letters to editors, thought pieces, etc. From there, I started in television and worked in two different studios, Warner Bros. and NBC Universal, before joining Banijay.

I've had a multifaceted career, covering everything from being a publicist to corporate communications, to doing events, and internal communications. Currently, I have a multifaceted role covering corporate communications, external communications, internal communications, event management, and social media. I don't do publicity anymore, but I understand the discipline well. Naturally, I've wanted to evolve my education, and I've always thrown myself into training to get better and learn new areas.

For example, we became publicly listed here two years ago, so the financial messaging became integral to the storytelling of the business and how we craft our news flow. I hadn't done much financial communications before entering this role. In this situation, you could put yourself on training courses, which I did, but ultimately, my best friend in the business, who can help in this situation, is the Chief Financial Officer. Having a great relationship with the

CFO means you can ask stupid questions! Building a relationship of trust is key, where you feel comfortable asking any question and know that the person is respectful of the fact that you are a partner and need to work closely on different types of projects, including building the financial narrative.

Again, it's about the relationship and leveraging those relationships when you need information so you can be the best you can, and deliver information in the best and most effective way. For example, I handle crisis communications regularly throughout the year. We produce reality TV, which naturally carries crisis communications under its hat. We're a global business and operate in many territories, which creates multiple crisis communications scenarios. In these situations, I need to partner very closely with our Chief Legal Officer, and again, if we already have a close relationship, in a fast-paced environment like ours, it means I can pick up the phone and get the answers I need quickly. It also means I have a good sounding board for how to best execute in a way that will safeguard the business. The same goes for when we have large events, and I'm preparing the CEO. I don't want to waste too much of his time on a briefing document that I can prepare with my boss, the Chief Strategy Officer, because they're plugged into every element of the strategy. It means when I take it to the CEO, it needs less time on his lap.

Tabita Andersson: You mentioned crisis communications is one of your key disciplines, and being in reality TV, it must give a whole other meaning to a crisis. Would you mind giving an overview of a crisis in your day-to-day work and why communications is so important to help manage those situations from a reputation and brand protection perspective?

Kate Humphreys: A lot of the work I do behind the scenes with our content teams and producers is about safeguarding. With a crisis comes prevention because you never want to find yourself in a crisis if you can help it. We do everything we can to avoid it.

Interestingly, this morning, I was looking at a welfare policy that had been put together by one of the content teams, and they asked for my input because I think about it from a different perspective. These types of policies run through my door before they are cemented. I don't draft them, that's done by a combination of our content or HR teams, but I play a role in overseeing all of them to ensure that they land in a way that could prevent us from a future catastrophe, particularly when you're dealing with reality TV where duty of care and behavioral management is key. We do a lot of work in this area, working on welfare pledges, codes of conduct, everything that can help you in the moment when you have to deal with those situations.

One public example that happened a few years ago, when I was working in a previous company, was about a reality TV show on Channel Four in the UK I woke up one morning and my phone was ringing off the hook. We had a plane crash while filming a series, and some of our crew were onboard. Two jets had already landed with our cast onboard, and thankfully, everyone survived by some miracle. Still, at the time, in the local environment, people were aware that we were filming on the ground and of the show's propensity in the UK, its reputation and wide reach. They also knew that lifeboats arriving on shore with crew would make for pictures that would sell globally, and they could make money from the footage. In that situation, you have an escalation process and policy, which means that people know who to contact, how to write the email, and who needs to be notified, so we can quickly stand up a working group.

That's exactly what we did. We assembled a team of the Chief Operating Officer, the Head of Unscripted, and all the producers into one committee, then carved out roles and responsibilities. For me, that involved gathering as much information as quickly as possible. What was the status? What were we dealing with? Were there any casualties? What was the severity of any injuries? What was the rescue operation? I had to get to the crux of the situation as quickly as possible to craft a reactive, up-to-date statement. I needed to get that to the COO and approved by the producers. At that point, I was ready to go.

Phase two is increasingly important. You need to get the text right. First, in the internal note that goes to all affected teams, and the central team who are familiar with the people involved, because they're our employees and part of the team. Drafting that note and getting it out as quickly as possible is key so the team is aware of what's happening, but you also have to be prepared that the note can be leaked to the media, so it has to be reflective of the external statement. After that, it's hourly progress calls.

Because this was such a high-profile crisis, pictures started to land quickly, so we had to call national media to have faces blurred and ensure there was no way of identifying team members. We then had to work with Heathrow Airport to ensure that when they arrived back in the UK, they had VIP access so the cameras couldn't get to them, and they were all treated with respect. And that was just the start.

After the initial situation, you proceed to the legal investigations, resulting in more statements and releases. At this point, you must also decipher which information you will release publicly from the investigation. This means working closely with the lawyers to decide if and how information needs to be released to the public and how we can best safeguard people and the business throughout the process.

This is why we work so heavily on preventative guidelines, policies, and other measures: to explain to the business that we have these things in place and can learn from each situation. The preventative side of crisis communications is to keep calm and cool in the situation, leverage those relationships you've spent time building, and be a strong partner for everyone in the business who needs you at that time.

Tabita Andersson: That's a great example. You mention some of the attributes that are important in a crisis. What are some of the other skills and attributes that good communications professionals need to be effective in?

Kate Humphreys: Ultimately, it will depend on your industry. I'm in the entertainment industry, and you need to be personable and resilient in this sector. We're in a creative environment, meaning you must deal with certain personalities and characters, and sometimes you need to say no to strong people. It means you have to be resilient, robust, and personable.

You must be outgoing in this specific environment because it's all about relationships. One aspect of the job is to build relationships with journalists, to the point where you can WhatsApp them or reach them quickly when something happens, or you have news. It's about being outgoing, networking, and building new contacts. If you're an ambitious communications person within an ambitious, growing company like ours, you'll constantly look at new ways to promote the business in new areas, like new conferences or new press. Also, I work across the global landscape and do the same activities in many territories, embedding myself in cultures, new spaces, and pushing further boundaries. Entrepreneurship runs through our DNA; we're all entrepreneurial here and are constantly pioneering and innovating.

Being inquisitive and open to new technologies and routines is important. When I joined Banijay, we didn't have a communications team; it was all outsourced, so I had to be brave and bold and prove the value of what we do. I also started building a team. It was just me and an intern to start with. We then acquired Endemol Shine Group, a significant transaction and a large-scale takeover I hadn't done before. Because I'm unafraid to ask for help, I hired an external agency that I knew could support me in the areas where I didn't have the skillset and from there, I knew I could do it on my own. Nothing is worse than making an error in the moment if it could have been avoided if you'd resourced the project correctly. Once the transaction had gone through, I inherited some team members from Endemol, and our department grew.

I've now got a team of six people centrally, along with communications outposts around our major territories around the world, with whom I partner. The team has grown through ambition, and as I'm fortunate to be in an entrepreneurial business, it means there's no box to your role. I've worked in some businesses where there's a ring around your role, and that's it, that's your role, and you're not allowed to go outside that ring. As long as you execute the plan, there's no need to push anything further or build anything else outside your ring. In this role, I've done everything from supporting the ESG strategy to setting up our business-to-business social media accounts, which are now fully in action. I've worked on strategy documents and supported on capital market days. Each day here is different, and because it's so entrepreneurial, it allows me to be much more ambitious as I'm not confined to a traditional box. Many people often ask me what communications is and what we do. I always say it's everything no one else wants to do!

Tabita Andersson: That's such a great way of describing the role! How do you think the role will change in the future? What trends do you see heading our way?

Kate Humphreys: Being in an entrepreneurial business is good because it teaches you to be more entrepreneurial in your approach, and the reality is that we're in an environment that's changing rapidly. In my industry, for example, YouTube is now the best-watched platform beyond Disney+, Netflix, and all the other channels. As a business, we face change, and as a communicator, we face change. It means we have to be agile, multifaceted, and multifunctional. It's not enough to say you just do communications anymore. I've gone from doing corporate communications to doing publicity to trying a lot of other disciplines within PR and communications. That's taught me that being agile in this role is key because new technologies like AI are coming down the track.

People in creative roles are terrified of AI, but I regard it as an opportunity. I believe we should leverage new technology because it can enhance our work and save time on tasks. If you're writing five pitches for a publication, you could use AI to inform your pitch and have it help you do a good first draft, saving you time. We probably write about 50 press releases every year about different versions of our shows, from MasterChef to Big Brother, and I'm sure ChatGPT could pull the same synopsis as one of my team members would have written five years ago. It seems sensible to use Microsoft CoPilot or Chat GPT behind a subscription wall to drive efficiency, deliver more, and to be more strategic because you can focus your attention on strategy and thinking outside of the box or think bigger better when planning rather than having to focus on a basic day-to-day task such as writing a press release. AI can do a good first draft, but you still need to work on it; you need to include the new details because AI only works historically, but it's a great starting point.

People who are not open to new technology will be left behind. We all have to get better at knowing more about the social environment. Some people are specialists in social media, and I'll leave them to that specialism! I would hire for paid social or social media campaigns if I needed that specialism. I'm also not a specialist in creating content for YouTube, so that's another area I'd hire resources for if I needed it. Still, I have a good understanding of what those channels require to be successful, so I can lead the team effectively.

As CCOs, we must be agile, and the role will keep expanding and evolving. There will be new platforms and tools for communication and different ways to reach different audiences. I dislike it when people say, "Oh, but we've always done it like that." That's not good enough in today's environment. To be a good communicator, you have to change, and you have to be progressive. You can't just be a follower; you have to be a leader. A lot of this is about self-education. Finding and learning new tools, new technologies, listening and learning from people like our Head of Digital, who's all over the new stuff. Spending time and not being dismissive when someone knocks on your door and shows you something new. Explore the tool, get underneath the bonnet and find out what's best for your business and your team. Visit conferences, listen and learn from your peers, but never say this is how you've always done it!

Tabita Andersson: That's such great advice. What would you say to the younger generation of communications professionals who are just starting out and aspire to become a CCO one day?

Kate Humphreys: I was recently invited back to the first business I worked in to speak to their new team during Women's Day. It was a young, inquisitive team, and I advised them that finding the right business for them is very important. It's a bit like dating. You must try a few companies to find the one right for you. You have to be self-aware and learn what you're good at and bad at. We're all bad at something! For example, I always struggled with my attention to detail. That used to be a major drawback years ago. Also, learn what makes you tick, what makes you want to come to work and do your job, and what makes you wake up every morning excited to go to work. This is all part of the journey. Yes, you need to do the training, learning, and listening. You need to be the best partner you can be to these companies. You need to be ambitious, take opportunities, and take more space than you have. Sometimes it's about being in the right place and time, but learn everything you can in every environment.

In my first job, I was listening, learning, and getting to know everyone in the agency, working on different accounts, so that I would understand the accounts. If someone asked for additional hands for an event, even if it wasn't for one of my clients, I would always be the first to put my hand up. You need to take space, not just wait for space to be given, or wait for the promotions to come, expecting it to come because you've been with a company for ten years, and therefore, you're entitled to it. Be self-aware and understand what you've done to earn that promotion.

I dislike bringing it up, but sometimes we have to be more aggressive as women. We have to take up space because often, space isn't given to us. We have to take a promotion, work hard, put our heads down, fight for it, and ask for it. Many of us as women have been affected by impostor syndrome at various levels over the years. Executive coaching taught me how to overcome it and avoid it when I feel it starting to creep in, as well as how to promote myself. It's not just about promoting the company you work for; it's about promoting yourself and being confident because that builds trust. If you're confident in your skills because you've learned them and put time and effort in, that buys you trust because you can be confident as an advisor, consultant, and partner, rather than just a PR or comms person.

Tabita Andersson: Agreed, sometimes, the biggest barriers we put up for elevating the roles stem from within ourselves.

Kate Humphreys: Age also plays a role. If I look at my career trajectory and my age and how quickly I've gone through the industry and been promoted, people will often say, "Oh, you're so young," and the moment you flip that sentiment to realize that's on them, not on you, that gives you a different perspective.

Opportunities don't come to us. We have to seize them. I was incredibly ambitious and wanted to climb, and I've put in time and effort. I've given up evenings and weekends to get there. I'm not saying that's the right way and you have to give up balance, but in these roles, the reality is that you are on call 24/7/365, all the days of the week. You have to be available on holidays, and you have to give up a lot. That will not change because of the nature of the role, but I've always committed fully to the roles I'm in and tried to learn and be the best person to the senior executives, despite any age difference.

Tabita Andersson: That's very wise advice. In these roles, you never know when something will happen, and you could be on holiday, it could be the weekend, and you have to be available to help. That's just the reality of the role.

Kate Humphreys: We talked about attributes earlier. Being calm is a key attribute to success in this role. I'm unflappable. You can't be flustered in a crisis.

It's an interesting area to work in because if you look at accounting, one plus one will always equal two. The Law will always be the Law. In HR, there are policies and guidelines. There may be some blending in these roles, but functionally, that's it. In the communications function, there's never a single right answer. If there's a new crisis, there's no rule book. We can't pick up a book and read about what to do in that specific crisis because there are too many variables. Being unflappable is key because if you pick up the phone, you never know what's happening at the end of the line. In that moment, you have to react quickly and go into action, into the field of the unknown. You have to provide an answer, which has to be right, but there is no right. And you have to be okay with working in that ambiguity.

Tabita Andersson: We haven't covered measurements so far. How do you measure success for communications within your organisation?

Kate Humphreys: When I started working in an agency, we measured success in many ways. We would measure coverage by the size of the spread on the page and then align it with advertising spending, which is ironic given there's no spending involved, which I firmly believe in. I don't pay to play ever. It's about having strong messages and a strong ability to build stories, and then you can cut through the noise, and you don't have to pay. I've never paid for an advertorial in this business, nor will I do so in the future. The strength of the message and storytelling is your job, and you should be able to land it effectively without having a guaranteed slot.

In the agency, we would also measure the number of pieces of coverage for each client. It didn't matter what the impact was; it was a numbers game.

Here at Banijay, we don't have formal measurements, primarily because I don't believe there's a tangible way to measure the sum of what we do. You can measure the success of individual pieces of coverage, look at whether the message landed in the way you needed it to, if there was a positive sentiment, and then reflect on what we can do better next time. I don't tend to count pieces of coverage throughout the year. We count how much we deliver, and it's a high volume because we're incredibly well-known in our industry. We've built the largest European studio and deliver huge amounts of content each year, most of it with a very high profile. I would argue that all the teams worldwide are doing a great job of leveraging the content, the business, and the communications. When I get to the end of the year and do my strategic review, and set the strategy for the next year, what I usually look at, is what new areas did we break into, did we hit a different stage this year, a different publication, how did we do that, and how did that land? How many new profiles did we land for our CEO? Were they strategic, and did they deliver external results? How much press did we get alongside him when he spoke at an event? That often reflects how well we delivered the message and how much value we get from the press. For me, measurement is not black and white; it's less about what we do throughout the year against what we said we would achieve, and more about the value of each piece.

I sometimes see how people fear asking for feedback, especially when doing events. For example, we started a new event last year, curating our internal leadership summit, where all the managing directors of our production companies come together, and we deliver the strategy. We tried a new format and gave it a go. Ultimately, I realized that the event had been a bit long and that we needed to cut it next time, but bringing people together had been a good idea. The first thing I did afterwards in the room was to ask everyone what they thought. Everyone's subjective, and everyone's got an opinion, but the greatest value for me comes from the feedback. You have to be open to taking and hearing feedback. What you do with that feedback is also important. We received so much feedback for this event at varying levels. We evaluated all the feedback and took some of it on board. We have a strong event planned for this year because we've recalibrated, shortened the event, and ensured it's laser-focused on the strategy. We think it will deliver us much more success than last year. Many people are terrible at receiving feedback, so being resilient and open-minded is important. You're not always going to like it, but it's what you do with the feedback that matters.

Tabita Andersson: What would you like your legacy to be as CCO for Banijay?

Kate Humphreys: I built something from nothing, which is probably not something many CCOs can say. You can join a business and change what the person before you was doing, and you can do it differently and better, you can innovate and build on it, but very few people can say that they genuinely built an entire department from scratch.

I'm proud of the relationships I've built. I have a huge global network, unlike those who concentrate in one territory. I've built an incredible relationship with our CEO, and I'm extremely proud that we go bigger and better, and do more each year. Not everyone is fond of doing communications, but thankfully, those in this business understand the value, and that's a huge legacy to leave behind.

Going from nothing to building that level of communications is not just about my legacy but the legacy of the business. The company was relatively unknown when I joined, and we've gradually built a reputation. The team has executed several transformative and label-led deals that have grown the business into what we are today. I feel fortunate to have been here for seven years, carving the story and the reputation, and crafting what this business is known for publicly. I hope this is not the end, and we can keep building in different environments and engage audiences on who we are and what we do. I believe there is so much opportunity to go much further. As a team, we're incredibly ambitious, and that collaboration has been key to my success in this role and building it into something amazing. It's great to look back and think that when I first started, I had to knock on the doors of all the trade journalists, and now we're approached proactively by established media each day.

Tabita Andersson: What advice would you give yourself if you could return to your early career?

Kate Humphreys: Be confident. Put your head down. Don't get involved in the politics, deliver what's needed, and you will get noticed. I've always loved the role. There have been challenges over the years and in different environments, but I keep coming back to the thought about finding the right place for you. I've always been quite entrepreneurial. I want to do more and more, and this is the place that lets me do exactly that, so I can be the best version of myself. Finding the right home for you is crucial because it's not just about being good at what you do. You can only be good at what you do if you have the trust and a safe environment to deliver. And a place where they will invest in your development.

This is why I'm still here after seven years: the business keeps changing. We've undergone so much transformation that it doesn't feel like the same business I started. I feel fortunate that I've had the keys to the comms for so long, so I have been able to carve this story and strategy and then plug in brilliant people on my team to help me deliver.

CHAPTER 23

Amy Bunn

Chief Communications Officer McAfee

Amy Bunn is the **Chief Communications Officer** for **McAfee**, a global leader in online protection for consumers. Focused on safeguarding people in an always-online world, McAfee's solutions adapt to user needs, empowering individuals and families with secure, intuitive tools. With 1,800 employees globally and customers in 182 countries, McAfee protects millions worldwide and frees them to experience more by making it simpler to be safe online, however and wherever they connect.

For more information about McAfee, visit mcafee.com.

Amy's LinkedIn profile: linkedin.com/in/abunn

Tabita Andersson: What are some of the external trends that are impacting you the most right now?

Amy Bunn: Some trends, such as artificial intelligence (AI), impact everyone, regardless of industry. AI is changing the game in many ways. In particular, for communicators, it impacts our external and earned media strategy. The value and impact of LLMs (large language models) is changing the strategy. Given their prominence and influence with consumers, I'm having conversations about how we can show up in meaningful ways within LLMs. For example, understanding how or if a news outlet allows an LLM to use their news stories as a source can influence the weighting and importance we apply to that outlet. As a result, part of our measure of success right now is not just gaining media coverage, but looking at how that coverage is translated and shows up in various AI searches. AI is starting to play a serious role in an already very fragmented industry and changing media landscape. Traditionally, we've wanted to go after tier-one news outlets and mainstream news. Now, the credibility of trade media and social content is increasing because of how they are starting to show up in some of these LLMs. Given the transformational shifts underway in our industry, it's an exciting and pivotal time to be in PR and communications.

For McAfee, we're paying attention to what's happening from a macro perspective in the political and economic climate. In addition, we're paying very close attention to what's happening on the cybersecurity landscape. There's a rise of misinformation and disinformation, so how can you tell what's real or fake? As a cybersecurity company, we offer protection against some of these challenges, but it's also interesting to see them from a media perspective. For example, when you look at social media, how hard is it to know if a news report is real or fabricated? How do you even start to navigate that? Trust is becoming more important than ever before. Can you trust what you are reading, watching, or listening to, and how do you decide the content or source that warrants your trust? Then, how do outlets and companies earn that trust?

Tabita Andersson: As a Chief Communications Officer (CCO), how can you help build that trust for an organisation?

Amy Bunn: This is when investing in your brand is so important because you need to ensure you're establishing that trust, whether it's with customers, employees, or other stakeholders. When they learn about your brand and company, your audiences need to think, "Does this feel right for this brand? Is this the way this company would show up? Is this something that McAfee would say?" Or when you think of large brands such as Walmart or McDonald's, how do they show up? What do you think about when you see their brands? You need to ensure that you've established a good brand presence and have a strong brand understanding with your customers and audiences so they know how the brand behaves, what they can expect from you, and your tone of voice. As a result, if a brand says or does something that feels off, audiences will recognise it and ask themselves if this is right. Is this really McAfee, Walmart, McDonald's, or whichever brand it is, telling you to do something? It will cut through impostor information when you've come to know and expect certain brand values, voice, and behaviors. It will also give your brand instant recognition.

Tabita Andersson: This means that in the world of AI with many LLMs, a trusted brand and reputation will become even more important, with communications functions leading the way to ensure the right information gets out into the right places.

Amy Bunn: Absolutely! You need to ensure you're influencing the right sources and considering what's being pulled through, so that your brand has a place in what people search and find. We live in a world with abundant information, so you also need to identify which sources to pay attention to.

Today, we're spending a lot more time looking at where we show up in places like Reddit and on social media, and not just when running campaigns or as part of our normal listening programs. Brands have to be aware of how and where they're showing up at all times. Are you mining the comments on your social content to better understand your audiences? Are you plugged into the conversations about your brand across forums or on YouTube? Being aware of what's out there is the first step. Then, what steps are you taking to mitigate, manage, or even fuel those conversations to drive consideration and brand affinity?

Tabita Andersson: That's a much more complex environment than a decade ago. As such, how do you think we, as communicators, can show the value of what we do? There seems to be a great opportunity for us to guide organisations on managing these challenges.

Amy Bunn: Yes, for example, if we look at earned media, there are some great advancements in measurement and analytics that help communicators demonstrate value. Our role is focused on maintaining or improving brand reputation and trust tied to certain strategic pillars, and I look at a range of metrics to support this goal. For instance, do I see an uplift in brand search queries or website traffic tied to campaign launches or news cycles we've created? I'm also layering into my analysis any changes within our brand health tracker and how these correlate to the work we're doing in PR.

The measurement tools are getting more sophisticated, and we should be looking more at those to prove our value.

Another way we show the value of what we do is by building a track record with our executives on how we advise and offer counsel, and how we exercise good judgment to drive positive results. For example, perhaps your company is rolling out a new initiative internally, and employees must be aligned and take action. Navigating the messaging, delivery, and tactics is critical, as is providing counsel to your CEO or leader regarding their personal brand, how they're perceived, and how they can connect. Truly understanding your leaders and your audience is key here, so you can help connect the dots between what leaders are saying and what employees are feeling. Our value is understanding how to meet a moment with thoughtful messaging that truly resonates and drives action. Earning and maintaining trust from your leaders is also critical to success.

Tabita Andersson: Trust is a key theme in communications between the CCO and the CEO, between the C-suite and customers, and, in publicly listed companies, between the C-suite and investors. Building and maintaining trust permeates everything we do. What is your advice to a CEO about how to best work with their CCO?

Amy Bunn: Trust is the key thing that makes the relationship work, and trust has to be earned. Be open and transparent, put your cards on the table and talk about how to partner and navigate the real challenges and situations together. Also, the CCO should be brought in as part of the decision-making, not just afterwards. The CCO can help you look around corners. We're the ultimate dot-connectors!

We can see, predict, and anticipate things the CEO might not know because of their operating altitude. We can pull together insights and knowledge across the employee base, customers, or media to be able to better predict how decisions will land, and then advise on whether they are the right decisions, or the timing is wrong, or they need to be rolled out in a certain way to land more effectively. I advise thinking through the strategy together vs. coming to the CCO or communications team post-decision, when everything is locked down, because you might not get the desired results.

Tabita Andersson: Being a trusted advisor is important for the communications function, so we can work most effectively. What are some of the critical decisions the CCO should be prepared to make?

Amy Bunn: A CCO makes decisions around communications strategies that support and drive the business strategy. You need to know what the strategy is, what the roll out is, the phasing, the timing, what success looks like and how to determine success. It's important to recognise the expertise that a CCO and communications team bring regarding understanding, honing, and crafting the message. What do we want people to go away with? What do we want people to consider after communicating this news or campaign?

The business needs to make and communicate decisions, and we have the expertise to do so in a way that lands the decisions and impacts audiences in the most effective way. I strongly believe the CCO should be in the room when decisions are made because the CCO often has a perspective that others don't. This means we're constantly thinking ten steps ahead and playing out various "what if" scenarios to ensure we plan for all possible outcomes. The CCO can add tremendous value in these situations.

Tabita Andersson: On the other hand, what mistakes have CCOs made in the last few years, and what can we learn from them?

Amy Bunn: Broadly speaking, if you have a CCO who's just a task-taker, that's not an effective relationship. It will never work out well for the CCO or the executive team. The value-added strategic partnership is key. As a CCO, you want to make sure you're not putting yourself in that position, and not thinking of yourself as someone who just goes and executes against a plan vs. being part of the decision-making process.

Part of that comes down to a CCO's willingness and ability to voice their opinions and stand up against things that might not be popular. You need to advocate for employees or customers, and how they might feel about certain decisions, and be their voice in the room. You need to understand that sometimes your voice might be different than others, and that's okay. That's your job. We are in the room to ensure that the people around the table consider different perspectives.

There are also the basic practices that every CCO should follow to mitigate risk. For example, crisis communications. Have you thought through different scenarios and do dry runs regularly, not just once every couple of years? Are you refreshing your crisis comms plan regularly, every time subject-matter experts leave the organisation, or when there have been leadership changes, so you know the plan will still work? You must stay on top of the basics, especially in a constantly changing environment. Planning and thinking through all of these situations is important.

The next mistake, and probably not a surprise, is that you will be left behind if you don't invest in and train your team in AI fluency.

Tabita Andersson: Let's pivot to talk about the structure and remit of your communications function at McAfee. What does it look like?

Amy Bunn: I report to our Chief Marketing Officer (CMO) and manage public relations, social media, content strategy, employee brand, employee communications, and corporate events.

Tabita Andersson: That's a wide remit. How do you integrate your work with other functions across the company?

Amy Bunn: My philosophy is to lead by example. I try to make sure that I signal to other teams how we should be working together. I do that by leaning in and leading myself. I believe in strong stakeholder management. For any project or initiative, this means identifying who needs to be made aware and bringing people along. I try to be very clear—this is the plan, this is what you can expect from us when we launch a product or campaign, or this is what you can expect to happen in employee communications that everyone should be aware of. I strongly believe in a transparent flow of information and a high degree of stakeholder management. You never want anyone to be surprised by a new initiative, and you want support and greater integration with your work.

I also believe we need to have visibility of everything that's happening. When I think of communications, I also think of it as air traffic control. You need to know how your brand is showing up internally and externally. It means working together and doing so with the best possible intentions and the same end goals. It's not the brand team doing something, and the paid team doing something else. Whatever we do as a company and as a team, we need to ensure tight integration. It's not different disciplines working in isolation. We will have a much stronger impact and success if we all come together, whether launching an internal initiative or an external campaign.

Tabita Andersson: Is there an advantage to reporting to the CMO and working closely with marketing?

Amy Bunn: Throughout my career, I've reported to different functions. I've run employee communications while reporting to the Chief People Officer, and I've done executive communications inside other departments, so I've seen different types of organisational design and different ways it can work. The advantage of being within the marketing organisation is the close alignment between brand, communications, and marketing. It means greater cohesion and understanding of the customer and improved visibility and collaboration around the brand message.

Typically, where communications sits often comes down to the organisation's structure. At McAfee, we believe in a flat structure and have a matrix organisation. In this environment, it comes down to the leaders, the departments, and the teams to work best together. For example, I meet frequently with our Chief People Officer. I'm part of the HR off-sites and leadership team meetings, so I'm very plugged into the business and our key audiences. We're also intentional about ensuring we have the right people in the room and collaborating on projects. It's about putting the people and expertise together and ensuring you have all the right pieces in the right place.

Tabita Andersson: You've mentioned a couple of your previous roles. Why did you choose communications, and what has your career path been like?

Amy Bunn: When I grew up, I always had a passion for writing and telling stories, so I went into Public Relations (PR) to write and create content. I spent much of my early career in PR agencies in London, UK. PR agencies are the best training ground for a career in communications, regardless of whether you end up in PR or move into different disciplines. The foundational knowledge you gain is invaluable because there are frameworks and practices that I learned during those early years that I still carry through today. It gives you a strong foundation because you manage multiple clients. You have an incredible number of deadlines to meet, you have to hone the art of what's compelling to media, you have to get clear about your pitch, learn what's interesting and what's not, so you're landing the right key messages.

I also ensured that I gained experience within different PR models. First, I worked as part of the UK execution for clients. Then I moved to gain experience working within a hub-and-spoke model in a European role where I managed thought leadership and issues management with different agencies across markets, ensuring we had a consistent narrative and reporting.

From there, I moved in-house, and there's a big difference. There's huge value in being around many like-minded professionals within agencies. You share your thoughts on media, communications, and storytelling, giving everyone great creative energy. When you work in-house, you often have to explain and position what you're doing and its value. When you switch from agency to in-house, you can quickly go from working with 100 PR professionals in an agency to only two or three people in an entire team.

I wanted a rounded experience across various communications disciplines, so I intentionally sought that out. For example, I worked as part of the European communications team at Intel and then moved into executive communications. It's good to do scary or unknown things—trust yourself and see the trust that others put in you. I spent a couple of years doing executive communications in EMEA. I then moved across to the United States when McAfee spun out of Intel, to run employee communications and corporate change management. That was in 2017. I've been in the United States for several years now, and I think gaining experience across different disciplines has made me more grounded, eventually leading me to my CCO role.

Tabita Andersson: What advice would you give someone younger, early in their communications career?

Amy Bunn: It depends on what you want to do and who you want to be. If you want to be a CCO, having a wide range of experience is important because you learn different things in each role. Those experiences become additive. For instance, I learned things in the exec comms role that I didn't learn when doing UK PR. When I moved to the United States, I gained different experiences working in HR communications and added corporate communications and social employer branding to my skillset. I've always had a mindset of mastering one particular discipline and then continuing to expand my skillset and expertise.

Solving problems and spotting gaps have been a big part of my career progression. I'm a big advocate for stretch projects, because where I learned new skillsets weren't necessarily as part of a role, but they were when I put my hand up. For example, when I was in the UK, the HR team ran an organisational insights project for employees, and I put my hand up to lead the EMEA project, although it wasn't strictly communications. It gave me new expertise around employee management that I didn't have beforehand, and I've been able to use that experience to move into different roles.

First, you have to figure out what you want to be. Do you want to be an employee communications leader or a social media expert? Those are perfectly valid careers in themselves, and if that's what you want to do, then it makes sense to focus on honing that craft, becoming the best you can be in that area.

Another challenge I've faced as a CCO is that sometimes you have to rely on experts in certain areas. You can't know everything about all areas, and they are constantly changing. Social media, for example, is constantly evolving. So, if I'm not on social media full-time, I need someone who can best advise me where we should be going and what we should be thinking about, and then help me design the strategy.

Tabita Andersson: That's so true. You have to find what you enjoy and what's right for you, and that might be employee communications, or PR, or you might like both. Finding what you're good at and what you enjoy, regardless of whether that's a specialism and you go deeper, or a leadership role where you need to be more of a generalist.

What skills and attributes do you look for when you hire new people for your team?

Amy Bunn: AI is the obvious one that everyone is looking at now, and it's worth ensuring you have a certain level of proficiency. Aside from the core competencies of the job, I look at attributes like how hungry someone is, how much they want to grow and learn, how curious they are about the world, and if they question things. Do they question why we're doing a newsletter a certain way, or how come we do town halls this way, if we've thought about other ways? I like people who question what we do.

I'm always telling my team that we should be challenging how we run things because there's always something we haven't thought of, so we want to ensure we're bringing new ideas to the table. Critical thinking is another important skill. It's a skill I worry about, especially with AI. AI has incredible advantages, but I'm very concerned about a potential dearth of critical thinking in the younger generation. We need to ensure we employ people with that skill, which takes us back to how communications experts shouldn't be just task-takers. We need to think critically about a situation, connect the dots, and provide recommendations and suggestions for improvement.

Tied to that, I always look for people who challenge the status quo. There's value in best practices and being able to rinse and repeat, but I get excited and try to motivate and inspire my team when we don't have to do things the way we've always done them. I love it when my team brings me fresh ideas and new thinking, new ways of doing things, because that's how we all develop and grow. Someone who's always thinking ten steps ahead, thinking about how to try something, and has the appetite to experiment and innovate, is key.

Tabita Andersson: That is highly relevant to the communications role because we have to be able to see around corners and anticipate outcomes. When working through a crisis or planning a scenario and working out the consequences, it's very useful to think about new ways of working.

Amy Bunn: That's one of the reasons I love my job, my career, and what I do. I always tell my team something is wrong if they do not love it! It's a great career and a great job to be in. I want my team to wake up every morning thinking it's great because they've seen the New York Times article we've worked on for months, or the social media campaign has launched, and the comments are on fire! We put so much time, energy, and thought into what we do, so to see it out there is always fantastic, and it's the same across all communications disciplines. For example, in employee communications, when you see the engagement survey data improve, the stats go up, and you see employees leaning in more, and you start hearing them repeat your message back to you. I love it when that happens; you know your work is working! Another reason being part of communications is so great is that you can see a quick impact of your work, so you get good job satisfaction. You can see results relatively quickly if you have a good strategy, plan, and solid execution. I like to look for people who get a lot of enjoyment from that as well.

Tabita Andersson: What is it about the role you love the most?

Amy Bunn: The ability to have an impact and to influence in a thoughtful, strategic way. Then see the work that you've done has improved something, like overall satisfaction for employees, because they better understand the work we're doing, the vision we have, and their role in that. So, you've done an excellent job connecting all the dots and uplifting employees, helping them feel more engaged and connected to their job and the company. The reward and satisfaction I get when I see the results is what I love the most. When I see the work out there, I can sit back and say that's us, our team, we did that, and it's having a positive impact.

Tabita Andersson: Considering our impact, how do you think employee communications can contribute to a company's culture?

Amy Bunn: Employee communications is the glue that connects all the dots in a company. You must have mechanisms in place to gather feedback and listen. It might be a leader rolling out a new strategy to ensure employees are getting behind it, or something new we want to communicate to all employees from the top down. At the same time, you need to ensure that you're surfacing what your employees are saying by having two-way feedback mechanisms in place. Employee communications play an important role in listening to all sides and being able to craft compelling and thoughtful messages that connect with people.

It's getting harder and harder because people's attention spans are getting shorter. I always think about how employees consume content and social media when leaving the office or workspace. They consume news differently than they do at work, and I have to think about how we can deliver news and information in a way that's more similar to how they're consuming it in their daily lives. For example, how can we make corporate videos that feel more human and heartfelt, to create authenticity? This is where a communications expert should coach whoever is delivering those messages because the channel and format are important. It might not feel important to the person delivering the message. Still, how you deliver a message and the level of authenticity will impact how employees feel about you, the company, and the culture. This is where employee communications has a very important role to play.

Tabita Andersson: Can you give an example of how you've started to change content to be more digestible and consumable in today's fast-paced world?

Amy Bunn: We're always working to improve in this area, and I often work with our IT team, asking them to help us navigate internal channels to better match the immediacy of social media. For example, we recently had a video from some of our leaders that we wanted to share with employees. I disliked how employees had to click through various layers to play it, so I challenged the team to work out how to make it autoplay from the email, or if we couldn't, how to design it better. Hence, it looked like an autoplay in the email, but it was a GIF that had been embedded and used as a teaser. However, the experience for employees when they open emails was the same as if it had been a "real" autoplay.

Another example is that I believe in human language. Being a cybersecurity company, what we do is extremely important, and we take our jobs seriously. Still, we don't need to take ourselves overly seriously, so how can we start to bring in what we're seeing in pop culture, with phrases and sayings that are now part of the language we're using every day, and how can we make that part of the information we're creating, perhaps borrowing formats for the message delivery too? When your news formats better mirror the way people consume information externally, it creates familiarity and a seamless and more digestible experience for your audience.

Tabita Andersson: With the explosion of information and the pace of change speeding up, how do you keep yourself informed and learn about what's coming so you can operate efficiently at the CCO level?

Amy Bunn: It's hard! I consume a wide variety of media, so I constantly read different news sources, both traditional and new. I also often listen to podcasts and vodcasts, and borrow their techniques when evaluating how we can create similar types of content.

When I look at outlets like Morning Brew, which does great skits for their top news, I see how they present news and share it across their social channels, so that's a great source for staying up-to-date. I try to be proactive in consuming different news outlets and subscribing to Substack newsletters and various industry outlets.

I also rely on my team. We share a lot of information, and I always encourage the team to try different ways of delivering a message or crafting it in another format, such as a video, or in a more fun way.

It's also about proactively learning about what's changing and how others use different tools, techniques, and new formats. Then experiment.

I have mentors and other communication leaders I've worked with previously, and I connect with them regularly to get a feel for what's happening in other organisations. Having a network of people to go to and be inspired by is helpful.

Tabita Andersson: Yes, it can be quite a lonely role; otherwise, if you haven't built a good peer network, having someone you can pick up the phone to when needed is very helpful.

Amy Bunn: I have a few people in my network whom I've worked with previously and who have gone on to do bigger roles, because I always support and feel proud when my team members grow in their careers. For many people I've worked with, I tell them I'm always here if you ever need to phone a friend, and that's because I, too, want to be able to phone a friend sometimes! There's a lot of value in being able to be each other's sounding boards and talk through different things. As you said, there can be a sense of loneliness in the role, so having the ability to have conversations with people who understand the pressure you're under is vital because sometimes just talking it out loud can be very helpful.

Tabita Andersson: What would you like your legacy at McAfee to be, and why?

Amy Bunn: That we left our company, our customers, and employees better off. We had a positive, tangible impact, and I helped the company evolve, transition, and grow into the brand we aspire to be and have the impact we want for our customers.

What we do and how well we do our jobs as a company significantly impact consumers' lives, protecting them against serious cybersecurity threats. We take that part of our job very seriously, so if I've been able to help customers understand the value and benefit they get from a company like McAfee, then I feel that's my job done well.

Internally, employees need to feel that they've had a role in our success and have a job where they can be the best possible versions of themselves, continue to grow, and feel like they have somewhere they can belong.

Tabita Andersson: What advice do you have for potential future CCOs?

Amy Bunn: One of my mentors told me to consider your career a lattice, not a ladder. When you make lateral moves, think about how you're adding expertise and acquiring knowledge, and using that to help you continue to grow.

Especially early in your career, you can often have a drive to constantly move up. If you've been in an agency in an account executive role for two years, you're keen to be an account manager, and then continue that climb up, but lateral moves can sometimes be very compelling. I've made multiple lateral moves in my career. I was a senior account manager at one point, but I moved to an account manager role because I wanted pan-European experience.

The other thing I've learned is to trust your instincts. We're dot-connectors; we pull together different insights daily, giving us a great perspective. Don't underestimate that perspective and the value you bring because you have a different vantage point than the CEO, CFO, or Chief Product Officer. Trust your instinct and lean in. You don't have to come in from an angle of saying they're wrong, but that you're bringing a perspective or critical data point to the table as part of a discussion. Back yourself and think through the value you are adding. We often have a perspective that no one else in the room has, and it's our role and responsibility to share that and make sure it's heard. Trust yourself, you're in that position for a reason, and you must share your perspective in the room.

Index

A

Academic research, 175
Accessibility, 126, 127
Adoption capability, 102
Advertising, 193
Advertising internship, 143
Advertising value equivalent (AVE), 213
Aging population, 127
Air traffic control, 267
Alm, Jessica
  brands, 17
  career path, 14
  challenges, 16, 22
  communications efforts, 20, 21
  crisis, 22
  expectations, 20
  functional expertise, 19
  growth, 19
  impact, 21
  LinkedIn profile, 13
  motivation, 23
  philosophy, 17
  priorities, 16
  profession, 16
  reputation, 19
  responsibilities, 17
  roles, 15, 22
  routine, 18
  scope, 15
  tactics, 21

Andersson, Tabita (interviewer)
  Alm, Jessica (Essity), 13–23
  Barrett, Paul (Davie Group), 219–228
  Brusca, Laura (Forbes), 137–148
  Bunn, Amy (McAfee), 263–274
  Burnand, David (Staffbase), 161–169
  Campbell, Heather (Eurostar), 111–123
  Charlton, Dan (Sussex Partnership NHS Foundation Trust), 171–182
  Curtis-Johnson, Ryan (The Valuable 500), 125–136
  Geldard, Andrew (Willmott Dixon), 37–49
  Green, Nicola (Virgin Media O2), 73–84
  Henry, Lucy (Avanti Communications), 209–218
  Humphreys, Kate (Banijay Entertainment and Banijay Live), 251–261
  Jones, Stacey (Honeywell), 85–97
  Kahn, Karen (Intel), 25–35
  Kontesi, Amalia (NIF), 99–109
  Lawson, Amy (Sage), 149–159
  Neebe, Katherine (Duke Energy), 229–240
  Sahl Taylor, Pernille (Handelsbanken UK), 51–58
  Schaller, Monika (SAP), 1–11
  Spence, Craig (IPC), 195–208
  Stein, Christian (Renault Group), 241–250
  Temple, Jennifer (HPE), 59–72
  Trout, Joanne (Omnicom), 183–194

© Tabita Andersson 2025
T. Andersson, *Chief Communications Officers at Work*,
https://doi.org/10.1007/979-8-8688-1856-1

Index

Artificial intelligence (AI), 9, 21, 42, 54, 67, 82, 122, 136, 138, 145, 156, 157, 164, 190, 205, 214, 233, 248, 249, 257, 263, 264, 270
Authentic engagement, 178, 180
Authenticity, 32, 272
Autism, 128
Automotive industry, 242
    advantages, 242, 243
    brand image, 243
    documentary, 245
    press types, 243
Avanti Communications, 209–218

B

Banijay Entertainment and Banijay Live (BNJ. AS), 251–261
Barcelona principles, 133
Barrett, Paul
    best practices, 225
    career path, 223–228
    contribution, 224, 225, 228
    LinkedIn profile, 219
    reputation, 220–222
    roles, 222, 223
BBC World Service, 226
Brand health tracker, 87
Brand reputation, 265
Brusca, Laura
    career path, 143
    challenges, 142, 143, 148
    culture, 147
    decisions, 146
    future trends, 145
    guidance, 142, 148
    insights, 139
    leadership team, 140
    LinkedIn profile, 137
    media brands, 137
    outcomes, 139
    problem solver, 147
    profession, 141
    recognition, 148
    recommendation, 146
    roles, 138
    skills, 144
    solving issues, 145
    suggestions, 144
    use cases, 140
    vision, 141
Buffett, Warren, 117
Bunn, Amy
    AI, 263
    approaching, 272
    business trust, 264
    career path, 268
    crisis/planning scenario, 271
    decisions, 266, 267
    expertise, 270
    guidance, 269, 270, 273
    impact, 265
    internal communication, 272
    legacy, 273
    LinkedIn profile, 263
    philosophy, 267
    reporting, 267, 268
    roles, 271
    strategy, 271, 272
Burnand, David
    business impact, 163, 164
    career path, 166, 167
    crisis, 168
    experimentation, 165, 166
    guidance, 169
    LinkedIn profile, 161
    motivation, 166
    overview, organisation, 162
    profession, 165
    roles, 162, 164, 165
    suggestions, 167, 168
    synergies, 162, 163
Business operations, 235
Business strategy, 19, 46, 87, 114, 150, 158, 163, 185, 266
Business-to-business (B2B), 60, 148
Business-to-consumer (B2C), 60, 148

C

Campbell, Heather
    career path, 111–114
    executive team, 118

Index

experience, 114
external factors, 120, 121
guidance, 114, 115, 123
leadership skills, 118
legacy, 123
LinkedIn profile, 111
metrics and measurements, 116
regions manipulation, 121
reputation, 117
resilient, 122
roles, 120
skills, 119, 120
tactics, 119
transferable skills, 122
trends, 121
trusted advisor, 115

Capitol Hill, 138

Career aspirations, 41

Centre for Health Communications Research program, 174

Charlton, Dan
career path, 176
challenges, 179
collaboration, 182
complaints, 172
culture, 181, 182
education details, 178
experience, 174
goals, 178, 179
guidance, 172, 175, 176
leadership, 180
LinkedIn profile, 171
profession, 172
reframing, 181
research, 174, 175
responsibilities, 174, 177
roles, 171
skills, 177
strategic function, 173
suggestion, 176, 177
tactics, 180
team size, 177

Chatbots, 53

ChatGPT, 145, 223, 257

Chief Communications Officer
Alm, Jessica (Essity), 13–23
Barrett, Paul (Davie Group), 219–228
Brusca, Laura (Forbes), 137–148
Bunn, Amy (McAfee), 263–274
Burnand, David (Staffbase), 161–169
Campbell, Heather (Eurostar), 111–123
Charlton, Dan (Sussex Partnership NHS Foundation Trust), 171–182
Curtis-Johnson, Ryan (The Valuable 500), 125–136
Geldard, Andrew (Willmott Dixon), 37–49
Green, Nicola (Virgin Media O2), 73–84
Henry, Lucy (Avanti Communications), 209–218
Humphreys, Kate (Banijay Entertainment and Banijay Live), 251–261
Jones, Stacey (Honeywell), 85–97
Kahn, Karen (Intel), 25–35
Kontesi, Amalia (NIF), 99–109
Lawson, Amy (Sage), 149–159
Neebe, Katherine (Duke Energy), 229–240
Sahl Taylor, Pernille (Handelsbanken UK), 51–58
Schaller, Monika (SAP), 1–11
Spence, Craig (IPC), 195–208
Stein, Christian (Renault Group), 241–250
Temple, Jennifer (HPE), 59–72
Trout, Joanne (Omnicom), 183–194

Citigroup, 1

C-level positioning, 93

Coherent strategy, 29

Commercial awareness, 29, 30, 107, 141, 150, 151

Commercial business, 119

Communications
accessibility, 126
AI, 248
association, 139
brand experience, 210
corporate affairs, 150
departments, 187
disciplines, 269
engagement, 177, 221
expert, 272
function, 151
human relationships, 249

Communications (*cont.*)
  marketing, 210
  organisation's structure, 268
  outposts, 256
  perception, 246
  professionals, 150, 172, 173, 233, 244, 245
  role, 247
  strategy, 253
  support, 168
  team choices, 169
  trust, 266
Communicators
  channels, 245
  external and earned media strategy, 263
  measurement and analytics, 265
  service deliverers, 247
Competence, 222
Construction industry, 45
Construction News, 43
Consumer technology, 193
Content creation, 156
Content generation, 156
Corporate affairs function, 224
Corporate communications, 17, 103, 114, 143, 227, 230, 233, 236, 237
Corporate economic press, 244
COVID pandemic, 44, 93, 94
Creativity, 202
Crisis communications, 75, 76, 93, 107, 113, 168, 235, 254, 267
Critical thinking, 270
C-suite, 63, 118, 131, 139, 188, 199, 207, 211, 247, 252
Culture, 207
Culture of transformation, 240
Curtis-Johnson, Ryan
  agency, 134
  apprenticeships, 131
  attention, reviews, 135
  brand overview, 125, 126
  career path, 128, 129
  comments, 136
  consuming content, 130
  culture, 135
  experience, 132
  LinkedIn profile, 125
  mission, 135
  network experience, 127
  opinion, 133
  press clippings, 133
  profession, 128
  progression, 131
  reputation, 126, 127, 133
  roles, 129, 130
  team structure, 128
  trends, 136
  trustworthy, 132
Customer proposition, 53
Cyber-attacks, 94
Cybersecurity, 264, 272
  threats, 273

D

Davie Group, 219–228
Davies, James, 221
Decision-making, 26, 54, 74, 206, 266
Deutsche Bank, 1
Digital advertising, 65
Digital channels, 184, 200
Digital content, 196
Digital formats, 245
Digital marketing, 56
Disabilities, 126
Disability organisation, 198
Disagreement, 179
Discourses, 175
Disruption, 32
Distractions, 30
Diversity, 28, 44, 123
Documentaries, 245
Down syndrome, 128
Drucker, Peter, 190
Duke Energy, 229–240

E

Economic development, 230, 231, 233
Economic pressures, 7
Ecosystem, 100
eMAP, 226
Embedding intelligence, 25
Emotional intelligence, 78
Employee communications, 267, 268, 271
Employee engagement survey, 20
Endemol Shine Group, 256
Energy infrastructure, 231
Energy modernization, 240
Enterprise-wide crisis, 237
Entertainment industry, 129
Entrepreneurial business, 256, 257
Essity, 13–23
Eurostar, 111–123
Executive coaching, 258
Executive leadership team (ELT), 33
Executive positioning, 86
External agency, 256

F

Financial communications, 86, 103, 253
Financial crisis, 227
Financial markets, 2
Forbes, 137–148

G

Garbage in, garbage out, 9, 54
Geldard, Andrew
    analytics, 40
    characteristics, 38, 39
    content change, 42
    growth, 40, 41
    guidance, 48, 49
    leadership team, 46, 47
    learning development, 47
    LinkedIn profile, 37
    navigation, 46
    profession, 43, 44
    reputation, 45
    responsibility, 49
    roles, 37, 38
Generation valuable, 126
Generative AI, 157, 184, 191, 248
Geopolitical movements, 94
Goldman Sachs, 1
Governance, 237
Govia Thameslink Railway (GTR), 113
Green, Nicola
    career path, 78–80
    communications team, 77
    creating environment, 77
    crisis, 75, 76
    decisions, 74, 81
    guidance, 77, 78
    insights, 82
    LinkedIn profile, 73
    navigation, 75
    open-mindedness, 74
    reputation, 74, 84
    roles, 73
    self-motivation, 80
    trends, 83
    work balance, 83
Grounded optimism, 178, 180
Growth mindset, 56

H

Handelsbanken UK, 51–58
Hard skills, 71
Henry, Lucy
    brand and reputation, 218
    guidance, 210, 211
    history, 216, 217
    ideas, 213
    interaction, function's control, 210
    learning skills, 214, 215
    LinkedIn profile, 209
    observation, 218
    outcomes, 212
    planning, 215
    priorities, 211
    roles, 209, 210, 214
    suggestion, 217, 218

Henry, Lucy (*cont.*)
    team functions, 212
    thought leadership, 211, 212
    upgrading, 213, 214
Hewlett Packard Enterprise (HPE), 59–72
High-performance computing products, 66
High-profile crisis, 255
Honeywell, 85–97
Host events, 130
Hub-and-spoke model, 268
Human-centreed approach, 55
Humphreys, Kate
    attributes to success, 259
    barriers, 259
    collaboration, 253, 254
    crisis, 254, 255
    future trends, 257, 258
    growth measurements, 259, 260
    guidance, 252, 258
    legacy, 261
    LinkedIn profile, 251
    public relations, 251, 252
    roles, 256, 257
    self-development, 261
Hybrid-powered ferries, 219

I

Icebreakers, 219, 224
Impostor syndrome, 33, 148, 258
Inclusion, 44, 123
Influencers, 83
Informal network, 188
Information flow, 253
In-house creative agency, 235
Integrated Agency Live, 193
Intel, 25–35
Intensity, 129
Interconnectedness, 168
Internal employee engagement, 210
Internal/external communications function, 235
Internal leadership summit, 260

International Paralympic Committee (IPC), 195–208
Investor-centric, 30

J

Jones, Stacey
    attributes, 94, 95
    career path, 90, 91
    crisis, 93, 94
    decisions, 96
    equity, 88, 89
    finance experts, 96
    guidance, 91
    issues, 92, 93
    learning, 97
    LinkedIn profile, 85
    narrative, 87, 88
    non-communications experience, 91
    overview, Honeywell, 85, 86
    professional services, 89, 90
    reporting, 87
    skills, 92
    suggestions, 96, 97

K

Kahn, Karen
    career path, 25–27
    challenges, 35
    commercial awareness, 29, 30
    crisis, 32
    guidance, 33, 34
    journalism background, 28, 29
    LinkedIn profile, 25
    mindset, 30
    motivation, 35
    narratives, 31, 32
    navigation, 34
    priorities, 30, 31
    roles, 32
    skills, 27, 28
Key performance indicators (KPIs), 11, 115, 116
Kontesi, Amalia
    career path, 102, 103
    commercial awareness, 107
    communications perspective, 102
    crisis, 107, 108

encouragement, 109
guidance, 104, 105
legacy, 101, 102
LinkedIn profile, 99
media relations, 104
mission, 100, 101
NIF overview, 99
profession, 105, 106
roles, 100

L

Landfill, 45

Lansons consultancy, 55

Large language models (LLMs), 263

Lawson, Amy
business strategy, 158, 159
career path, 150–153
communications knowledge, 149, 150
contribution, 157
crisis, 152
data points, 154
decisions, 153
guidance, 151
legacy, 159
LinkedIn profile, 149
opinion, 155
profession, 151
roles, 152
skills, 153
trends, 157
trusted sources, 156
working balance, 154

Leadership, 4
building trust, 252
communication, 21
enterprise, 26
external controversy/campaign, 239
management issues, 268
positivity, 178
team meetings, 268
transparency, 88

Learning disability, 171

Liner Shipping Network, 226

Local Government Chronicle, 226

London Gatwick Airport, 112

London Heathrow Airport, 113

M

Major maintenance projects, 43

Marketing organisation, 268

MasterCard, 192

McAfee, 263–274

Media clipping agencies, 200

Media environments, 142

Media quality scores (MQS), 234

Media relations, 46

Media traction, 220

Mental health trust providers, 176

Microsoft Copilot, 9, 257

Mini-LLMs, 157

Minor capital works, 43

Moore's Law, 25

Multichannel campaigns, 164

Musical industry, 38

N

National Health Service (NHS), 171, 173, 176, 178, 180

NATO Innovation Fund (NIF), 99–109

Neebe, Katherine
AI impact, 233
career path, 229
confidence, 232
contribution, 235, 237
crisis experience, 237
criticism, 239, 240
destiny, 240
guidance, 236, 239
learnings, 230
legacy, 240
LinkedIn profile, 229
opinion, 238
perspective, 234
reputation, 231
roles, 230, 235, 236
skills, 238
stability, 231, 232
tactics, 234, 238
team structure, 235
trends, 232, 233

Net promoter score (NPS), 234
Net zero, 43
Neurodevelopmental services, 171
Neurodivergency, 127
Non-clinical corporate services, 182
Non-profit organisation, 125, 201

O

Omni AI, 184
Omnicom, 183–194
One-track relationship model, 252
Optimism bias, 39
Organisational change, 178, 179, 181
Organisational culture, 75, 235
Organisational design, 268
Organisational structure, 74

P

Paralympic Games, 196, 197, 201, 204, 205
Paralympic symbol, 197
Pension scheme, 113
Perceptions, 44
Performance analytics, 67
Personalization, 244
Planning, 96
Polar Max, 219, 221
Policymakers, 231
Political activities, 127
Political environment, 168, 187
Pragmatic approach, 6
Proactiveness, 48
Problem-solving, 62
Procurement Act, 39
Procurement system, 221
Product marketing, 64, 65, 163
Professional credibility, 249
Professionalization, 172, 175
Prozac leadership, 179
Public affairs, 76, 103, 120, 227, 230, 235

Public relations (PR), 52, 79, 117, 133, 140, 143, 152, 157, 163, 167, 184, 190, 191, 193, 251, 252, 268
Purpose-driven business, 45

Q

Qualitative measurements, 66
Quality control, 9
Quantitative measurements, 66

R

Renault Group, 241–250
Re-skilling program, 164
Resource-constrained environment, 182
Resource plans, 232
Responsible, accountable, consulted, and informed (RACI), 95
Reverse mentoring program, 126
Rewarding profession, 84
Risk mitigation, 267
Rugby Football League, 202

S

Sage, 149–159
Sahl Taylor, Pernille
    career path, 55
    communications management, 52
    customer connection, 53, 54
    data collection, 54, 55
    decisions, 56
    experience, 55, 56
    growth, 54
    learning, 58
    LinkedIn profile, 51
    marketing, 52
    priorities, 58
    reputation, 57
    roles, 57
Sales/marketing, 242, 243
SAP, 1–11
Sapphire, 5
Satellite communications, 211
Satnav analogy, 208

Index

Schaller, Monika
  advisory capacity, 3
  career path, 1, 2
  challenges, 7, 10
  crisis, 3, 4, 6
  discourse, 6
  experience, 1
  external reality, 8
  guidance, 4, 6
  impact, 8
  LinkedIn profile, 2
  metrics, 10
  mindset, 5
  motivation, 11
  profession, 3
  reputation, 5, 7
  responsibility, 9
  self-motivation, 2
  targets, 5
  traits, 4
  transformation, 6, 8
Self-disclosing, 127
Self-education, 258
Self-sustaining, 144
Shareholders, 155, 235
Ship-building industry, 219
Sideris, Harry, 235
Small and mid-sized businesses (SMBs), 149
Social media, 145, 189, 270
  business-to-business accounts, 256
  conversations, 140
  forums, 153
  metrics, 154
  specialists, 257
  training, 247
Social networks, 244
Soft skills, 72
Software as a service (SaaS), 162
Spence, Craig
  career path, 202
  communication evolutions, 200
  communications function, 204, 205
  culture, 207
  decisions, 206, 207
  future trends, 205
  guidelines, 196, 197
  interaction, 199
  LinkedIn profile, 195
  mistakes, 206
  organisation issues, 199
  reputation, 197, 198
  roles, 195, 196, 198, 199
  sports, 204
  strategic plan, 201
  suggestion, 202, 203
  team functions, 196
  team skills, 203, 204
  thoughts, 201
  thriving, 207, 208
Sports organisation, 198
Staffbase, 161–169
Stakeholders, 4, 5, 16, 32, 48, 74, 75, 83, 100, 101, 113, 117, 143, 154, 155, 184, 188, 210, 211, 220, 223, 224, 231, 243, 246, 249, 267
Stein, Christian
  AI impact, 248
  best practices, 247, 248
  career path, 241
  challenges, 246
  concentration, 249
  crisis, 244
  decisions, 247
  experience, 242
  guidance, 249, 250
  LinkedIn profile, 241
  reputation, 243, 244
  responsibilities, 248
  skills, 244, 245
Stereotypes, 44
Storytelling, 25, 26, 126, 243
Strategic planning, 104
Subject matter expertise, 60
Sussex Partnership NHS Foundation Trust, 171–182
Sustainability, 9, 14, 46, 103, 126, 231
Sustainable development, 45
Swedish Agriculture University, 14
Systemic quality problems, 179

T

Target audiences, 16, 52–54, 116, 139, 243, 245
Targeted marketing campaign, 54
Team culture, 4
Team sports, 204
Technical literacy, 213
Temple, Jennifer
    career path, 59, 60
    challenges, 70, 71
    content generation, 67
    convictions, 69
    decisions, 72
    expectations, 71
    experience, 65
    guidance, 62
    insights, 67
    learning business, 63
    learning client service, 68
    LinkedIn profile, 59
    marketing, 61, 62
    mistakes, 68
    non-crisis situation, 69
    opinion, B2B and B2C, 61
    reports, 64, 65
    reputation, 69–71
    roles, 63, 64, 72
    scenarios, 63
    shared relationship, 72
    skills, 71
    tactics, 66
Thought leadership, 86, 211, 212
Tiger Aspect Productions, 216
Trade-offs, 63, 154
Traditional product press, 244
Transport industry, 120
Trout, Joanne
    best practices, 191
    brands, 183
    career path, 191, 192
    challenges, 185
    company culture, 189, 190
    company structure, 184
    crisis, 187
    decisions, 186
    discipline, 193
    experience, 187–189
    growth, 193
    guidance, 193
    insights, 188, 189
    job descriptions, 191
    LinkedIn profile, 183
    planning, 186
    profession, 188, 190
    reporting, 186
    reputation, 185
    roles, 183, 184, 187
    suggestion, 192

U

UK national budget, 39
Unconscious bias, 39
Unsigned musical talents, 37

V

Value-added strategic partnership, 266
Value chain, 158, 242
Values-driven organisation, 56
Video briefings, 40
Virgin Media O2, 73–84
Visibility, 6, 10, 27, 31, 48
Visual content, 245

W, X

Webinars, 39
Welfare policy, 254
Wildfires/geopolitical situations, 146
Willmott Dixon, 37–49
Women's leadership network, 39
Work-life balance, 44, 130
World Wildlife Fund (WWF), 229

Y

Yorkshire Water, 208

Z

Zero waste, 45

GPSR Compliance

The European Union's (EU) General Product Safety Regulation (GPSR) is a set of rules that requires consumer products to be safe and our obligations to ensure this.

If you have any concerns about our products, you can contact us on

ProductSafety@springernature.com

In case Publisher is established outside the EU, the EU authorized representative is:

Springer Nature Customer Service Center GmbH
Europaplatz 3
69115 Heidelberg, Germany

www.ingramcontent.com/pod-product-compliance
Lightning Source LLC
LaVergne TN
LVHW021956060526
838201LV00048B/1592